Dramas of Dignity

Looking beyond the shiny surface of Potsdamer Platz, a designer micro-city within Berlin's city center, this book goes behind-the-scenes with the cleaners who pick up cigarette butts from sidewalks, scrape chewing gum from marble floors, wipe coffee stains from office desks and scrub public toilets, long before white-collar workers, consumers and tourists enter the complex. It follows Costas's journey to a large yet hidden, four-level deep corporate underworld below Potsdamer Platz. There, Costas discovers how cleaners' attitudes to work are much less straightforward than the public perceptions of cleaning as degrading work would suggest. Cleaners turn to their work for dignity yet find it elusive. The book explores how these cleaners' dramas of dignity unfold in interactions with co-workers, management, clients and the public.

JANA COSTAS is Chair of People, Work & Management at the European University Viadrina, Frankfurt (Oder), Germany. She is the co-author of *Secrecy at Work: The Hidden Architecture of Organizational Life* (2016).

Dramas of Dignity

Cleaners in the Corporate Underworld of Berlin

JANA COSTAS
European University Viadrina Frankfurt (Oder)

CAMBRIDGE
UNIVERSITY PRESS

University Printing House, Cambridge CB2 8BS, United Kingdom

One Liberty Plaza, 20th Floor, New York, NY 10006, USA

477 Williamstown Road, Port Melbourne, VIC 3207, Australia

314–321, 3rd Floor, Plot 3, Splendor Forum, Jasola District Centre, New Delhi – 110025, India

103 Penang Road, #05–06/07, Visioncrest Commercial, Singapore 238467

Cambridge University Press is part of the University of Cambridge.

It furthers the University's mission by disseminating knowledge in the pursuit of
education, learning, and research at the highest international levels of excellence.

www.cambridge.org
Information on this title: www.cambridge.org/9781108475846
DOI: 10.1017/9781108608572

First published 2022

A catalogue record for this publication is available from the British Library.

Library of Congress Cataloging-in-Publication Data
Names: Costas, Jana, author.
Title: Dramas of dignity : cleaners in the corporate underworld of Berlin / Jana Costas, European
    University Viadrina Frankfurt (Oder).
Description: Cambridge, United Kingdom ; New York, NY : Cambridge
University Press, 2022. | Includes bibliographical references and index.
Identifiers: LCCN 2021044719 (print) | LCCN 2021044720 (ebook) | ISBN 9781108475846
    (hardback) | ISBN 9781108469166 (paperback) | ISBN 9781108608572 (epub)
Subjects: LCSH: Cleaning personnel–Germany. | BISAC: BUSINESS & ECONOMICS /
    Organizational Behavior
Classification: LCC HD8039.C442 G336 2022 (print) | LCC HD8039.C442
(ebook) | DDC 331.7/616480943–dc23/eng/20211006
LC record available at https://lccn.loc.gov/2021044719
LC ebook record available at https://lccn.loc.gov/2021044720

ISBN 978-1-108-47584-6 Hardback
ISBN 978-1-108-46916-6 Paperback

Contents

Figures

Acknowledgments

My acknowledgments go to Chris Grey (Royal Holloway, University of London). His interest, support and feedback throughout this project were of tremendous importance. I am particularly thankful to him for reading all my chapters and providing me with detailed comments that greatly improved the text.

I am also grateful to Gideon Kunda (Tel Aviv University) for all his encouragement, input and excitement about my ethnography. He provided me with valuable support during my fieldwork and encouraged me to engage in more freestyle writing about my ethnographic experiences.

Thanks to my former and present colleagues at the European University Viadrina Frankfurt (Oder). Mona Florian, Philipp Arnold and Birke Otto provided me with helpful suggestions and inspired my thinking. My current secretary, Frau Hübner, and former secretary, Frau Gdowska, and various student assistants supported me by taking care of administrative duties and by transcribing voice recordings. I am thankful for institutional support from, and insightful conversations with, colleagues at Freie Universität Berlin, Copenhagen Business School and the European University Viadrina Frankfurt (Oder). Thanks go to my former colleagues at the Freie Universität Berlin, specifically Markus Helfen, who invited the human resources (HR) manager, Ludwig, from CleanUp (both pseudonyms) for a talk at our university – an introduction that opened the door for my ethnography.

I would like to thank Günther Ortmann for so attentively collecting and sending me articles on dirt and the cleaners in recent years; Alexander Martin for his theoretical suggestions; Oana Albu for sharing with me her insights on the latest developments in surveillance studies; and Dan Kärreman for commenting on and encouraging me to write this book. Gregory Jackson brought much excitement to the project by using passages of the text in his musical compositions.

My office community in Kreuzberg was a frequent source of inspiration. Thanks to Mads Pankow for creative input on my chapter titles.

The organizers and participants of various workshops and conferences, including the 2014 EGOS Colloquium in Rotterdam and LAEMOS conference in Cuba, the 2015 Ephemera conference in Moscow and the 2014 Hans-Böckler-Stiftung conference of the research network "personal, arbeit, organisation" in Flensburg, all provided me with opportunities to present my ideas and receive helpful feedback.

Acknowledgments go to Paul Festa for editing the text, particularly for his help in finding the right English words to convey the world and the language of the cleaners.

I am thankful to Valery Appleby at Cambridge University Press for her support and feedback on the manuscript, as well as to the reviewers, among them Melissa Fisher and Damian O'Doherty, for their insightful comments.

Thanks also to my family for their encouragement and support: to my mother for commenting on my chapters, my father for challenging my thinking and my sister for sharing with me her experiences of Potsdamer Platz's upperworld. My partner, Martin, helped me make sense of the cleaners' pop culture references.

Finally, this book would not have been possible without the unique access CleanUp and, in particular, Ludwig granted me. It relies significantly on the cleaners themselves, who welcomed me into their world and shared their working lives with me. In so doing, they gave me far more than I could hope to repay.

Below Potsdamer Platz
Introduction to the Minus Area

"Jana in the underworld," muses Norbert, a foreman with the major German cleaning company CleanUp,[1] when I tell him I will study cleaning work at Berlin's Potsdamer Platz. For the cleaners, this large, four-level underworld is the nodal point of their work. Cleaners spend much of their time in what is also known as the "minus area": windowless storage and break rooms, labyrinthine corridors, stairways and elevators that descend to the lowest point – garbage collection. In the underworld's tunnels and interstices, cleaners move around and interact with fellow workers. This underworld is the setting for my ethnography of the cleaners' largely invisible work life.

Norbert's use of the metaphor "underworld" is apt, given its Greek-mythological origins. In the κατο [under] κοσμο [world], the god Hades, whose name means "the unseen" or "invisible," rules over the dead.[2] Potsdamer Platz's cleaners are far from dead, of course, and they regularly emerge aboveground. But the River Styx of concrete and steel keeps this underworld hidden.

Potsdamer Platz is a significant place for Berlin: a privately owned, corporate designer micro-city right in the city center, close to the Brandenburg Gate. Potsdamer Platz has become one of the iconic places seen in the background of tourist photos, advertisements and movie scenes depicting the "new Berlin." The *crème de la crème* of international architects, funded by large corporations, rebuilt Potsdamer Platz to restore its prewar importance, overshadow its Nazi and Cold War past and create the ideal "city for the twenty-first century."[3] The skyscrapers of Renzo Piano, the redbrick Art-Deco-reminiscent tower of Hans Kollhoff and Richard Rogers' glassy

---

[1] To ensure anonymity and protect sources, I use pseudonyms for CleanUp, its employees and all the other participants I encountered in the field.
[2] Hard (2004: 107).
[3] https://potsdamerplatz.de/en/mythos-potsdamer-platz/ (accessed June 2017).

complex with yellow blinds and green atria together make Potsdamer Platz a futuristic standout in the cityscape. With its Arkaden shopping mall, five-star American chain hotels, entertainment centers, casinos, cinema complexes and luxury apartments, Potsdamer Platz has become a hub for cosmopolitan residents, professionals, consumers and tourists.

On arriving at Potsdamer Platz, I enter both strangely familiar and unfamiliar worlds. Berlin-born and -raised, I've visited the complex many times; but I've known nothing about its corporate underworld and the people working there. Cleaning work is also new to me. Entering the underworld, therefore, feels like visiting a remote place in the middle of my native city.

An encounter more than fifteen years ago, during my work as a strategy consultant, helped spark my curiosity about cleaners and their work life. Responsible for a project's data calculations, I was spending a late night in the consultancy's Munich office. Around 9 p.m., the office became quiet. I could hear the last steps of departing colleagues, doors closing and the hallway lights automatically switching off. Absorbed in my spreadsheet, I was startled by the sudden presence of a young woman in a cleaning uniform. After a perfunctory greeting, she went to the next room to start cleaning. I found myself mulling our brief encounter. What was it like for her to clean the empty hallways and offices at night? What did she make of me, a lone female worker like her, yet dressed differently and engrossed in work with higher pay and status? Which one of us wanted less to be working here so late? When did she sleep and see her family? Did she have a family? Did she have children? Where did she live? How did she end up in cleaning?

Our encounter made me aware that the hotel bed I sleep in, the office I enter in the morning, the streets I walk to work, are all cleaned before and after me by the absent-present workers. They are present in that the absence of cleanliness would be noted and absent in that their presence is normally unheard, unseen and unfelt. So our lives are both intimately connected – the cleaner's work is scheduled around the consultant's – and kept separate. Until the moment I join the cleaning workforce and descend into the Potsdamer Platz underworld, cleaners have only entered my life when serving me.

Despite reading all I can about CleanUp, and speaking to foremen and account managers at training workshops, I worry I am not prepared for my first day. The night before, I toss and turn, anxious that

I won't wake up with my 4 a.m. alarm, or that my presence in the field will backfire – what if the cleaners won't talk to me or even acknowledge my presence? But after a fitful sleep, I am brimming with excitement and anxious curiosity as I cycle to Potsdamer Platz at dawn.

Before 5 a.m. on my first day in the field, Norbert and Tom, the account manager at Potsdamer Platz, welcome me in their thick Berlin accents. Tom walks me through the formal introduction for new cleaners: safety and cleaning guidelines, the Potsdamer Platz map and the confidentiality rules regarding client information.

A tour of Potsdamer Platz and its architectural highlights follows. At one point, in a dusty construction elevator, Norbert warns me using the formal German "Sie": "Careful, don't lean against it and get dirty!" On this introductory tour, I am still a visitor, one with nice clothes and contacts at headquarters. Ludwig, CleanUp's human resources manager, has granted me wide access, acknowledging the company's interest in raising public awareness of cleaning work. For Tom and Norbert, I am someone from "the university," a remote institution where none of them has ever set foot except perhaps to clean it. While I have decided to be transparent about my academic background and motivation, I certainly don't want to emphasize my university pedigree, for example pointing out my title of Prof. Dr., which would only reinforce the cultural, social and economic gap between them and me. (Later, once I am well immersed in the field, cleaners will ask about my title and react with laughter and disbelief when they learn that I – a thirty-year-old half-Greek female who expresses herself colloquially – am a professor. They'll demand to see my ID.)

After showing me around, Tom and Norbert introduce me to Michaela, a sixty-two-year-old cleaner from the former East Berlin. Following a brief greeting, Michaela trains me. She shows me how to clean the toilets, using a brush and a particularly strong cleaning fluid. To my surprise, she works without gloves. These wouldn't let her "adequately feel" what she touches. No gloves for her, no gloves for me, I decide, and so begins my first shift.

During the 9 a.m. break, I sit at a table drinking coffee and eating breakfast with Michaela and other cleaners. Cleaners exchange curious looks in silence; I should introduce myself. "My name is Jana," I say. "I'm here from the university to study cleaners. I am simply interested in learning what it means to work as a cleaner."

Michaela is the first to respond. "Well finally," she says. "Finally somebody is coming here to pay attention instead of taking us for granted all the time."

I am relieved to find people so welcoming. To some degree it surprises me that cleaners like Michaela take my presence there as a sign of appreciation and respect. I am, after all, a person who comes from the "upperworld" that generally tends to overlook if not look down on cleaners. Indeed, not everyone reacts like Michaela. Some cleaners keep their distance, half-jokingly referring to me as a management "mole."

Overall, however, cleaners open up to me more than I expected, perhaps because I work alongside them. Admittedly, I report for work two to four times per week, not five or six. Nor do I have fixed shifts. Instead, I change shifts every two to three weeks to get to know different cleaners and gain insights into the varied nature of cleaning services: from cleaning private apartments, offices, lobbies and shopping malls to window and post-construction cleaning. Still, I work full shifts at Potsdamer Platz, from 5 a.m. to 1:30 p.m., and do my best to do the job as the others do it: brushing toilets without gloves, sweeping staircases, picking up cigarette butts from the street and mopping up urine. I present myself as an assistant who wants to learn and help and who is generally curious to understand cleaners' take on things.

Cleaning from the Outset: Invisible Dirty Work at the Bottom

Cleaners conduct what the literature terms "dirty work."[4] They deal with the "physically disgusting,"[5] that is, matter that people prefer not to see, smell or touch. This makes cleaning a prototypical example of a stigmatized occupation, one that enjoys little, if any, prestige or respect.

There is a further reason why cleaning work seems undignified. Both cleaners and their work remain largely invisible. When work is invisible, people tend to value it less, both symbolically and materially.[6] At Potsdamer Platz, cleaners are made invisible in different ways. They commute more than an hour from Berlin's more affordable outer

---

[4] Hughes (1984/2009); see also Ashforth and Kreiner (1999), Bolton (2005), Kreiner et al. (2006), Ashforth et al. (2007), Paetzold et al. (2008), Baran et al. (2012).
[5] Hughes (1984/2009: 344).   [6] Crain et al. (2016).

districts to begin their work at 5 a.m. By the time white-collar workers, consumers and tourists enter the complex, cleaners have already ful-filled the bulk of their day's shift. They have extracted scraped chewing gum from marble floors, wiped coffee stains from office desks and scrubbed toilets. To keep the cleaners out of sight, their shifts are scheduled to minimize contact with the public.[7] Compared with the European average, German cleaners work odd hours: in the evening, at night or early morning.[8]

At Potsdamer Platz, cleaners inhabit a hidden corporate underworld. Like a building foundation, the underworld is as indispensable as it is invisible. Only with a special key card can one go from the gleaming upperworld to the dark labyrinth below, where low ceilings trap air thick with the smell of waste. As the magazine *Potsdamer Platz* explains, the services and activities of the workers are "discreetly sunk" into the minus area,[9] where they will not "disturb" above-ground residents. This reflects the broader trend in architecture and urban planning of "vertical growth"[10] in which higher towers for the elite are accompanied by lower basements with service centers, garbage collection points and workers.

The fact that the cleaners work for and report to CleanUp, rather than to individual clients, compounds the problem of their invisibility. In recent decades, organizations increasingly outsource service work[11] like cleaning in order to cut costs and increase flexibility. The outsour-cing of private household service work has also been on the rise.[12] The German cleaning market, the biggest in Europe, has shown high growth rates.[13] The resulting corporate work arrangements of cleaners

---

[7] My study thus adds the dimension of temporality to Hatton's (2017) analytical concept of invisible work, which focuses on sociocultural, spatial and legal dimensions. On nightwork, see also Müller (2019).

[8] In Germany, 50 percent of cleaning services take place in the evening, 5 percent at night and 30 percent in the morning, leaving only 15 percent for daytime cleaning. The European average of daytime cleaning is 25 percent Grömling (2007) in ArbeitGestalten (2017).

[9] https://potsdamerplatz.de/en/discreetly-sunk/ (accessed June 2017).

[10] Graham (2016).

[11] This is part of the general trend toward the "market rationality" paradigm driving much management thought in recent decades (Kunda & Ailon-Souday, 2006; see also Aguiar and Herod [2006] in relation to the cleaning industry).

[12] Farvaque (2013).

[13] https://die-gebaeudedienstleister.de/die-branche/daten-und-fakten (accessed September 2021).

minimize direct contact with service recipients. In addition, cleaners' work does not need to be "consumed" and "produced" simultaneously; in fact, it is easier to clean in the absence of clients.[14] Not just the cleaners' presence but the work itself can easily be overlooked or taken for granted. The importance of cleanliness is often best appreciated when things get dirty.[15]

Cleaning also sits near the bottom of the labor market hierarchy in terms of skill and pay. It is regarded as "servant labor," a kind of "low-skilled work that is done for others who could perfectly well do it themselves."[16] Although CleanUp introduced an hourly minimum wage before German law enforced it in 2015,[17] cleaners' income remains low, especially for those who work only a few hours per day. Germany's social safety net protects cleaners. [18] Nevertheless, income inequality persists.[19] At Potsdamer Platz, a cleaner is paid around €10–11 per hour whereas the lawyer in the cleaned office more than twenty times that amount.

Altogether, cleaning at Potsdamer Platz combines a lot of features that make this work unpleasant and degrading and place it at the low end of the employment spectrum: cleaning means dealing with filth, being made invisible and conducting low-skilled, low-paid labor. It seems to be a job people do for financial necessity alone. There seems to be little, if anything, that is dignifying about being a cleaner.

[14] While customer service is commonly understood to constitute interactive service work (e.g. MacDonald & Korczynski, 2009), cleaning amounts to non-interactive service work.
[15] Karafyllis (2013: 18).   [16] Sayer (2007: 577).
[17] Depending on the German state (former East versus West), in 2020 this ranged from €10,55–€10,80 for interior and maintenance cleaning to €13,50–€14,10 for glass cleaning (https://dgb.de/schwerpunkt/mindestlohn/hintergrund/branchenmindestloehne#GEBÄUDEREINIGUNG accessed September 2021).
[18] To this extent, they are not the so-called working poor, unable to provide for basic needs like healthcare, as is commonly the case with service workers in the United States(AMJ Editors, 2010; Leana et al., 2012). The cleaning work and the cleaners I am studying therefore differ from the service work and the working poor studied by Ehrenreich (2001).
[19] Especially from 1999 to 2005, income inequality grew in Germany (Krause, 2015). While it is leveling off now, it is still significantly higher than it was twenty years ago. In comparison with other EU countries, Germany's income inequality is just below the EU average (www.boeckler.de/de/soziale-ungleichheit-18291-ungleichheit-geht-kaum-zurueck-4416.htm accessed September 2021). The rise of inequality in Germany has also been related to the expansion of low-wage work (Bosch and Weinkopf, 2008).

Perspectives from the Corporate Underworld

At Potsdamer Platz, cleaners' attitudes toward their work prove to be less straightforward. Of course, they do it for the money – but there's more to it. What troubles the observer, cleaners may in fact welcome.

As I work alongside the cleaners, I'm struck by the care they take in the job: Michaela, for example, refusing gloves in the service of precision. Rather than feeling disgusted by filth, some cleaners seem to derive excitement and even pride from dealing with the worst of it (dead animals, human excrement). Cleaning can be dismal and repetitive, yet cleaners may also find it fun, varied and conducive to a certain degree of autonomy. As the long-serving cleaner Ali puts it: "I enjoy my work. You know I am my own boss here." Cleaners are quick to point out that there is more to cleaning than just pushing a mop or emptying the trash. Interior and exterior cleaning, glass wiping and maid service, all require different skill sets and experience.

In service work like cleaning, educational and work-experience barriers to entry are low; workforce diversity is correspondingly high. At Potsdamer Platz, I encounter cleaners who are young and old; female and male; West German, East German and foreign; black and white; educated and uneducated; trained and untrained. What they all share is that they come from the social underworld. Histories of unemployment, immigration, criminal records and homelessness run through their lives. For these people, cleaning comes with the pride of work, the hope of belonging to a community and the promise of becoming a full-fledged member of society. At the boundary of employment and unemployment, of integration and exclusion, cleaners regard their work as more than just an undignified job.

During my fieldwork, I also become aware that the corporate underworld is a zone of mixed blessings. It provides cleaners with little sun or air, fosters conflicts and, indeed, reinforces cleaners' lack of recognition by the upperworld. But the underworld also allows them to earn a living, find a refuge from surveillance, elude encounters with upperworlders and build coalitions with other workers.

All of this suggests that public perception of cleaners and their work does not necessarily reflect how cleaners see themselves. The value system of the upperworld does not completely dominate and determine that of the underworld.[20] On the contrary, the cleaners at Potsdamer Platz also seem to approach their work as a source of dignity. But how can cleaners develop and maintain this dignity at work? How do CleanUp, coworkers, clients and upperworlders generally shape cleaners' dignity? What happens when others deny cleaners respect or recognition?

Dramas of Dignity

Dignity is about the state of being worthy. It entails both developing a sense of self-worth and being treated as worthy by others.[21] In the case of the cleaners, these two sides of dignity are often in tension: cleaners seek to derive a sense of worth from their work, yet when they interact with others, they are often denied respect and recognition. As a result, they face what I will term *dramas of dignity*.

This notion captures the emotional intensity and tension involved as cleaners struggle to attain and maintain dignity. Indeed, dignity is not something one can casually do without. As the sociologists Richard Sennett and Jonathan Cobb argue in *Hidden Injuries of Class*, it constitutes "a compelling human need."[22] Dignity may be thought of as inherently fragile, a fragility that manifests itself differently in the life of a cleaner and, say, a university professor. The latter belongs to an institution that confers high status, starting with a title. Cleaners' dignity finds little if any institutional anchor. While the professor may be more vulnerable to the loss of dignity, cleaners have to work much harder to gain it in the first place.

The dramas of dignity I observe in my research bring into focus the significance of social interactions at work. The sociologist Everett Hughes has referred to the "social drama of work" to capture how "every kind of work takes place in a social matrix and involves social interactions."[23] In order to understand work, it is not enough to focus on the "technical tasks" people perform. One has to "understand the roles of the various people involved in it."[24] For Hughes, it should therefore be "[o]ur aim ... to *penetrate more deeply* into the personal

---

[20] Hall (1992: 273). In this regard, Lamont (1992) and Hall (1992) criticize Bourdieu's approach.
[21] Hodson (2001), Sayer (2007).   [22] Sennett and Cobb (1972: 191).
[23] Hughes (1951: 123).   [24] Hughes (1976: 2).

and social drama of work, to understand ... [how] men [sic] make their work tolerable, or even glorious to themselves and others."[25]

For this reason, we should approach cleaners' struggles with dignity as dramas that unfold in a social context. It is not enough to look at how workers develop a sense of self-worth. It is also necessary to explore how and whether their sense of worth is undermined or maintained when they interact with others.[26] Focusing on social interactions, this book aims to show how cleaners are not passive, but are rather actively involved in these dramas. This is not to deny that they also face challenges and severe constraints, such as those posed by their role and working conditions.

By exploring cleaners' dramas of dignity, I will point out how we, the upperworlders, are directly or indirectly involved. These workers mainly cater to us, the mall shoppers, the office workers and the tourists. Their work is vital to our organizations, the economy and society as a whole. Yet workers like the Potsdamer Platz cleaners receive too little recognition from the upperworld.

Research may perpetuate the problem. Work, workers and organizations at the low end of the employment spectrum have received little attention.[27] If invisibility does, indeed, correlate with being less valued, then the lack of research attention to cleaners and other low-end workers represents a significant problem.[28] The line of research that looks at "dirty work" can also be problematic.[29] When Ludwig at CleanUp HR hears about the so-called "dirty work" literature, he

---

[25] Hughes (1958/2012: 48; emphasis in original).

[26] As Collins (2000: 18) has also argued, "[o]ccupational prestige can only be realistically understood if we can survey situations of occupational encounters and judge the actual situational stratification which takes place."

[27] *AMJ* Editors (2010), Leana et al. (2012).

[28] As a side note, the often dark history of service work, particularly domestic work, is also frequently overlooked not only in popular claims about the supposed shift from industrial to service economies, but also in dominant social and economic histories. It does not play a role, for example, in E. P. Thompson's prominent *The Making of the English Working Class*. This neglect may arise from the fact that, from Adam Smith to Karl Marx, service work has fallen under "unproductive" or "reproductive" labor. Such work takes place in the domestic realm, employs women and isn't unionized. By the middle of the twentieth century – earlier in Germany – such service work declined when women entered the industrial workforce and demanded more rights, among other reasons.

[29] E.g. Ashforth and Kreiner (1999), Bolton (2005), Kreiner et al. (2006), Ashforth et al. (2007), Paetzold et al. (2008), Baran et al. (2012).

shakes his head with chagrin; it is precisely this labeling that reinforces the stigmatization of occupations like cleaning. It also risks prioritizing theoretical assumption over lived experience, assuming that people, by default, suffer from doing "dirty work" and must develop coping strategies against stigmatization. While the cleaning occupation undoubtedly struggles with stigmatization, we should resist the temptation to reduce every cleaner's work life to this, lest we foreclose the possibility of developing a sense of worth more robust than a mere defense against the "dirty work" stigma.

Bearing in mind the difficulties inherent in questions of representation, authorship and authority,[30] I hope to give voice to those who remain otherwise invisible and "inaudible"[31] to academe and the broader public. This ethnography aims to acknowledge people who reside and work at the bottom – in the corporate underworld. Of course, this does not mean that cleaners, or any other workers for that matter, should be approached in an uncritical manner. There is nothing to romanticize about cleaners, especially how they interact with each other. Discriminatory and racist attitudes are not uncommon among the cleaners. Nonetheless, they deserve a work life with dignity.

A Preview

Chapter 1 sets the scene of the cleaners' work life. It provides a tour of Potsdamer Platz, its history and space. I will start with Potsdamer Platz's upperworld before descending into the underworld to introduce cleaners' presence from below.

Chapter 2 introduces four characters from the corporate underworld, the young German trainee Alex, the Turkish veteran Ali, the Mozambican newcomer Luisa and the East German dropout Marcel. It also provides an overview of the cleaning occupation, its history and status, as well as CleanUp management's human resources approach. The stories of the four cleaners illustrate different paths that lead people into cleaning. In contrast to the negative public perception of cleaning, the chapter shows how their work can also represent to all four cleaners a portal to dignity.

In Chapter 3, the focus turns to the various ways in which cleaners experience and approach dirt. Dirt matters in their everyday work life

---

[30] Clifford and Marcus (1986).   [31] Hochschild (2016: xiv).

not just symbolically, but also in its very materiality. In exploring how working with dirt brings about a whole mix of experiences – frustration and satisfaction, disgust and fascination, freedom and servitude, humiliation and pride – I argue for the need to move beyond the common assumption of dirt as merely a source of shame.

Chapter 4 looks at relationships and interactions among the cleaners. I analyze how cleaners show little interest in defining themselves as a group. Instead, alliances and divisions mark their microcosm. These come about as cleaners produce and enforce markers of difference to establish a status hierarchy among themselves. However, while cleaners seek to differentiate themselves from each other, a sense of negative equivalence, of belonging to a stigmatized group of "anyones," persists and poses a great threat to their sense of worth and the status hierarchy they seek to construct.

In Chapter 5, I discuss what happens to cleaners' dignity as they enter the upperworld and interact with clients and other upperworlders. While cleaners can experience appreciation and derive a sense of exclusivity from their access to the upperworld, more often than not cleaners feel looked down upon or simply ignored. Cleaners deal with the threats to their dignity in the upperworld in different ways, from debunking the upperworld and confronting it to withdrawing back underground.

Chapter 6 develops how surveillance shapes cleaners' everyday work life. It studies how cleaners feel being watched by clients, security guards, CleanUp management and sometimes even coworkers. Such surveillance may amount to an attack on cleaners' sense of worth to the extent that it represents distrust in their work abilities and efforts, and the resulting need to control them. I explore how cleaners counter surveillance by engaging in various tactics, from turning against, off and away from surveillance.

The concluding chapter brings together the main findings of the book to explicate cleaners' dramas of dignity. It discusses whether the presence of invisible service workers in corporate underworlds marks a return of the servant society. The chapter ends with a reflection on the presence of two images – the Statue of Liberty and Harold Lloyd – in Potsdamer Platz's underworld.

1 | The Corporate Micro-city Potsdamer Platz
Cleaners' Presence from Below

On my early morning commute, I cycle through the still sleepy streets of my middle-class, residential neighborhood to the rougher and livelier thoroughfare Potsdamerstraße, which will take me directly to Potsdamer Platz. I bike past social housing where satellite dishes picture children or national flags; I pass Turkish grocers, kebab stands, chain bakeries, casinos, hostels and brothels. The smells of vomit and urine mix with those of freshly baked bread and endlessly turning kebab sticks (see figure 1.1).

The city shows itself differently at dawn. On the usually congested Potsdamerstraße, a few taxis bring home drunken partiers while trucks drop off wares for the coming day. Women in tight pants and high heels swivel their hips under washed-out streetlights and whisper to the occasional passer-by. Paperboys with wrinkled faces deliver the news and uniformed workers rush to their shifts.

Potsdamer Platz cuts a sharp contrast with not just dingy Potsdamerstraße[1] but all its immediate surroundings. Against a dark dawn sky, soaring above the city's predominantly low-rise skyline, the futuristic creations of international starchitects gleam, signaling at a distance that from the center of Berlin rises a luxurious and cosmopolitan micro-city (see figure 1.2).

Privately owned and operated, Potsdamer Platz fits anthropologist Marc Augé's description of a non-place.[2] Little "organic social life" manifests in this corporate complex with its tony hotels, restaurants, shopping malls, cinemas and offices. Catering to tourists, suited professionals and monied residents, Potsdamer Platz represents the ongoing marketization and gentrification of Berlin. It is a designed space, "cleansed" of both undesirable things, like garbage and graffiti,

---

[1] Potsdamerstraße is in fact gentrifying with the opening of galleries, fancy bars and shops.

[2] Augé (1995); in relation to Potsdamer Platz, see Göttlich and Winter (2004: 95), Nowobilska and Zaman (2014: 15).

Figure 1.1 Cycling through Potsdamerstraße at dawn.

Figure 1.2 Potsdamer Platz from afar at dawn.

and the undesirable poor and homeless people common on the city's less-regulated streets.[3]

The destitute aren't the only locals Potsdamer Platz keeps out of sight. Beneath the complex's street-level profile lie the four levels of a

---

[3] See also Bublitz and Spreen (2004: 147).

labyrinthine underworld, an invisible realm that houses the backstage service functions of the complex. It bears little resemblance to the upperworld it serves with its dark, often malodorous and sticky spaces hemmed in by low ceilings, infinite corridors and concrete stairways.

This chapter explores how the spatial segregation of Potsdamer Platz is not an incidental matter of architectural design, but rather a particular social mapping that interrelates with status.[4] Indeed, space is not what social theorist Henri Lefebvre calls a "neutral container" existing in the background of our lives.[5] Instead, he famously argues, "social relations ... project themselves into a space, becoming inscribed there, and in the process producing that space itself."[6] What social relations does the vertical segregation of Potsdamer Platz establish between the upperworld and underworld? How do the architects, investors, politicians and the media market the complex? Do the cleaners even figure into how it is marketed? If so, how? And how do the cleaners and their management relate to and experience Potsdamer Platz?

Potsdamer Platz: "City for the Twenty-First Century"

Residents and visitors alike know Potsdamer Platz thanks to its central location and striking appearance, and also because it markets itself as a territory of symbolic importance – the "heart of the capital."[7] A few blocks away in one direction are the Brandenburg Gate, the Holocaust Memorial and the Reichstag (the German Parliament). In the other direction lie the National Library, the Philharmonie and the Tiergarten, the city's signature public park. Emblematic of Potsdamer Platz's distinctive architecture, the Sony Center's whimsical roof suggests an off-kilter circus tent, and the peak of the Atrium tower glows like a cubic, turquoise flame on a rectangular candle. Designed by a team of internationally celebrated architects, both foreign and domestic,[8] this showy skyline is more typical of North American than

---

[4] See also Zerubavel (1993), Massey (2007), Richer (2015), Wasserman and Frenkel (2015).

[5] Lefebvre (1974/1991); see also Massey (2005).   [6] Lefebvre (1991: 129).

[7] https://potsdamerplatz.de/wp-content/uploads/2015/08/ForumTower_Teaser_150914_RZ_EN_Lowres.pdf (accessed February 2018).

[8] The German architecture office Hilmer & Sattler and Albrecht was responsible for the overall urban planning. The architects of the different buildings include Renzo Piano, Christoph Kohlbecker, Hans Kollhoff, Richard Rogers, Arata Isozaki and José Rafael Monea.

Figure 1.3 The facade of the Kollhoff Tower.

European cities (see figures 1.3 and 1.4).[9] The diversity of architects
represented here produces a variegated cityscape, however planned,

[9] The official description of the Kollhoff Tower, named for its architect, Hans
Kollhoff, acknowledges the New World debt: "POTSDAMER PLATZ
1 combines the appeal of an international landmark with all the benefits of
tomorrow's business world. Prof Hans Kollhoff's stunning masterpiece builds a
transatlantic bridge, bringing the unmistakable colour and design of America's
classic skyscrapers to the German capital." (https://potsdamerplatz.de/en/offices-
at-potsdamer-platz/potsdamer-platz-1/architecture/ accessed February 2018).

Figure 1.4 The atrium inside the Kollhoff Tower.

suggesting that the modern Potsdamer Platz has served as a testbed for architectural innovation.

When the postwar reconstruction of Potsdamer Platz began in the 1990s, the barren parcel became the biggest construction site in

Europe.[10] Heavily bombed, almost all of its buildings reduced to ashes during World War II, Potsdamer Platz in the postwar period was an abandoned, fallow, a non-place with no-go zones, all under military observation in the east. In the western part, a platform let tourists glimpse the German Democratic Republic, or GDR. The Wall ran straight through the present-day Potsdamer Platz complex.

With the fall of the Wall in 1989, these sixty-eight hectares became a prime real-estate development opportunity, controversially sold to two large-scale investors: Daimler AG and Sony.[11] The political goal was to make Potsdamer Platz an icon of the newly reunified German capital.[12] Although markedly different from each other, all buildings were designed as "an impressive testimony to the transition to the twenty-first century."[13]

Concerted design effort went into attracting consumers, tourists, wealthy residents and businesses alike. Potsdamer Platz is therefore emblematic of the city's desire to market Berlin as both an attractive site for corporations[14] and a culturally creative metropolis.[15] Indeed, the tenants of this privately owned, thus non-public complex include Sony, Deutsche Bahn, Daimler Financial Services, PricewaterhouseCoopers and Freshfields. The coworking brand WeWork set up offices here.[16] Potsdamer Platz is designed to become a hotspot of creative workers, in addition to the professionals already ensconced there. The glassy towers, typical of corporate architecture found in urban centers worldwide,[17] have been the exception rather than the rule for Berlin with its comparatively light and aging industrial footprint.[18]

---

[10] The complex was erected by construction workers, especially from Eastern Europe, working under difficult conditions and at times for "dumping wages" (*Der Tagesspiegel*, 1997).

[11] Today Potsdamer Platz is largely owned by a Canadian real estate investor (*Der Tagesspiegel*, 2016).

[12] Nowobilska and Zaman (2014).

[13] https://potsdamerplatz.de/wp-content/uploads/2015/08/ForumTower_Teaser_150914_RZ_EN_Lowres.pdf (accessed February 2018).

[14] Fischer and Makropoulos (2004).   [15] Colomb (2011).

[16] Berliner Zeitung (2017).   [17] Resch and Steinert (2004), Watson (2006).

[18] Since the World War II, little industry and few major businesses established themselves in Berlin, which is a comparatively poor state by comparison with others in Germany. Famously, the city's unofficial motto is "poor but sexy." In 2016, Berlin had the highest percentage of people on state unemployment benefits compared to other German states (www.destatis.de/DE/PresseService/

Figure 1.5 The Arkaden shopping mall.

But for the 100,000 visitors that Potsdamer Platz can welcome on a daily basis, the area offers more than just office space:[19] 370 rented or owned apartments, many of them second homes; luxury hotels like the Ritz-Carlton; specialty stores and the Arkaden shopping mall (see figure 1.5); restaurants, snack bars and cafés; a casino, a theater, large cinema chains and a dance club.

Various cultural and urban events make their home here, most famously the annual Berlin International Film Festival, or Berlinale. Against the backdrop of swarming fans, press photographers and TV cameras, film stars walk the red carpet on Marlene-Dietrich-Platz – a name chosen to evoke the racy glamor of the Weimar Republic. Indeed, the modern reinvention of the complex harks back to the 1920s, when Potsdamer Platz was a hub of department stores, entertainment centers and hotels, like the "Haus Vaterland," catered to the emerging mass consumer and cultural markets,[20] and the ten-story office building "Columbushaus" as well as Europe's first traffic light

Presse/Pressemitteilungen/2017/08/PD17_298_122.html accessed February 2018; https://de.statista.com/statistik/daten/studie/4275/umfrage/anteil-der-hartz-iv-empfaenger-an-der-deutschen-bevoelkerung/ accessed February 2018).
[19] https://potsdamerplatz.de/en/facts-and-figures/ (accessed February 2018).
[20] Adorno and Horkheimer (1944/1997), Kracauer (1963/1995).

set up at Potsdamer Platz which marked the city's ambition to position itself as a world-class metropolis.[21] Nothing of the area's Nazi past remains; the swastika flags that hung from monumental buildings and the Columbushaus offices of the Nazi "T4 Euthanasia Program" – along with those of the anti-Nazi Leninist resistance movement "New Beginning" – bear no marker or memorial.[22]

The selective presentation of history[23] at Potsdamer Platz fits with the image and experience it aims to cultivate. As an icon for Berlin, if not all Germany, Potsdamer Platz is meant to represent the future as the "city for the twenty-first century"[24] where one finds an "incomparable blend of high-class entertainment, shopping, restaurants and culture, harmoniously combined with living and working opportunities."[25] But Potsdamer Platz predominantly caters to those who can afford such "high-class" entertainment, shopping or housing, or who work for one of the marquee corporations anchored here. Furthermore, although people do work and live at Potsdamer Platz, it mostly caters to visitors; it seems more conducive to buying and consuming things than to settling here and living one's daily life.

Potsdamer Platz's proliferation of high-rises exemplifies the increasing verticalization of cities. The geographer Stephen Graham notes how such "vertical growth" is promoted by "city leaders and development agencies keen to engineer glitzy, futuristic skylines as a means of building urban 'brands' that compete with other so-called world or global cities for investment, tourism, media exposure and the 'creative class' (mobile and well-educated high-tech elites)."[26] This goes hand in hand with the privatization of urban space and the displacement of lower-income groups from city centers – another trend Potsdamer Platz epitomizes.

In her study of New York, sociologist Sharon Zukin shows how consumer-oriented contemporary cities become increasingly exclusive (both economically and culturally), homogeneous and therefore "soulless."[27] Potsdamer Platz, the nonpareil "non-place," exemplifies the

---

[21] Makropoulos (2004: 161), Resch and Steinert (2004: 123).
[22] For a more detailed discussion of the history of Potsdamer Platz, see Fischer and Makropoulos (2004), Nowobilska and Zaman (2014).
[23] Sandler (2003), Tölle (2010), Colomb (2011).
[24] http://potsdamerplatz.de/en/history/new-beginnings/ (accessed May 2015).
[25] https://potsdamerplatz.de/en/history/ (accessed February 2018).
[26] Graham (2016: 176).   [27] Zukin (2010).

phenomenon. Not only is the complex "formed in relation to certain ends,"[28] namely for consumption purposes of an exclusive group of people, and its history selectively staged and marketed, but its transnational design provides little in terms of identity. Diverse as they may be in terms of style, the buildings could stand in any other cosmopolitan city.

As a corporate micro-city, Potsdamer Platz illustrates a pair of correlated trends: the rise of service workers who maintain these corporate cities and serve their exclusive clientele,[29] and efforts to make these workers and their labor invisible. Priced out of the city center, these employees live far from Potsdamer Platz, and once at work, they're kept belowground and out of sight. Below the skyscrapers one finds basements deep under the ground with service centers, garbage collection points and workers.[30] If the overseers, investors, politicians and architects behind Potsdamer Platz are right that the complex represents the future of city life, we must examine the implications of this segregation. Who works here, and what does it mean for them and for the society that they are kept out of sight underground?

CleanUp's "Prestige Object" Potsdamer Platz

A range of service employees reports to Potsdamer Platz for work: security guards, garbagemen, cloakroom and counter attendants, waiters and kitchen staff, tailors, salespeople and cleaners. Some service workers spend their workday aboveground, but the corporate underworld is where most goods are delivered, stored and sorted, where garbage is collected and clothes laundered and tailored. Among the service workers, cleaners occupy a unique position as they enter virtually every space in the upperworld – offices, apartments, shops, public areas – even when the world belowground remains the nodal point for their work.

Service workers, including cleaners, are not directly employed by the corporate tenants of Potsdamer Platz but by a service-work provider; in the cleaners' case, CleanUp. Every few years, Potsdamer Platz management invites bids for various service contracts. Given its size and

---

[28] Augé (1995: 94).   [29] Sassen (2001).   [30] Graham (2016).

prominence, Potsdamer Platz is a major client in the portfolio of service companies, a "prestige object" for CleanUp.[31]

The CleanUp management promotes the image of prestige and exclusivity Potsdamer Platz seeks to project, thus boosting its own image. It comes as little surprise, then, that the director of CleanUp Berlin decides to place me at the complex. In addition to showing off CleanUp's success and size within the industry, Potsdamer Platz lets the account manager, Tom, advertise the good relationship the company has cultivated with its prestigious client. CleanUp's operations here run relatively smoothly – an outcome that is by no means guaranteed. Account managers often struggle with demanding clients who ask for services beyond the contract or condescend to them. Tom, however, speaks about Potsdamer Platz positively and with some pride.

Potsdamer Platz is our prestige object. We do everything, from glass and building to external cleaning here. It is the company's biggest object in Berlin, a complex that, of course, everyone in Berlin knows. And if you look around, very high-profile people live here, and you find exclusive shops and the offices of distinguished doctors.

Though Tom may be motivated to toe the company line and paint an unduly positive picture, his enthusiasm for the company seems genuine. At twenty-five, Tom is young for his position and he looks it. He wears a fixed dental brace, and his tanned round face, marked by a scar on the right cheek, bears the flush of youth. Some cleaners attribute the scar to his weekend job as a bouncer, others to a flight of stairs after too many drinks (the police once confiscated his driver's license on suspicion of drunk driving). What gives Tom a more managerial appearance is his attire: pink dress shirts (some with a CleanUp logo affixed to the left collar) tucked into designer jeans, brown leather shoes and a heavy silver watch on his right hand.

Tom's office is located in a futuristic office building, designed by Richard Rogers, whose proportions and complicated whimsical exterior suggest an update of Rogers' Pompidou Centre in Paris. From his office, Tom has an unobstructed view of the Berlin skyline, prefaced by the manicured meadow of Tilla-Durieux Park with its steep artificial rise. Apart from a martial arts trophy and a photo of his infant son, the office is dominated by CleanUp corporate messaging: the logo, slogans

---

[31] In cleaning industry terminology, object refers to the site to be cleaned.

and stickers, images of smiling cleaners on his desktop screensaver and CleanUp mugs decorated with generic figures of cleaners, a prominently displayed corporate mission statement.

Tom has ambitions to enlarge the scope of his responsibilities by acquiring more buildings within Potsdamer Platz. A map of the complex denominates its different areas, from A to D, and buildings, for example A1, A2, B1, B2 and so on. Tom refers to the map in our first conversation.

Look how large Potsdamer Platz is – it's over 550,000 square meters. During the day more than 150,000 people are here, at night less, of course, around 90,000. All these buildings are part of it and we are responsible for A1 and B1. Recently CleanUp was able to acquire more objects, like the Canadian Embassy and parts of the Sony Center.

Potsdamer Platz's high volume of visitors has direct implications for cleaning, as does its architecture. "There are areas and surfaces to clean, and then all this glass. It is a very work-intensive place. Here we need to constantly keep up the cleaning," Tom says.

Potsdamer Platz boosts both CleanUp's image and Tom's standing within the company. On my first day at Potsdamer Platz, Tom and his colleague Norbert bring me to the Kollhoff Tower. We take "the fastest elevator in Europe" to the twenty-fourth floor, where we tour the Panoramapunkt roof terrace (see figures 1.6 and 1.7). In each direction, Tom points out objects in the CleanUp portfolio. For Tom, Potsdamer Platz represents the achievement of having risen from cleaner in its murky underworld to manager overlooking a prestigious empire of objects.

While Tom's office places him within the Potsdamer Platz upperworld and spatially manifests his elevation within the CleanUp hierarchy,[32] the foremen's office is located on the second floor of a building where the cleaners' room is underground. It functions more as a space for storing materials and processing paperwork than one representing the company to the public or the marketplace. The foremen's office is small and plain, with barely more than a rudimentary desk and chair for furniture. Detergents and cleaning materials are stacked here; the foremen hand these out by request only, otherwise, supplies have a tendency to go missing.

---

[32] See also Strati (1999).

Figure 1.6 View over Berlin from the Kollhoff Tower's Panoramapunkt.

In contrast to Tom, who reports to work around 9 a.m., the foremen start working when the cleaners' shift begins at 5 a.m. In limbo between the upperworld and underworld, they spend much of their days en route from building to building, floor to floor. For the cleaners, the foremen are the main contacts. They are responsible for day-to-day management: instructing cleaners, checking their work, providing them with the necessary equipment, allocating shifts and, when necessary, stepping in and cleaning. The foremen dress more like the cleaners than like Tom or

Figure 1.7 View over Berlin from the Kollhoff Tower's Panoramapunkt.

the typical Potsdamer Platz professional, and report to work in CleanUp-branded work pants, thermal jacket and baseball cap.

Tom approaches Potsdamer Platz through the lens of business opportunity and career advancement. For the foremen, however, the prestige object with its slick and soaring towers represents a recipe for overwork: a large, difficult "territory" to oversee combined with high client expectations: working at Potsdamer Platz means dealing with "fussy, rich" upperworlders. On top of that, the size of the building complex and the number of objects make the foremen's work intense. "I walk eight kilometers back and forth under Potsdamer Platz every day," Norbert says. Stress and sleep deprivation are engraved under his eyes and on his forehead. It does not surprise the cleaners when for almost half a year Norbert takes sick leave due to overwork and high blood pressure. With the added work during his absence, Anton seems to get paler and thinner almost by the day, to the point that cleaners worry that he, too, might be at risk of overwork. As for Anton, he betrays a note of pride in "surviving" the stressful work life of a foreman.

Potsdamer Platz from Below: The Cleaners

Modern city-dwellers are no strangers to environments like Potsdamer Platz; such corporate micro-cities can be found around the world, from

Hamburg's HafenCity and New York's Hudson Yards to the Archipelago 21 development in Seoul. These upperworlds are frequently visited, read about and photographed. And apart from the occasional stack of cleaning materials, Tom and the foremen report to typical corporate offices. By contrast, the corporate underworld of Potsdamer Platz, designed to be hidden, is almost immune to representation.

The cleaners spend a great deal of time underground. They are responsible for cleaning certain basement areas, and both the garbage collection point and their basement utility room are underground. Potsdamer Platz regulations state that after 9 a.m. cleaners may not walk with their cleaning cart through aboveground spaces, such as the shopping mall, and instead must use the basement level to move around. Thus, cleaners are spatially and temporally made invisible to the upperworld.[33]

The Labyrinth

The Potsdamer Platz underworld is an enormous territory of four subterranean levels, each almost the size of the aboveground footprint. Natural light does not reach the minus area; daylight, street life, hustle and bustle are the hallmarks of another world. One day an older cleaner named Bertha asks about the weather. "I haven't seen the sun today yet," she says. "I've been in the basement all day."

Some parts of this corporate underworld are so cold I need a jacket and scarf in order to work – to the amusement of my fellow cleaners. "A bit brisk?" teases Christian. "Well, once you have warmed up, you can come and clean." When I can't tolerate the cold at the garbage collection point, Matthias nicknames me "Madame." Other underground areas are hot and stuffy. While passing through certain tunnels, one notices the airlessness that cleaners regularly contend with. Conditions change according to both location and season. "You have to see how it is in the summer, really sticky," my cleaning colleague Michaela says. "You don't get enough air. And in the winter it is really cold."

The smells under Potsdamer Platz verge on the unendurable. The upperworld's waste converges here to be concentrated in grease

---

[33] See also Star and Strauss (1999), Crain et al. (2016), Hatton (2017).

Figure 1.8 Corridor to the garbage collection point.

collectors, garbage cans and waste pickup points. Cleaners transport garbage cans through gray empty corridors and service elevators to the minus-four level where the garbage collection point is located (see figure 1.8). These paths are imprinted with the smell of waste. In the large hall of the garbage collection point, the waste is separated into containers to be driven off by trucks.

Compared to the shiny malls, spacious lobbies and open-plan offices above, the Potsdamer Platz underworld is stifling and poorly maintained. The ceilings are low, the gray or off-white walls often marked with bumps or streaks where carts have collided with them. (Steering a fully loaded garbage cart in a straight line through a corridor is harder than it looks.)

Even for cleaners with years of experience navigating this underworld, it is a baffling maze that connects a dizzying array of enclosed spaces.

"So, now we get to the labyrinth," says Lena, a trainee, as we make our way through the supply passages to mop their concrete floors. "You see one door, then another – endless doors."

An unserious but telling rumor has it that some underground spaces here have yet to be discovered. The labyrinth is a seemingly endless succession of interlaced paths, unexpected corners, dead-ends of iron doors, gates and walls. Staircases, elevators and tunnels extend throughout the underworld and up into the backstage areas of the upperworld. It's not difficult to get lost – or trapped.

"Everything is so full of nooks and crannies, and for everything you need a key," Benjamin says. "And if you close the wrong door behind you, you can't get back."

I suspect this represents some hyperbole until experience proves otherwise. Sent to clean a toilet one day, I take a wrong exit on my way back. All the doors are identical, and I have only a vague memory of my route. When a door closes behind me, I find myself in a small room in complete darkness. I can't go back the way I came because the door has locked behind me, and from here only one door opens: to the emergency staircase (see figure 1.9). I go up and down the stairs, checking for open doors – to no avail. Eventually, I pick up a cell phone signal and call a colleague to come liberate me.

Remembering one's keys and maintaining a good mental map amount to survival skills for cleaners in the sparsely populated territory under Potsdamer Platz, though elsewhere in the minus area workers confront congestion. The service elevators to the garbage collection point are in heavy demand, and waiting for an empty one, I notice that faces are becoming familiar. Nearly every morning Michaela and I come across a flirtatious handyman. "The sun comes up, the ladies again!" he greets us, sometimes producing chocolates or candies from his uniform's pockets. At the garbage collection point, a man who claims to be the longest-serving worker at Potsdamer Platz will detain his coworkers to chat.

In the minus area, the upperworld shops store wares and receive deliveries. The tailors work in the minus-two level below the shopping mall, sitting between clothing piles in carrels whose high metal grids bring prison bars to mind. Matthias and Benjamin often go out of their way in hopes of encountering a particularly beautiful and curvaceous Brazilian tailor there. Benjamin calls her "Conchita."[34] Matthias blames Benjamin for these detours. "Because of her we have to do these hallways twice a week and hang out in the minus area, even though it should only be once a month!" For all their utility and

---

[34] This Spanish name has acquired some extra currency in the German-speaking world since the 2014 victory of Austrian drag artist Conchita Wurst at the Eurovision Song Contest.

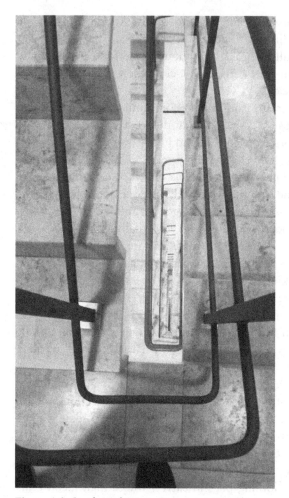

Figure 1.9 Stuck in the emergency staircase.

discomfort, the minus areas nevertheless serve another purpose as a social stage and cruising area.

The Basement Room

Dark, stuffy, windowless and low-ceilinged, the cleaners' basement room sits at the minus-two level under the mall. It functions as a storage space, laundry facility, break room and changing area. The workers call it variously A2 (its official designation on the Potsdamer Platz map), the maintenance room, the storeroom or the cleaning room. Thanks to its versatility, the room is usually full.

On the left side in the front, cleaning carts are lined up next to the ride-on floor scrubbers, which cleaners drive to mop large areas (see figure 1.10). The carts carry all the equipment needed for a shift: feather dusters, brushes, mops, hooked poles for gathering hard-to-reach trash and so on. These supplies hang from the wall above the cleaning carts, and detergent bottles are stacked on shelves beside the entrance. Near the front of the room, cleaners empty dirty water into a drain in the floor, then retrieve fresh water from the adjacent tap (see figure 1.11).

Toward the back of the basement room, a narrow door opens to a tiny unlit room where bundled electrical cables are plugged into wall sockets. For cleaners, the little chamber meets two needs. First, it serves to hide equipment from other cleaners – a secret Marcel shared with me while stashing a new broom. Heavily used brooms smell and work less well; and newer equipment is in short enough supply that cleaners wind up competing over it.

Cleaners also use the room to change clothes before and after a shift. Since the room lacks a place to put a change of clothes, one has to hold them under one's arm. And because the cables prevent the door from properly closing, one has to simultaneously guard the door while changing and holding clothes. Some male cleaners skip the balancing act and just change in front of their coworkers.

In the basement room, cleaners have lockers where they can secure their belongings (see figure 1.12). Above the two rows of lockers, cleaners stow their buckets and other equipment. A cabinet next to the lockers holds the keys cleaners will need for their shifts, and a bulletin board updates those shifts on a weekly basis. Bigger and higher lockers are more desirable and usually taken. On my first day, the only locker left is a small one in the lower row. Michaela advises me to bring a padlock. That same day, I leave my jacket on a chair in the room during the shift. It's gone when I return.

Despite the presence of a little fridge, the cleaners prefer to keep food in their lockers. One day Alexey, a cleaner from Kazakhstan, opens the fridge only to immediately slam it shut again. He warns me not to use it: I'll find God-knows-what bacteria and rotten food there. On top of the fridge, an old water kettle splutters throughout the 9 a.m. break to produce coffee, taken black (given the fridge, milk seems ill-advised).

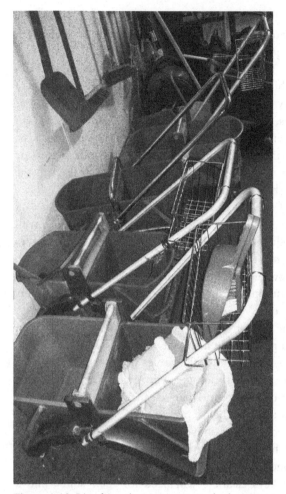

Figure 1.10 Lined up cleaning carts in the basement room.

Cleaners bring their own cups and cutlery and use hot water from the kettle to rinse them. The tap next to the fridge has only cold water, and dishwashing liquid is usually in short supply, as is hand soap, particularly when Michaela – or "Mutti" (mommy), as some of the younger men call her – is on leave. Among this group, only she demonstrates any care about keeping the basement room clean.

Industrial washing machines and a dryer as well as buckets and mops crowd the back of the room. The machines run most of the time, although at

Figure 1.11 Drain in the basement room.

Figure 1.12 Lockers in the basement room.

least one of them is usually out of order. But even with only a few working, the washing machines make a racket, and the dryers emit such thick hot air that it can feel, Matthias complains, like 80°C (see figure 1.13).

The focal point of the room is a large white table in the back, graced by a stool with peeling paint and four chairs in varying states of

Figure 1.13 Washing machines, the dryer and mops in the basement room.

disrepair salvaged from garbage collection points around Potsdamer Platz. "Where else are we going to sit?" Michaela asks.

Since there are far fewer chairs than cleaners, seating privileges at 9 a.m. are a source of tension. Some cleaners try to reserve seating. "This chair is reserved for Mrs. Naller!" Maria scrawls on a note she leaves on a backrest. On the back of another chair, a note reads "Director." Such property claims are routinely ignored – chairs, like lockers, are first-come, first-served.

Overall, the basement room provides little to accommodate a comfortable social gathering or leisurely time-out from work. Packed with equipment, shelves, lockers and at times people, the room is often noisy and hot from the machines and redolent of filth from the mops, saturated with dirt, from the drain and the nearby garbage room. Unless the basement room's heavy metal door is closed and the garbage containers are emptied, the stench is overwhelming. No wonder the cleaners don't regard this space as theirs, or, apart from Michaela, do more to help maintain it.

Yet the basement room remains central in cleaners' work life as a space to meet, talk and relax. At times, A2 feels like a chaotic stage play, with comedies and dramas unfolding around me. Especially before the start of the morning shift at 5 a.m., during the half-hour break at 9 a.m. and at the end of the shift around 1:30 p.m., cleaners gather in this room. They come and go, change clothes, collect gear, change the water of their buckets, take a coffee break, take a bite from a homemade sandwich, look at the schedule of shifts or fill out a timesheet. At times the room is so crowded that people in chairs must constantly move them back and forth to make way for the others.

Cleaners tell me, and a foreman confirms, that the basement room became the main place for cleaners to sit and socialize after they were banned from the second-floor social room. During one 9 a.m. break, a client had passed through and subsequently complained to management that the cleaners were too loud and made off-color jokes. The only other space designated to the cleaners is the second-floor smoking room. But not every cleaner is a smoker, has the necessary access card or wants to be seen by the foremen, whose office is across the hall – especially if they take a long break. Indeed, there is always a good reason for cleaners to find themselves in the basement room, even during the shift, since all the equipment is there.

Cleaners in Potsdamer Platz's Upperworld

While Potsdamer Platz's underworld constitutes a nodal point, cleaners and other workers are also present aboveground. In the very early morning, when the upperworlders are yet to populate the streets, the cleaners are still allowed to freely move around Potsdamer Platz. Junction points where the paths of workers frequently cross, or where people smoke and take breaks, become busy sites. Over time I begin to associate familiar faces with the various corners of Potsdamer Platz where I encounter them.

At one of the shopping mall's side exits, groups of cleaners often gather to take last puffs before a shift. One important coordinate in the cleaners' mental map is the Potsdamer Platz McDonald's. It's open twenty-four hours, the coffee is affordable and the staff is prone to handing out freebies to cleaners, especially the younger ones. I buy my coffee from the same young woman most mornings, exchanging smiles and a few words. A few months in, she starts giving me the occasional free cookie, or a large coffee for the price of a small.

The first time Marcel takes me on his cleaning tour through Potsdamer Platz's outdoor area, two scaffolders, one old and one young, approach us.

"Who's the hottie?" the older one asks Marcel.

"My intern," Marcel responds with a broad grin.

Their eyes travel back and forth between Marcel and me.

"I am not searching for a girlfriend," Marcel clarifies.

"Are you gay?" the old man demands.

"Nah, I'm no ass pirate – that's this guy," Marcel says, indicating the younger scaffolder.

"No! I am not!" the younger scaffolder snickers.

Some days later I pass the scaffolders again.

"So alone here," the old man observes. "Where's the boss?"

At first, I am taken aback by such patronizing flirtations but after a while I get more used to such exchanges, which aim to open the floor for provocative jokes (also refer to Chapter 4). I also realize that women are not the only recipients of unwanted sexual attention amongst Potsdamer Platz service workers. The checkout girl Clare at McDonald's is so infatuated with Marcel that he routinely gets free burgers. "I ordered four hamburgers and she just added two Big Macs and everything was free," Marcel says. "It's too much." Everybody at CleanUp knows about this and therefore goes to McDonald's when Clare is on duty. Marcel is perplexed when random CleanUp workers start coming up to him to say, "Yo man, thanks!" They all benefit from Clare's infatuation, as Clare herself tells other cleaners, "You can thank Marcel for this."

Free food and drinks at McDonald's are not an exception. These are part of an economy of gifts and flirtations amongst Potsdamer Platz service workers. The receptionist Jasmin brings Paul his morning coffee unbidden, the gay bar owner treats Marcel to cocktails in the afternoon and Lena is always excited to pass by the ice cream parlor: "I get free ice cream if he is there – but shhh!"

Cleaners are part of the service workers' scene at Potsdamer Platz – a scene with its expressions and rules of interaction. Loitering in front of McDonald's, especially in summer when the basement room is too hot, cleaners and other workers amiably hassle each other. A handyman banters in passing, "I'd like to work for your company!" – implying that we're always on break. Having heard this expression many times before, Marcel has a ready answer: "But they don't take everyone!"

Apart from the area around McDonald's and those designated for smoking, most of the upperworld consists of workspaces for the cleaners. Yet cleaning a lobby, stairwell and roof terrace also provides the opportunity to pause and observe the hustle and bustle – to "consume" life, if only in a voyeuristic sense. Cleaners keep tabs on a man and woman who regularly meet at a certain hidden spot to kiss and hold hands. A clandestine love affair? One cleaner reports catching a glimpse of the man's wedding ring.

Male cleaners also occupy themselves ogling women. "In the summer, it's like a punishment," Marcel groans. When a group of young women walks past, Marcel stops, stares and aims a feckless pelvic thrust in their direction. "Oh, to fuck her now!" The miniskirts, bare legs and low-cut necklines provide much fodder for unfulfilled desire and sexist commentary.

Streets at the edge of the complex, along with inner courtyards of Potsdamer Platz apartment buildings, provide cleaners with opportunities to leave work behind. However, this can only be done on the sly – no easy task given the prominence of glass and surveillance cameras in this high-density development.

Though rooted in the corporate underworld, the cleaners' scene at Potsdamer Platz extends aboveground. When cleaners look at the architecture of Potsdamer Platz, they see more than a layout of buildings to be cleaned. It is also a place for observing the world and hanging out: a stage for social encounters.

Cleaners' Presence from Below

The Potsdamer Platz upperworld is shiny and spacious; the underworld dark, labyrinthine, cramped and malodorous. These worlds have distinct populations: shoppers, tourists, white-collar workers and wealthy residents above; cleaners, garbagemen, tailors and other service workers below. A one-way membrane separates the worlds: cleaners have access to the upperworld, mostly for the purpose of cleaning it, but the people from above cannot descend. Indeed, while the upperworld predominantly shapes the image of Potsdamer Platz as the "new" Berlin, the "city for the twenty-first century," the corporate underworld usually remains hidden from representation, buried not only spatially, but also discursively.

Potsdamer Platz is designed to minimize the cleaners' visibility. Rules set by the Potsdamer Platz management reinforce this erasure, for example the rule that cleaners may not move freely aboveground after 9 a.m. and, if they do, they must present themselves in ways that do not disturb the upperworld: they may not speak too loudly or joke in ways that might cause offense.

Potsdamer Platz is designed to reinforce status hierarchies that help separate the upperworld and underworld.[35] It's apparent within CleanUp how closely status hierarchy and building design interrelate: Tom's office sits in one of the "prestigious" buildings, the foremen's office is stacked with cleaning material, the cleaners occupy a rank dungeon on minus-two. Among the cleaners too, hierarchy emerges: according to who has what access card and key, who knows the labyrinth well enough to navigate it, who has a bigger locker in the upper row, who gets to sit in a salvaged chair.

The Potsdamer Platz cleaners constitute what we might call a "presence from below." I borrow the idea from the historiographical notion of "history from below," namely that ordinary people's experience and perspective matter to history at least as much as the role of "great men."[36] Cleaners are well aware of their status as "minus men," as the cleaner Matthias puts it – and minus women, he does not think to add. Yet this doesn't mean that these workers experience Potsdamer Platz only according to how this space and their position in it has been designed.[37]

Cleaners consciously struggle with the problem of invisibility, yet they do not perceive themselves merely as invisible figures.[38] They are part of a scene above- and belowground in which workers interact with and recognize each other. For them, the underworld can be more than just a dark, dingy and cramped "space"; it can also be a "place"[39] of social encounters, of taking breaks and withdrawing from the gaze of managers and clients alike. Similarly, cleaners find and make room for themselves in the upperworld. In Lefebvre's words, the same spaces that are "abstract" – designed toward homogeneity and coherence – may, at least temporarily, become "differential" – enacted and lived in alternative, heterogeneous ways.[40] Despite its meticulously designed

---

[35] See also Richer (2015), Wasserman and Frenkel (2015).
[36] For a discussion of such an understanding of history, see Lynd (2014).
[37] See also de Certeau (1988).   [38] See also Crain et al. (2016).
[39] The literature on space makes a distinction between space and place. Whereas space is non-specific, place denotes an organized space (Cresswell, 2004), to which actors attach certain meanings and a sense of stability (Tuan, 1977).
[40] Lefebvre (1991: 408); see also de Certeau (1988).

nature, the space of Potsdamer Platz is therefore more "essentially contested" than it may appear.[41]

Apart from the basement room, cleaners are not tied to particular spaces; nor can they claim them. Cleaners are constantly on the move, making both work and leisure space dynamic.[42] Here we do not find the divide between what have been termed "dominant" spaces of work, such as the office, the desk or counter and "liminal" spaces, such as toilets and stairwells.[43] Similarly, cleaners' spaces of work cannot easily be separated into "front-stage" spaces – where cleaners are visible to clients and managers – and more private "back-stage" spaces.[44] For cleaners, the liminal and back-stage spaces can be work-spaces as much as those typically considered as the dominant and front-stage ones.

Descending into the corporate underworld of Potsdamer Platz from the upperworld where I otherwise belong, I discover – "with all [my] senses, with the total body," as Lefebvre puts it[45] – a different facet of the complex. It no longer seems a non-place, a transitory, overde-signed, artificial and homogeneous corporate environment devoid of meaningful interpersonal relations. The more time I spend in the workers' world, the more the crafted prestige, slick architecture and tailored suits aboveground fade into the background, eclipsed by the increasingly familiar faces of my underworld colleagues.

As my perceptions change, so does the way I am perceived. I become more visible to workers than I had been as an upperworlder. My borrowed identity follows me even as I cycle home on now-congested Potsdamerstraße after my shift. Still wearing the CleanUp uniform, I elicit a response from cashiers at the Turkish supermarket where I stop to shop. "Already off work? Any weekend plans? Partying

---

[41] I borrow the notion of "essentially contested" from Gallie (1956), who developed it in relation to concepts whose meaning and therefore application is a matter of dispute. Rather than applying this notion to the theoretical realm, I use it to capture how the ways spaces are used and lived can diverge from how they were conceived. I thank Chris Grey for this idea.

[42] Best and Hindmarsh (2019).

[43] Following Shortt (2015: 634), dominant spaces, compared to liminal ones, are "those spaces that are defined by mainstream uses, that characteristically have clear boundaries and where the practices within them are interwoven with social expectation, routines and norms."

[44] Goffman (1959/1990); see also Dale and Burrell (2008), Courpasson et al. (2017).

[45] Lefebvre (1991: 391).

tonight?" I sigh that I'm too tired, up since four. One well-built middle-aged man in jeans and a black sweater points at my company shirt: "You work for CleanUp!" he says with a grin. "Me too!"

By the same token, I become intermittently invisible in the upper-world. Colleagues from the university and an old school acquaintance fail to recognize me in my uniform; they pass me by without a word, a reminder that cleaners are overlooked, ignored, made socially invisible. Cleaners in the upperworld remain minus men and women.

2 | Characters from the Corporate Underworld

Alex, Ali, Luisa and Marcel

At the outset of my fieldwork, Ludwig, the HR manager, asks whether I'll present myself as a bona fide cleaner and conceal my university background. I could pass as a Greek student in flight from my country's economic crisis, for instance, someone who needs to clean for extra income. The prospect is unthinkable: not only would the subterfuge be unethical, but I couldn't sustain it. Indeed, people in the field can tell right away that I am not one of them. At one workshop, an account manager points out how cleaners would not express themselves the way I do; they are simpler people. And Potsdamer Platz cleaners aren't surprised when I tell them I come from the university, though they think I am a student, not a professor. To them, I don't look and act like a typical cleaner. But who is a typical cleaner?

During my fieldwork, I don't encounter "the cleaner" – a particular profile and path leading into cleaning. Instead, the Potsdamer Platz underworld seems like a catch basin for a variety of people. Cleaners range in terms of age, training and experience. They include men and women, East and West Germans, locals and foreigners. People from different walks of life and with different motives become cleaners; but in one way or another, all of them share origins in the social underworld. Criminal records, addiction, immigration or unemployment, among other things, often mark their lives. What does it mean for people from society's margins to work as cleaners? How do they respond to the stigma of their work? What role does CleanUp play in how cleaners see themselves?

Alex, Ali, Luisa and Marcel are CleanUp employees whose stories illustrate four paths into cleaning, and four ways of looking at the job. All derive from it a sense of worth, one that surmounts the negative public perception of cleaning work. To put their stories into context, this account begins with an overview of the stigma associated with cleaning as an occupation, followed by a look at CleanUp and its approach to human resource management.

The Occupation of Cleaning: An Overview

As the social anthropologist Mary Douglas has observed, cleanliness and ideas of purification define most religions and societies.[1] Cleaning as paid work represents a more recent phenomenon, dating back to the late nineteenth and early twentieth centuries.[2] Leaving aside black-market labor, two strands developed within the occupation[3] that still matter today: cleaning as domestic service work that mostly young, working-class women perform in bourgeois households; and the cleaning of building exteriors – the facades and glass surfaces of factories, department stores, administrative and public institutions – mostly done by working-class men. In the course of German industrialization, cleaning was recognized as a trade; occupational associations were formed and training was offered. This professionalization of cleaning peaked during the Nazi regime when cleaners were obliged to become members of a trade association. After the war, efforts to organize the cleaning occupation ended, and untrained women increasingly worked in interior and so-called maintenance cleaning.

Starting in the 1970s, West German public institutions, municipalities and private organizations began to outsource cleaning services to cut costs. This led to the rise of cleaning companies, especially in maintenance cleaning. Another major change came in 2004 when cleaning became an unprotected trade, making it no longer necessary to be a master craftsman in order to incorporate a cleaning company. This loosening of the market led to an explosion in the number of cleaning firms.[4] Today the German cleaning market, the biggest in Europe, is saturated.[5] It is characterized by price competition, the increasing diversification of services and market polarization: a few large facility management companies – CleanUp among them –

---

[1] Douglas (2002).   [2] Latzke (2015).

[3] Following Hughes (1984/2009: 287), "[a]n occupation consists in part in the implied or explicit *license* that some people claim and are given to carry out certain activities rather different from those of other people and to do so in exchange for money, goods, or services." For a recent overview of the literature on occupations, see Anteby et al. (2016).

[4] From 2003 to 2010, that number quintupled (ArbeitGestalten, 2017).

[5] In 2019, the aggregated turnover of the German cleaning market amounted to roughly €20 billion (www.die-gebaeudedienstleister.de/die-branche/daten-und-fakten/ accessed March 2017).

generate almost half the turnover.[6] Overall, around 850,000 people in Germany work for cleaning companies.[7]

The majority of cleaners overall are women,[8] though in exterior building cleaning the majority are male.[9] More than one-quarter of cleaners are foreigners, most of them concentrated in former West Germany;[10] even more have a migration background. Compared to other occupations, this share is high. In terms of age, cleaners are typically between forty-five and fifty-four years old.[11] More than half the workforce has not finished any training in cleaning or another occupation.[12]

To become a journeyman requires three years of occupational training; to qualify as a master craftsman requires still more, plus there are facility management studies at a polytechnic.[13] Occupational training is mostly done by young men who go on to work in exterior building cleaning, where qualification requirements are more stringent than in interior work. Yet the number of trainees has dropped steadily over the past decade, and companies like CleanUp have begun to introduce other training programs for their largely unskilled workforce. Overall, this shows that while the typical cleaner is female, German (perhaps with a migrant background), older and unskilled, differences persist between the former West and East Germanies as well as between interior and exterior cleaning.

These differences include working conditions. Here the picture is mixed. To prevent wage dumping, an hourly minimum wage existed throughout the sector before it became statutory across Germany in 2015.[14] That means wages aren't lower than in other low-paid

---

[6] Latzke (2015), ArbeitGestalten (2017).

[7] ArbeitGestalten (2017), https://de.statista.com/themen/1673/gebaeudereinigung/ (accessed March 2018). Of course, this does not include cleaners who do not work for a cleaning company or those paid "under the table," for example, in private households.

[8] ArbeitGestalten (2017).　　　[9] Bosch et al. (2011).

[10] According to Bosch et al. (2011), there are 31.3 percent foreign cleaners in West Germany, and 8.7 percent foreign cleaners in East Germany.

[11] ArbeitGestalten (2017).　　　[12] ArbeitGestalten (2017).

[13] www.die-gebaeudedienstleister.de/beruf-und-karriere/ausbildung/ (accessed March 2018).

[14] Bosch et al. (2012) in Latzke (2015). Cleaners who do not fall under the minimum wage are those selling their labor through online platforms as self-employed workers.

occupations – unless the company illegally pays them less.[15] There are some caveats to this positive picture. Cleaners endure increasing time pressure as they have to clean more in less time.[16] In addition, as is the case at Potsdamer Platz, working hours can be extreme. In order to keep cleaners out of sight, shifts mostly take place either in the evening or early in the morning.[17] As a result, the work is often fragmented, and cleaners are only employed for a few hours per day.[18]

Compared with workers in other occupations, a large number of cleaners work only marginally: They work too few hours to support themselves and are dependent on government aid and/or second jobs.[19] This is particularly the case for women. Whereas the majority of women work in so-called minijobs for only four hours per day or have part-time positions, male cleaners usually hold full-time positions.[20] Short-term contracts are common. The estimated number is up to 50 percent in the five biggest cleaning companies.[21] While cleaning represents a job opportunity to many people who otherwise have little chance to find employment, such as untrained, foreign or older women, it often fails to provide a secure, long-term income or a pension.[22]

Cleaning is a stigmatized occupation.[23] One explanation for this is that cleaners deal with filth and carry out tasks widely regarded as "physically disgusting."[24] Cleaning is a prototypical example of what the literature terms dirty work.[25] However, in the case of cleaning, the stigmatization goes beyond the work's association with filth. It also has to do with the lack of skills and knowledge associated with the work. It is not perceived as a "real" occupation but as something anyone could do if they had to. As sociologist Andrew Sayer puts it, "[o]ther things being equal, a skilled job brings more respect and is a stronger source of dignity than one which anyone can do."[26]

---

[15] Millmann (2014).   [16] Latzke (2015), ArbeitGestalten (2017).
[17] ArbeitGestalten (2017).   [18] ArbeitGestalten (2017).
[19] ArbeitGestalten (2017).   [20] Bosch et al. (2011).
[21] ArbeitGestalten (2017).
[22] ArbeitGestalten (2017); see also Schürmann (2013).
[23] Millmann (2014), Latzke (2015), ArbeitGestalten (2017).
[24] Hughes (1984/2009: 343).
[25] E.g. Ashforth and Kreiner (1999), Bolton (2005), Kreiner et al. (2006), Ashforth et al. (2007).
[26] Sayer (2007: 577).

Related to this is the association of cleaning with "low pay, poor conditions of employment, domestic unemployment and an 'outsider' status"[27] – attributions that further stigmatize the occupation and the cleaners. In the case of cleaning, the stigmatization derives from the work itself and the groups of people perceived to do it:[28] unskilled, older, female workers with migrant or foreign backgrounds, for example, Eastern Europeans, Turks and nowadays refugees from Arab countries or Africa. These people are regarded as outsiders who would otherwise be unemployed as they have little opportunity to find another job. Cleaning is seen as a job that people wouldn't take unless they had to. The cleaners are "tainted, discounted"[29] persons because of both their work and their social, cultural and economic backgrounds.

Stigmatization is a problem for the cleaning industry, of course, making it difficult for companies to charge higher prices or attract more qualified employees. There have been various attempts to foster a more positive image. The trade union IG BAU introduced "Building Cleaning Day" to raise awareness regarding cleaning as an occupation and increase the visibility of cleaners.[30] *Der Bundesinnungsverband des Gebäudereiniger-Handwerks*, the federal cleaning trade association, has sponsored image campaigns that advertise career opportunities and position cleaning as a "service trade" akin to those practiced by skilled German industrial craftsmen. Finally, the big cleaning companies, including CleanUp, have launched their own initiatives to counter stigmatization.

CleanUp: Appreciation through Professionalization

CleanUp is a large facility services company with operations throughout Europe. It is a family-owned business that started as a cleaning service provider and in recent decades has expanded its range of services. CleanUp today employs more than 30,000 people, the most in the industry. Influenced by the founder's political beliefs, the company takes a social market approach, which seeks to reconcile market

[27] McCabe and Hamilton (2015: 107).
[28] Ashcraft (2013); on the relation of gender, sexuality and dirty work, see also Tracy and Scott (2006), Slutskaya et al. (2016).
[29] Goffman (1963/1990).
[30] Only about 7 percent of cleaners are members of the trade union (Staab, 2014).

logic with social needs. CleanUp strives to emphasize professionalism[31] in its marketing in an attempt to correct what Ludwig calls "the distorted perception of cleaning services." He asserts that "the tasks of cleaners are at least as demanding as those of the industrial crafts- man, if not more so."

CleanUp aims to "engage staff, strengthen the self-confidence of each individual, inspire everyone to the reach common goals and instill pride in the company and its achievements" (Ludwig cited in a CleanUp leaflet). Only if the employees conduct the work with pride and confidence, goes CleanUp's rationale, will they see themselves as professionals, thus letting clients approach them as such. In its official value statements, CleanUp stresses that it stands for appreciation of its employees, for commitment to the work and for being "colorful." The statements, accompanied by illustrations of a diverse workforce, adorn company walls, cups and leaflets.

CleanUp seeks to present itself as an attractive workplace for people of different ages, sexes and educational, cultural, religious and occupational backgrounds, a company that provides its employ- ees with recognition and opportunities for career advancement. The company promotes cleaning work as what I term an *Auffangbecken*, or catch basin, a notion that captures the heterogeneity of the workforce CleanUp recruits. *Auffangbecken* comprises the verb *auffangen*, with connotations of catching someone or something before it falls. Indeed, for many workers, cleaning constitutes a way out of unemployment and poverty. Ludwig stresses that espe- cially for low-skilled workers, "working at CleanUp is actually an opportunity."

However, *fangen* also means to capture or ensnare, which reflects the difficulty people have in moving out of cleaning work once they get into it. In part to counter this difficulty, CleanUp HR makes an effort to promote internally – the route Tom took to become Potsdamer Platz's account manager.

As part of its efforts to boost employee self-confidence, CleanUp has also launched a training and development program for its employees, particularly those who moved laterally into cleaning. Workers at

---

[31] Here professionalism does not refer so much to expert knowledge (see Abbott, 1998) but rather to a particular behavioral conduct (Grey, 1998; Fournier, 1999).

different levels of the hierarchy go through different types of training. Cleaners receive online lessons at the CleanUp regional headquarters. The foremen and account managers are trained in workshops lasting as long as three days that take place in hotels across Germany. Whereas the cleaners' training program primarily deals with technical aspects, the foremen and account managers' workshops also focus on how to deal professionally with clients[32] and how to manage staff. The whole training program is built on the idea of train-the-trainer, whereby superiors become trainers of subordinates. After each training session, employees receive an official certificate.

All this is supposed to provide cleaners with a sense of appreciation and the confidence that they are skilled professional service workers. As I overheard Ludwig explain to one participant in an account manager workshop:

Do you know why we started the training with the employees in the lower ranks? Because we wanted to empower them. It's all about appreciation. The managers further up were actually jealous. But we deliberately did it this way.

Note that CleanUp's strategy differs from those of the federal trade association and trade union, which maintain that cleaning is a craft that requires government-certified occupational training. Instead, CleanUp promotes its own program to train its diverse and largely unskilled workforce. Its approach is therefore in line with the trend toward eliminating occupational entry criteria and giving work to a diverse set of people – such as Alex, Ali, Luisa and Marcel, to whom we now turn.

On Being Cleaners: Alex, Ali, Luisa and Marcel

At Potsdamer Platz, different paths have led people to become cleaners. There are skilled cleaners, like Alex, who enter the occupation through the traditional route of occupational training. These cleaners often have backgrounds where parents, other family members, neighbors or friends work as cleaners too. There are also trained, skilled workers, like Ali, who have worked in other occupations, serving as everything from heating technicians and factory workers to Bundeswehr soldiers

---

[32] This shows the "disciplinary logic" (Fournier, 1999) involved in discourses and practices of professionalism (see also Grey, 1998).

and hairdressers. They "slid into" cleaning, as Benjamin, the former heating installer puts it, because they couldn't find work in their original occupation and/or because cleaning offered them better opportunities. Then there are the unskilled workers. They often enter cleaning as newcomers to Germany, as in the case of Luisa, or as "dropouts" from German society, like Marcel. While what it means to be a cleaner differs among them, they share origins in the social underworld – something that significantly shapes their sense of worth as cleaners.

All in the Family of a Trainee: Alex

Alex is a second-year trainee in his late teens. He hadn't planned to follow in the footsteps of his parents, who have been cleaners for more than twenty years. Alex grew up and still lives with his parents in Wedding, a working-class neighborhood in West Berlin, home to a large number of Turkish, Arab and African immigrants. When I first saw Alex, he was assigned to work alongside Ali, the veteran Turkish cleaner, and I thought he, too, was an immigrant. Despite his German background, he uses immigrant youth slang. His skin is tanned from regular visits to the solarium, and his brown hair is cut stylishly short. Alex clearly cares about cultivating a cool appearance, typical for immigrant teenagers. He wears the gray cleaning pants in a baggy, hip-hop style along with fashionable sneakers, a tight-fitting hoodie and a backward Nike cap. From years of soccer, Alex's body is slim and athletic. When he was younger, he dreamed of playing professionally, but knee problems prevented him from pursuing it.

Alex tried to prove himself in the criminal underworld. He grew up in Wedding, where gang violence was part of everyday life, and manifestly enjoys telling me stories of his neighborhood, how tough it is and how tough it made him. He shows me a picture on his phone of a Palestinian girl he dated for three years. Her brother, who opposed the match, first beat her up, then Alex. Alex knows the young Turkish men who beat a teenager to death in a random street fight in Berlin's city center – an incident that received nationwide attention. They live on his street. "That's really sick," he tells me. "You see them every day and say 'Hello' and then this. They have to go to jail, but it isn't going to help. The German state is much too lax. People get away with everything."

Alex, too, has been in trouble with the law. With a friend who worked at a local post office, he "raked" thirteen credit cards and the bank correspondence with the PINs and spent more than €5,000 on clothing and electronics. He got caught in a random search during which the police found all the credit cards with him. Alex was imprisoned but only for a week and "this wasn't a problem." An apprenticeship in a Best Western hotel promised a new start. Yet after three weeks, Alex decided it wasn't for him, as did the manager who trained him. Alex still remembers her telling him, "You are very well built and look good in a suit, but the hotel business is not for you." The idea of directly serving customers does not appeal to Alex with his rebellious nature and sense of pride. That's when he signed up for occupational training at CleanUp.

Alex's parents are his role models. In his view, they achieved success within the cleaning world. They are skillful, committed and hardworking. "My father really works his butt off. When my parents do stairs, they look great!" Alex says his father is anxious to start work even on the weekend. "He doesn't finish his coffee" and runs out to work. Like his father, Alex describes himself as obsessed with cleanliness and order. "I am the most extreme one in the family. If the curtain is not folded right, that's a no-go." Alex proudly speaks of all the objects for which his parents, his father in particular, are independently responsible. "My father always works alone, he is his own boss." Although Alex looks up to his father, he is also acutely aware that this over-commitment comes with a price: "My father is always called for everything and can never switch off. Physically he has destroyed himself. He's already had three heart attacks. This work can make you really sick. But he can't do without it."

Among the three children, only Alex followed in their parents' footsteps. His sister is an assistant to a veterinarian and his brother works in construction, occupations Alex regards as worse than cleaning. His brother lays pipes and has to "constantly be in the shit down there – that's really disgusting." Alex takes much pride in cleaning. Cleaning is not just an occupation for him but a vocation:[33] work he does for reasons beyond making money. Contrary to its stereotypical feminine image, he equates cleaning with a physical,

---

[33] Weber (1946/1991).

masculine job. For him, office work is emasculating, irreconcilable with his self-understanding:

You know, I am a real man. I used to play soccer. I have to move. I can't just stand around. I am sure office workers get €3,000, lots of money per month, but I would not like to do that. In this weather, they always sit inside. Fair enough, they have air-conditioning, but even so, the whole day sitting at the desk and paperwork – that's not for me.

When referring to office jobs, Alex has in mind his brother-in-law, who, after finishing his bachelor's degree, took a job in the office of a large car company. Alex once visited him there and did not like what he saw. Pretending to be sitting at a desk and typing away, Alex shakes his head. "My sister wears the pants around the house."

Alex is attracted to cleaning for economic reasons too. In his view, finishing the occupational training will enable him to quickly make money and become independent. Although still living at home, Alex does not receive any additional support from his parents: "I get nothing from my parents, what do you think?" Alex exclaims, possibly insulted at the suggestion. Once he graduates with a journeyman's certificate from CleanUp's training program, Alex can count on a higher salary, especially if assigned to glass cleaning. Another option is going back to school. Alex only has a *Hauptschulabschluss*, the lowest German secondary-school qualification. The journeyman's certificate would allow him to enroll in advanced high school. For now, finishing the occupational training to make "money, money, money" is most important to him.

Despite its advantages, however, life as an apprentice challenges Alex's dignity, his sense of pride and his independence. He struggles with the notion that *Lehrjahre sind keine Herrenjahre*: An apprentice is not his own master. On the contrary, "as an apprentice, one is a slave. You feel constantly observed and get only small shitty jobs. You always have to wait for Anton [the foreman] to tell you what to do."

Consequently, Alex frequently rebels. One summer, the foreman Anton assigned him to clean toilets at a Saturday night rave. It was unfair, Alex felt, that of all the trainees Anton picked him. He found cleaning toilets and serving "junkies" degrading. So Alex left the site without informing the other cleaners or Anton. As a result, Alex received a warning letter. (Three warnings are grounds for dismissal from the training program.) He cares more about the preservation of his dignity than the letter. "Nobody can tell me anything, not even Anton! I am a human being and I am going to speak out. I can't do that slave work, I'm not a prostitute."

Working with Alex is not always easy. It makes him furious, he confessed to me, when cleaners, especially untrained ones and those who know the shift less well than he does, treat him in a high-handed way. At times Alex questions Ali's instructions, especially when he thinks that Ali offers more services than necessary to satisfy the client. Again, Alex does not want to be a "slave" – not to Ali, and certainly not to a rich, arrogant client – some "snotty brat." Alex considers most of the female trainees and cleaners "lazy" and "incapable." In his eyes, they lack the required physical – masculine – strength to be good cleaners. He never bypassed an opportunity to tease me about mistakes I made. If I forgot to wipe a table in the café, for the rest of the shift Alex would call me Nicole, the name of the overweight trainee he most looked down on.

His rebelliousness and temper, however, do not undermine his status at CleanUp. Male cleaners especially look up to him for his attitude. "I like Alex, he reminds me of myself when I was younger," Marcel says. "He won't be bossed around." Others, who regard him as a good worker, meticulous and diligent, are forgiving and even try to educate him. Ali, who treats Alex like a younger brother, told him to control his temper and "hold back." Management, aware of his abilities, likewise overlooks his rebelliousness. Anton considers him "our best trainee."

Aware of his standing, Alex isn't worried about finishing the trainee program. Rather, for him the bigger question is whether he will be able to work all his life as a cleaner. On this matter he is of two minds. His injured knees constantly hurt him, and then he starts considering whether he is better off doing military service: "If you are good [there], you can retire early and make a lot of money. But he questions his options: "What job is good for the knees?" and "Whatever! I cannot sit around. Anyways I don't want to get old – nobody in my family gets." And if he makes it as glass cleaner later on, he will also "earn a lot." Indeed, Alex believes that compared to other occupations, jobs are secure in cleaning. "Cleaning will always be needed. You can always make money here." So, Alex stays, the advantages of cleaning, at least for the time being, overcoming its disadvantages.

Overall, Alex regards cleaning as a vocation for a craftsman – an understanding in line with the federal trade association rather than CleanUp with its emphasis on professional service work. He entered cleaning from the social underworld, with a criminal record, an unfinished apprenticeship and the lowest German school qualification. Given his family background, Alex derives a sense of worth from being a cleaner; it allows him to display his physical strength, devotion to cleanliness and hard work, and also promises a secure income and independence. At the same time, however, Alex finds his dignity under threat: serving clients, following orders and working with untrained, especially female, workers who run counter to what being a cleaner means to him. In addition, the prospect of physical decline weighs on him – an anxiety he shares with Ali.

From Industrial Worker to Cleaning Veteran: Ali

Ali is in his late thirties. Although born and raised in Berlin, he still holds Turkish citizenship. His family came to Berlin with the wave of *Gastarbeiter* – so-called guest workers – from Turkey, Italy, Spain and other Southern European countries in the 1970s. His father used to work in a factory as a machine fitter, while his mother stayed at home, taking care of Ali and his other three siblings. His family lived in the poor eastern parts of Kreuzberg, a densely populated immigrant area of Berlin. Though gentrified, the district still has its mosque, its Turkish supermarkets and cafés where men drink strong black tea and play "tavla," backgammon. His family belongs to a wider network of cousins, uncles and aunts, and the local Turkish community. In the late nineties, his father lost his job and never worked again. Today, his aged parents have partially resettled back to their village in Turkey, living part of the year there.

Like his father, Ali started off as an industrial worker. He finished his training as a "machine operator," but never found a job in the profession. Rather than staying unemployed, Ali moved into cleaning, like his brother. Among Ali's siblings, only his two sisters pursued higher education; they became teachers. Though he enjoyed school and particularly math lessons, he speaks German with Turkish slang, typical for people with a migration background in Kreuzberg, Neukölln or Wedding. For example, Ali addresses Alex always as "brother." At some point during his youth, he became too preoccupied with "other things" to continue with his education (when I asked him what these are, he declines to tell me). Thus one path to social mobility, limited to begin with for Germany's immigrant working class, was foreclosed.

Like Alex, Ali got into cleaning to "quickly make money." Rather than living off state benefits, as his father did for years, Ali is proud to have an independent income. Bringing money home is a serious issue for Ali. He has three children with his East German wife. Note that even thirty years after reunification, the cultural affiliation and economic differentiation between the East and West persists. Ali's wife works six hours per day in a well-paid job at the front desk of a BMW garage. They bought property outside of Berlin, and now try to save money to build a house without having to pay off a large loan. At times, Ali struggles with the "German" way of being, and with ignorance about the Turkish culture, food and music that he extolls throughout his shift.

"People don't know how great Turkey is," Ali tells Alex and me. "They just see the Turks here. Come, Alex, let's go to Turkey. I'm inviting you and if you can't pay the airfare, I'll pick it up," – an offer he later on extends to me.

Ali now lives a life that is distant and different from that of his family and community. After a shift one day, he invites me to a chicken restaurant in Kreuzberg. Here he seems in his element, speaking Turkish to the waiters, greeting others on the street and telling me stories about his upbringing and his concerns with his current life. That Ali opens up to me has something to do with how he regards me as a Greek person. "So, you know what I mean," he says. "Greeks would also never do this. We are not like the Germans." Ali sounds variations on this theme when describing German behaviors that upset him, for example when German cleaners fail to reciprocate after he invites them to socialize.

At work, Ali proudly speaks about his children and their achievements. Freshly shaven and dressed up, he went to his oldest daughter's middle school certificate celebration. She was second-best in her class and, in contrast to both her parents, got into the academic high school from which she can progress to university. Ali does not want his older daughter to be a cleaner. "One has to work too hard," he says. "And

I see how shitty they are to the trainees. No, I would not want that."
He hopes that his children, rather than following his path, will ascend
through the ranks of German society through education.

  This does not mean that Ali struggles with being a cleaner. He
regards himself as a skilled worker as he completed a vocational
training. "Jana, I might be, or maybe you think that I am dumb,
because I am a cleaner, but I am actually smart. I've finished training
as a machine operator." He is proud of his income. "I am not ashamed
to be a cleaner," he says. "For me, it's important to make good
money." And cleaning can "even be fun."

Ali is not just any cleaner at Potsdamer Platz, but practically an
institution. He has been working there for fourteen years (only the
garbage man working in the minus-four area has been there
longer – something Ali doesn't wish to be reminded of). He is well
connected among management and workers alike. Ali is even
prouder of his relationship with the bosses of the client company
at Potsdamer Platz. He greets them personally, they invite him to
lunch and he attends the annual Christmas party at the café
he cleans.

These personal connections, which date from his first job there
cleaning the head office of Daimler, Potsdamer Platz's first owner,
clearly matter to Ali; they account for the fact that Ali is still there.
Management of the operating company insists that no matter which
cleaning company is contracted, Ali's job is secure. Indeed, four
cleaning companies have cycled through during Ali's tenure, but Ali
remains. Alex notes how Ali "is loved by the people here," and
CleanUp benefits from this, as Ali has helped the company acquire
objects, such as the café in the Kollhoff building he cleans.

That Ali managed to cultivate this degree of independence at
Potsdamer Platz has a lot to do with how conscientiously he fulfills
his duties. Among the cleaners and the CleanUp management, Ali is
regarded as hard-working, honest and reliable. Ali works in what he
calls "his own building," where neither Tom nor the foremen come by
to check his work. Instead they sometimes join Ali in the morning for
tea or coffee, which the café manager allows him to make before
starting his shift.

Some time ago, CleanUp promoted Ali to foreman, but he quickly
gave it up. He found the perpetual phone calls, demands from all sides
(account manager, client, cleaners) and the responsibility for the

workers much more stressful than his current position. It allows him to be his "own boss."

Yet there is a price to his career that Ali feels the more his short dark hair turns gray, the more his waist expands. The years of hard labor are taking their toll: there's a worrisome pain near the belly, and back pain, impediments to carrying buckets of water downstairs, to bending. Picking up Ali's slack, Alex complains with his usual refrain: "I am not a slave!" This makes Ali more upset; he treats Alex like a brother. He worries about his future: "This is backbreaking work. The other day I was in the head office, and some guy came in, an older man, and I asked myself, how much longer I can keep going?"

His cousins and sisters are asking the same thing. "Brother," they say, "we want you to be well." They suggest he get a taxi license, join their taxi business and drive for them. While Ali admires their business success – "they make enough money to spend lots of time in Turkey" – he is not ready to leave cleaning. Working for the cousins does not seem as attractive as his independent position at Potsdamer Platz. And he doesn't relish the prospect of sitting all day in a cab and gaining still more weight; Ali still enjoys working physically. "As long as I still feel good, then cleaning is actually not a bad job." At the moment, he's making good money. What will happen in the future, how much pension he will receive, is not worth thinking about now. "You don't know how old you'll get and if you'll even get a pension. Anyway I don't trust the German pension. Suddenly we have to work until 67, some even say until 70!"

Ali's story reflects trends in the growing service sector and in the decline of industrial work (though in Germany a comparatively high number of employees still work in the industrial sector).[34] On the one hand, Ali derives a sense of worth from being trained as an industrial worker, especially when confronting the stigma of being a cleaner. On the other, cleaning has let Ali become an independent and income-generating family man who averted the indignities of his father's unemployment and dependence on the state. Like Alex, he emerged from the social underworld, in Ali's case from unemployment and an immigration background, and this helps explain the worth he attaches

---

[34] www.destatis.de/DE/ZahlenFakten/Indikatoren/LangeReihen/Arbeitsmarkt/lrerw013.html (accessed March 2018).

to being a cleaner, a working man. Ali takes pride in being, for most practical purposes, his own boss at Potsdamer Platz. He owes his special standing to his service ethic toward the client – a devotion CleanUp management would like to instill in all the cleaners. But as the wear and tear of the job accumulates, Ali's future in cleaning becomes uncertain.

Cleaning as a Starting Point for the Newcomer: Luisa

When thirty-seven-year-old Luisa arrived from Mozambique two years ago, the German job center, responsible for the unemployed and refugees, placed her with CleanUp. Luisa came to Berlin not as a refugee but as the wife of a blue-collar employee of a manufacturing firm here. The transition to German life has been a struggle for Luisa. In her native Mozambique, Luisa styled the hair of local celebrities; now it is only her own hair that she styles, with little braids tied at the back of her head, straight extensions or curls. Her German language skills are still basic. She cannot form full sentences, mixes up "he" and "she" and often responds to others with a friendly but quizzical facial expression. Her pronunciation can be comical, for instance when she says, as she often does, "scheeiiiiisse" (shit). Language amounts to a barrier between Luisa and her colleagues.

Perhaps for this reason, Luisa spends much of her time at the Universal Church of the Kingdom of God, a Christian church founded by a Brazilian businessman. Clad in a suit, a birthday present from her husband, she visits the church every Sunday and, if possible, during the week. Here she finds a community of other Portuguese-speakers as well as a place to sing, dance and share grievances and hopes.

Luisa relies heavily on this support network amid difficulties at work. She has never worked in cleaning before. On the contrary, in Mozambique, she herself had a cleaner for her large apartment. Her family is solidly middle-class. One brother works for the parliament, another just finished his law degree – something that the family wants to celebrate with a big party, for which Luisa saves money to send home. For Luisa, as for many immigrants and refugees, entering German society means moving down the social ladder.

But the income she and her husband generate here is far higher than what they would earn in Mozambique. In addition to regularly sending money, clothing and electronics (mobile phones, an electric kettle, a plasma TV) home, she and her husband save up for an annual trip home, where they are building a house. Luisa showed me pictures, praising its size and beauty. It's certainly a step up from their run-down apartment, which I saw on two occasions when she invited me over after we shared a shift cleaning the shopping mall. Like Alex, she lives in Wedding.

At Potsdamer Platz, Luisa works from 5 to 9 a.m., six days per week. She has a minijob, an employment classification the government introduced to help the unemployed find work. "Minijobbers" can earn no more than €450 per month. In addition to her CleanUp position, Luisa also cleans in the afternoon, in a hotel or private home. Without her husband's income, Luisa's financial situation would be extremely precarious.

Luisa's status among her fellow cleaners is low. They frequently express frustration because she easily misunderstands things and does things wrong. Ali complains that she uses the wrong "chemistry," or cleaning liquid, or does not clean all the surfaces. She's somebody "you can forget about," Hans says. Thorsten calls her "stupid." She's an object of scorn, an example of how not to clean. "Everybody has their own technique," Matthias says of putting a mop head on a stick. "Only Luisa bends down to pick it up." Cleaners are often impatient and irritated with her. When Luisa uses the wrong word to ask for the CleanUp scheduling sheet, Bertha sharply corrects her: "You mean sign in, not subscribe!" Such reproaches make Luisa even more hesitant to speak.

But Luisa, too, is capable of issuing a correction. During the shopping mall shift, she will wipe railings Bertha has just cleaned and show black dust on her cloth. "Must perfect be, perfect!" These corrections don't win her any friends. She can also be pushy, even aggressive. One day, showing me what to clean, she prods me in the ribs. When I reciprocate the gesture, she harrumphs. Over time, we learn to communicate with one another, and I become one of her few allies at Potsdamer Platz.

What does it mean for Luisa to work as a cleaner? On the one hand, she often describes the work as "scheiiiiiiiiiss Arbeit" – "shit work." On the other, Luisa carries herself with pride. "Work not difficult for me," she says, and claims that both Anton and Tom recognize her abilities. "Boss not looking. He knows, I good." Anton does indeed appreciate her. "Luisa may not understand German," the foreman

says, "but she does her work." Furthermore, having an income independent of her husband's allows her to pay for extras, like new
hairstyles, and to send money home. "Money sent parents Western
Union," Luisa often proudly announces to me.

But Luisa regards her life here as far from settled. She wishes to have
a child, hopes to secure visas to bring more of her family over, and
aspires to find a better-paid and less strenuous job. Instead of
remaining, like her husband, in a subordinate position, she wants to
open a café or shop one day where she can sell African goods and be
her own boss. To fulfill these goals she knows she must first learn the
language and get a driver's license. This is "difficult, with work," and
her minijob has prevented her from attending language courses. For
now, her life revolves around waking up at dawn, cleaning, going to
church and finding her way into Potsdamer Platz's underworld.

Luisa's story reflects those of most maintenance cleaners who are
unskilled, foreign and female, and receive low and insecure incomes
with which they can barely support themselves. For them, cleaning
constitutes one of the few options for entering the German job market,
be it because they have been housewives so far,[35] because their foreign
qualifications are not officially recognized here, because their language
skills are limited, or, most likely, some combination of these factors.

For Luisa, cleaning stands for both moving down the social ladder –
compared to her Mozambican life – as well as climbing it in Germany.
Like her more integrated colleagues, Luisa finds herself in the underworld of German society. For her, cleaning offers the opportunity to
escape from the societal margins and become at least somewhat more
independent from both her husband and the state. Luisa is proud to
earn an income that allows her to send money and gifts back to
Mozambique – something that enhances her status within her community. Whereas Luisa regards cleaning more as a job than a vocation,
she also seems devoted to her work. Given her lack of formal qualifications or special connections to clients, the recognition from within
CleanUp seems the more important to her – perhaps especially because
of her poor standing among the cleaners. Luisa hopes to fulfill her
aspirations to become her own boss, yet the more time that passes
without any improvement in her German skills, the more she fears that
cleaning might turn out to be an endpoint.

[35] See Latzke (2015).

A Dropout Cleans Up His Act: Marcel

Such is the case for Marcel, who entered cleaning as a dropout from German society. Marcel is slightly terrifying. His hand is covered with a black tattoo of a gun. On the back of his neck, two pointy silver studs are notched into his skin. He shaves his black hair on the sides, and leaves it longer, gelled and combed to one side on the top. Endless smoking has darkened his teeth. He looks unhealthily thin; after-work beer-swilling and weekend pot-smoking and pill-popping are a regular part of his life and have been through most of his thirty-eight years. Years ago, his mother put him into rehab along with, in his words, "junkies injecting drugs under their fingernails." He left with the doctor's prediction of a "98 percent chance of relapse" and the warning that he would not reach forty. He does not "give a fuck about this."

Nowadays, however, Marcel has things better under control. His time at rehab and the "bullshit psychotherapy" he underwent there are the source of amusing stories to share with coworkers, like the time his therapist told him to imagine his parents as animals. "What kind of animals would they be?" Among the cleaners, there are running jokes about Marcel's background. Ali suggests he's not actually East German but Romanian: "His mother got him from an orphanage where he played with shit." Another banters, "Marcel is a prison child. His father was named Walter" – the name of the very manly acting female protagonist in the German TV series *Hinter Gittern – Der Frauenknast* (Behind Bars – The Women's Prison).

These jibes reflect a dark reality. After his parents' divorce, Marcel grew up with his two brothers, their mother and her changing partners. The father was imprisoned for assaulting a woman and her husband when the latter found the two of them in bed. Marcel recounts how police pictures showed blood all over the couple's flat. Behind bars, the father got together with the prison madam; he died shortly after his release. Marcel's mother, who struggled to make ends meet waitressing, has been divorced three times. She always chooses "pricks," says Marcel, who fought with them all. He moved out when he was fifteen and became the self-described black sheep of the family.

Despite growing addiction problems, however, Marcel managed to graduate from middle school. He worked as a chef and later as a geriatric nurse. Despite a promotion to sous chef, the kitchen job bored him. Working in a nursing home was too difficult. Puréed food forcibly "shoveled into people" and bedridden elderly "lying in their own shit" are among the scenes he describes with disgust. Three years ago, his brother found him a position at CleanUp, where he worked at the time.

"People think cleaning is the pits," Marcel reflects. "But I actually make good money here." Marcel makes around €1,500 per month, depending on his hours. "And nursing – that was much worse, really disgusting." Significantly, his mother is finally proud of him for having the job. "Everybody thought that nothing would become of me," he says. "For years I did nothing but drugs. Everyone's glad things worked out this way."

Marcel lives in a small apartment in Bernau, just outside of Berlin in the former East Germany, although cleaners joke that he probably just sleeps on a bench – "the third one on the market square." Marcel prefers being alone to dating. "Can't be bothered to have a missus, rather go to Poland for a fuck once a week." He spends his free time with friends in Bernau, and except for work barely enters Berlin, much less the rest of the country.

In Bernau, the extreme right is active, and Marcel and his friends share their views. They listen to right-wing musicians and play war-simulating paintball in uniform (he invited me to join them, but I declined after seeing the bruises it left on his arms). He delights in a photo of a baby with a fake Hitler mustache. His buddies scorn him for friending "a nigger" on Facebook and he cancels the request.

The racism and militarism go hand in hand with nostalgia for a lost past: life in the GDR, with its "Free German Youth" organizations and "real values." Marcel even valorizes his grandfather's service in an SS death squad in Stalingrad. "My granny has a picture of him in uniform with a skull," he says. "I really want to have this." He nevertheless gets along with immigrants and foreigners at work, regularly spending his break with Ali whom he lightly calls "our token Turk." He chitchats amiably with the older African cleaner Viola in the storage room.

Life has made him what he calls an "optimist as a pessimist." He does not expect much, as it is easy to "fuck things up" and be disappointed by others. At times, however, he also sees how things can turn out better than expected. Marcel speaks of himself as a misanthrope, one who hates children especially. He casually describes picking up teeth and mopping up blood after a suicide at Potsdamer Platz, or removing a bunch of headless pigeons from the gutter. Yet he speaks and carries himself in such an ironic manner – for example when he makes a muscle and declares, "I am king of the Platz!" – that it's hard to know whether these stories, along with the right-wing tendencies and the rest of his darkness, are not, at least to some degree, part of an act.

Indeed, for a misanthrope, Marcel is quite solicitous of the young homeless man who walks around Potsdamer Platz during the day – he often gives him cigarettes or food. He's popular among the CleanUp staff, respected for his hard work and meticulousness. Cleaners will tease him on this score: Ali's standard joke is to point out an isolated cigarette butt and scold Marcel that the "Platz looks like shit."

Marcel is capable of self-parody as well. Assigning me some streets to clean, he says, "Don't let me hear any complaints!"

"No, that won't happen," I say, playing along. "I give my best."

"Well, sometimes that's not enough," he replies.

"But I give a hundred and twenty percent!"

"That," Marcel says, mock-patronizing, "is what I like to hear."

Tom admires Marcel. "I take my hat off to him for all the things he achieves here," he says, noting that Marcel will clean up just about anything (human excrement, dead animals) without batting an eye. He'll work overtime and pay no attention to how others – the upper-world people – perceive him. All that matters is to do a good job.

Some time ago, Tom promoted Marcel to foreman. Marcel gave it up after a while, slapping down the keys on Tom's desk. He didn't like the paperwork, or having to manage others, or fielding calls after work. "It really made me want to throw up," Marcel recalls. He's happier now. "I have my freedom, my territory" – the large outside area he's responsible for. Marcel feels comfortable in his position as a cleaner and has no desire to be promoted, regardless of the money. It is "really shit, for €9 to get fucked," he says.[36] Depending on his mood and the state of his relationship with Tom, Marcel talks about applying to other cleaning companies. At one point he asks Anton and Tom for a reference letter. But they are in no mood to write it – Marcel is too conscientious and hard working.

On the whole, Marcel's experience is emblematic of German society's dropouts, the "failed existences," as he puts it, who reach

[36] At the time of the study, the hourly wage was €9.

cleaning work from a world of troubled families, addiction, domestic abuse and other violence, homelessness and prison. The dropouts are typically unskilled in cleaning or any other occupation. For them, working as a cleaner represents an opportunity to get both work and life on track. For Marcel, that means having a regular income and a structured day; it means making his mother proud.

His story parallels Luisa's in certain respects. For her, cleaning also means the chance to enter the German labor market and society. Yet while Luisa does so as a new arrival, Marcel re-enters as a dropout. He exhibits the dignity of someone who doesn't pay attention to the upperworld's stigmatization; what matters to him is being respected and recognized by his peers as a hard-working, fearless and meticulous cleaner. Like Ali, Alex and Luisa, he takes working independently in his "own territory" as a marker of success. But while the others show ambition to rise above their role as cleaners, Marcel is content for this to be the end of the line.

Cleaning Work as a Portal to Dignity

After a workshop for account managers in Leipzig, Ludwig gives me a ride back to Berlin and asks my impressions of the workshop and its participants. It struck me, I tell him, how seriously people take their jobs. This launches a conversation about the meaning of work for people in cleaning. Cleaners, Ludwig says, "cannot afford to be cynical" – a remark that puzzled me until I entered Potsdamer Platz's underworld and got to know cleaners like Ali, Alex, Luisa and Marcel.

Their stories reflect diverse paths into cleaning. They show how cleaning work constitutes a catch basin for a variety of people of different ages; skilled and unskilled; German and foreign; male and female. For some, cleaning is a vocation, an occupation they are devoted to. For others, it's just a job. The different cleaners do not share an occupational or a working-class culture,[37] nor do they embrace the company culture.[38] Cleaners like Alex, Luisa and

---

[37] E.g. in contrast to Paul Willis' (1997) "lads" who share a masculine working-class identity.

[38] This is typically assumed in the dirty-work literature, as McCabe and Hamilton (2015) have also pointed out.

Marcel do not primarily regard themselves as professional service workers in the way CleanUp seeks to construct them. Only Ali displays a service ethic that has allowed him to develop relationships with clients and enjoy special status and a degree of independence at work. But while CleanUp's professionalization efforts may have limited impact on cleaners' understanding of their work and role, all wish to be recognized for their work, to display a strong work ethic and to work independently.

Sociologist Max Weber famously established how the Protestant work ethic constituted the fertile soil for the rise of capitalism.[39] In the Christian tradition, hard work, self-discipline and asceticism are marks of piety and worthiness, while idleness breeds sin and sickness.[40] This fusion of work with moral values continues to shape German society.[41] Employment status is associated with having a healthy attitude more than with job availability. As former German Chancellor Gerhard Schröder put it, "There is no right to sloth in our society." It is the responsibility of the individual to be employable and to find work.[42]

This valorization of work and simultaneous condemnation of unemployment assumes particular importance among the cleaners. Their background frames their choices, their path and the meaning they attach to cleaning, which stands for a way out of an undignified life.[43] In the words of Tanja, a CleanUp account manager, "Some people collect welfare and think, why should I work for so little money? But the cleaners here don't want to sit around at home and be dependent on the state. They are too proud for that."

Put another way, the cleaners, lacking education and wealth, feel they must earn their place in society through physical labor, honest work; it is their path out of the social underworld.[44] This explains Ludwig's observation that cleaners "cannot afford to be cynical."

---

[39] Weber (1930/1976). From a Marxist point of view, Weber failed to take into account the material forces driving capitalism. Others have critiqued the focus on Protestantism, noting that capitalism developed similarly in Catholic regions (see e.g. Grossman, 2006).
[40] Wulf (2016). [41] Lessenich (2013).
[42] See also Garsten and Jacobsson (2004). [43] See also Newman (2000).
[44] See also Lamont (2000).

This current of optimism and even idealism explains the degree to which the cleaners' sense of self at work withstands the occupation's associations with degrading, unskilled, undignified labor.[45] A value system exists in Potsdamer Platz's underworld,[46] whereby being a cleaner, for all the associated stigma, can be a source of satisfaction and pride.

---

[45] See also Léné (2019) on the significance of the employment history for how people evaluate their work.

[46] See also Hall (1992) on the need for moving away from a holistic understanding of a social space and status hierarchy and instead allowing for "multiple and incongruous values and distinctions [to coexist] that cannot be reduced to another" (1992: 264).

3 | From Feces to Flowers

The Sweat, Shame, Disgust, Pride and Fun of Working with Dirt

When I'm scheduled to work with Marcel on his shift outdoors, the others issue ominous warnings.[1] His face in a twist, Alex recalls how Marcel once removed fifteen headless pigeons from a shaft. I find this image so disturbing that I neglect to ask if anyone knows how the fifteen birds became separated from their heads, or if there's any chance Marcel might be prone to embroider his stories.

In any case, Bertha says animal carcasses are the exception on Marcel's rounds; the rule, she reassures me, is mostly cigarette butts and vomit.

Still, Marcel is surprised when I join him, and skeptical.

"Are you going to watch or work?" he asks.

"Work," I answer. Then, hedging my bets: "Or what do you think?"

He sizes me up, finds me worthy. "OK," he says. "Let's get to work."

Out on the street, leaning sidelong and slightly stooped, he expertly brooms cigarette butts into a dustpan, scanning the pavement for errant chewing gum, coffee cups or spent Capri Sun pouches. Try as I may, I can't master his broom technique. I'm struggling to coax a cigarette butt from a concrete crevice when Marcel announces, "There's some shit. You want to get it?"

Fearfully, I look around but don't see or smell the target. Marcel laughs. "I mean shit from the tree," he says, and indicates a handsome litter of birch flowers.

Even apart from the pleasure of lightly tormenting a visiting academic, Marcel appears to enjoy his rounds. For me, they crystallize the degree to which dirt itself plays a central role in the work lives of all the cleaners. Dirt is what they do – they search for, capture and remove it. They confront dirt in every variety, from single-use food packaging

---

[1] Depending on the shift, cleaners are exposed to different amounts and different kinds of dirt (see also Baran et al., 2012; McCabe & Hamilton, 2015).

that will never biodegrade to rotting food and animal carcasses and human excrement and fallen blossoms. What does it mean for all this to be the substance of one's work?

Like the cleaners, this chapter pursues the dirt. We follow their sequence: first we examine the hunt; then the encounter, the physical labor of cleaning and its larger significance in these workers' lives; then how they experience the relentlessness of their fight against dirt as well as the gratification of prevailing over it, however temporarily; and finally the consequences of this tension for the cleaners' dignity.

"The Easter Egg": Dirt Detectives

Marcel has a playful, if infantilizing, way of drawing my attention to litter: "I spy with my little eye ..." If it's a contest, I have no chance against his finely tuned litter radar. It's famous among the cleaners, all of whom learn to anticipate dirt everywhere – anything they miss is a potential source of complaint. The amount and kind of dirt they find determine how much time and effort an area will cost them. It also matters where they find it. In the shopping mall, a single banana peel on top of a pillar occupies a group of cleaners for nearly twenty minutes. By the time it's captured, the rest of the mall must make do with a light dusting.

The search for dirt has an element of treasure hunt. Cleaners train their antennas to find the valuable in what others have deemed garbage. As Mary Douglas in her landmark study *Purity and Danger* writes, "There is no such thing as absolute dirt: it exists in the eye of the beholder."[2] Luisa particularly has made a name for herself as a scavenger. "The black one collects everything," Michaela says. "You won't believe your eyes." Luisa buys herself a new Samsung Galaxy smartphone on the proceeds of bottle and can deposits, which bring in as much as €20 per day in the peak summer season. She finds a discarded leather handbag, Wolford stockings and a full tube of hand cream in the shopping mall. Coins and notes she takes to be good omens. Others are more selective than Luisa. Marcel only picks up deposit bottles worth more than twenty cents. Others won't do it at all, it's beneath their dignity. Matthias calls it "a badge of poverty."

---

[2] Douglas (2002: 2).

Even worthless garbage and outright filth have their share of interest. Like detectives, cleaners treat what they find as evidence. Greasy
spots at eye level on a glassy elevator wall suggest hair gel to Christian.
"Again with these office workers," he says. "So tired at the end of the
day, they fall asleep standing up."

"Look here," Michaela says at the entrance hall to a club. "That's
where they stand around spitting. These young people have nothing
better to do." Porn magazines in a trash bin inspire another round of
underworld storytelling.

And then there are the rude surprises. On our way to an apartment,
Susanna compares cleaning a woman's toilet with breaking open an
Easter egg. "You never know what you're going to get," she says. "But
you can be sure it won't be pleasant."

Images of toilets seen or described are permanent fixtures in cleaners'
minds. Entering a bathroom and opening a toilet lid, I always hold my
breath and stand back. But while some of us are repelled by what we
find, for others, this is where the fun begins.

"Eyes Has Fear, Hand Does It": Anxious Encounters with Shit, Vomit and Rotten Meat

"Garbage, waste, is uncanny for the cleaners," according to Ludwig,
the HR manager. His use of the word "uncanny" recalls Sigmund
Freud's sense of it as the confrontation with something that is strangely
familiar but should be kept hidden.[3] Such uncanniness may arise as
cleaners come uncomfortably close to other people's dirt, especially the
one to which the English word *dirt* owes its derivation: the Old Norse
drit, or excrement. Encounters with shit risk transgressing ancient
religious and civilizational prohibitions,[4] and they rank high among
the cleaners' occupational anxieties.

As Susanna's remarks illustrate, women's toilets are regarded as the
"most disgusting." They call to the cleaner's mind disturbing images:
toilets where "people did their business and filled the toilet brush and
everything with shit to the top," where "women tried to flush their
tampons instead of putting them into the bin," where "women had

---

[3] Freud (1919); for a discussion of uncanniness in organization studies, see Beyes
(2019).
[4] Elias (1939/1996), Baier (1991).

thrown their sanitary napkins behind a radiator," where cleaners found "blood up on the ceiling like a woman took out her tampon and purposefully smeared it there." It's not just these sights and smells but the need to reach into the toilet to clean it that cleaners find disgusting. Some find public toilets, even cleaned ones, so repulsive that they won't use them; they call themselves "home shitters," a kind of purification practice.

But no such practice can prevent dirt from entering the cleaners' bodies. Scent is formless and infiltrates the defenseless body. Cleaners' ability to smell constitutes a central asset in their work. With it, they detect both hidden and invisible dirt. But the olfactory sense is also a curse of the job. On his shift cleaning the corridor next to a restaurant, Alex breathes through his mouth to avoid inhaling the fumes from some unidentifiable "poisonous" source.

Cleaners' skin inevitably comes into contact with filth, and such contact can be frightening. Alexey recalls his struggle to overcome fear when faced with cleaning up two large cans of rotten meat. "I thought, I can't," he says. "But then I somehow did. How shall I say – eye has fear, hand does it."

This remark points to the significance of affect when encountering disgusting dirt.[5] Disgust goes beyond the cognitive realm and reaches the corporeal:[6] it requires "reference to the senses. It is about what it feels like to touch, see, taste, smell, even on occasion hear, certain things."[7] Disgust marks "the experience of a nearness that is not wanted."[8] It is an affective rejection of a boundary violation, of what is felt to transgress social norms and order.

At times even Potsdamer Platz's upperworld fills with stenches; these cut a remarkable contrast with the fancy buildings. The grease separators, which collect leftover fats from the restaurants, release smells that can contaminate whole regions of the complex. Then there's the

---

[5] It is beyond the scope of this work to engage with the burgeoning studies and theories of affect. For a discussion, see Thanem and Wallenberg (2015), Beyes and De Cock (2017), Pullen et al. (2017), Otto and Strauß (2019). Note, however, that the notion of affect here does not presume that the body and discourses are separate realms (e.g. Massumi, 1995), but rather follows the line of research suggesting that these are relational toward one another.

[6] This also suggests the need to go beyond the predominant cognitive focus of the dirty work literature (for a similar critique, see Simpson et al., 2012).

[7] Miller (1997: 36).   [8] Menninghaus (2003: 1).

stink that may suddenly emerge through vents or shafts, pervading large areas above and below street level. Insufficient ventilation makes the underground garbage collection points infernos of stink.

CleanUp's basement room, the nodal point of cleaners' work life, is situated directly next to a garbage room.

"How can you sit here and eat?" Patrick marvels. "It's so disgusting! I'm going to end up with nose cancer."

"After twenty years of giving women perms," Michaela – a former hairdresser – replies, "I can't smell anything anyways."

Indeed, a weak nose is an asset if you want to hang out in the basement room. Most cleaners either avoid it or attempt to mitigate the smell by closing the door. This inevitably renders the room airless.

Most of the time, there's no door to close between cleaner and dirt. Refusing to confront dirt can result in disciplinary action. One account manager recalls her response to a cleaner who refused to clean something: "Downstairs in my office is a dismissal letter with your name on it." Yet management does not expect cleaners to handle extreme cases, for example dead animals, though cleaners like Marcel welcome such tasks.

At Potsdamer Platz, one way to avoid particularly repulsive tasks is to get a coworker to do them. Sometimes, in my case at least, they even offer.

"If it's too nasty, tell me and I'll do it," Alex says when it's my turn to clean a toilet.

I thank him, but do it myself, having resolved to clean whatever the others do. But when Marcel asks me to clean up vomit, I reach my limit. Perhaps he's testing me; if so, I fail. The sight and smell of the slimy, half-digested mess sickens me.

"But how would you remove it?" Marcel asks.

"I don't know," I reply. "Why don't you show me?"

Without hesitation, Marcel gets to work. "You get the bigger pieces with the broom," he explains, sweeping them up. "Then you hose it down."

Perhaps I should be ashamed of my cowardice, but I am only relieved, despite Marcel's chivalry and bravado.

In this proximity to filth, cleaning tools and detergents take on the utmost importance. The worse the mess, the more the cleaners rely on the use of water, aromatic substances, the various cleaning agents referred to generally as "chemicals." Following Ludwig, cleaners tend to use more "chemicals" than needed – something that is problematic both for their health and the environment (see below). Ludwig tries to put environmental considerations on the CleanUp agenda by addressing them in training programs for cleaners, foremen and account managers. However, he also notices and I observe as well, that practice is proving somewhat different as both clients and cleaners equate a strong smell of detergents with cleanliness. Cleaners also use strong detergents, as they believe it makes it easier to clean dirty surfaces.

The necessary tools are sometimes in short supply, and their quality varies, so the cleaners wind up competing over them. At the end of a shift, Michaela always replenishes the lower drawer of her cart with all the mops, rags and glass cleaner needed for the following day.

"But look!" she exclaims. "Something always goes missing. People just take stuff."

Gloves are a hot topic under Potsdamer Platz. Cleaners complain that the CleanUp gloves are not up to the job.

"These blue gloves are no good," Michaela says. "They fall apart immediately."

Indeed, after the first half-hour of our shift in the mall, Luisa's gloves shred; she stops using them altogether. Some of the others bring their own box of heavy-duty black gloves (see figure 3.1). These are treated like a precious commodity. Marcel secures his supply through Paul's mother, who works in a hospital. When we work together, he offers me a single glove, explaining, "You only need the right one."

Cleaners take CleanUp's failure to supply them with necessary equipment as a sign of neglect, even contempt. "It's pretty sad," Alex says, "that you have to buy everything yourself."

Even with all necessary supplies, the barrier between cleaner and dirt remains thin and porous. Dirt contaminates everything in the cleaning process: clothing, equipment, cleaning agent, water.[9] Alex picks up the dirty mops from the garbage room floor only with a plastic bag. Despite such precautions, his pants are covered with permanent stains. Impatiently awaiting a new pair, he is furious at CleanUp for making him "run around like a bum."

---

[9] Karafyllis (2013).

Figure 3.1 A box of black gloves.

Nor am I immune to dirt's depredations: after a few weeks in the field, Michaela draws my attention to the stains on my pants. "You got to really wash them," she admonishes me. My dirtiness violates a code of cleanliness that helps workers like Michaela and Alex separate themselves from the matter of their work: from the dirt. For them, the CleanUp uniform doesn't carry shame unless it compromises their self-image as being clean.

Facing and touching the disgusting constitutes a "danger to [one's] purity"; it means that one "did not escape contamination."[10] This does not mean that cleaners necessarily perceive themselves as impure; instead, their disgust "admits [their] own vulnerability and compromise even as it constitutes an assertion of superiority."[11] Dirt may make the cleaners "despair of humanity," an expression I frequently overhear; but they do not, by default, despair of themselves. Primarily when they lack the appropriate tools and clothing from their employer does their dignity start to suffer.

"I Find It Hot": Fascinations with Dirt

Breakfasting in the storage room over the pages of a tabloid, Matthias shares the highlight of his morning shift.

[10] Miller (1997: 204).   [11] Miller (1997: 204).

"Outside McDonald's I noticed some paper on the floor," he recounts. "I picked it up and then I saw it everywhere – human shit."

His delivery is dry, but he's clearly enjoying the story, particularly my shock and disgust.

"But who would do something like that?" I ask.

"Who knows?" Matthias says. "Bums, the homeless, people like that. It happens all the time."

Not everyone agrees that the culprits are street people; others suspect the party crowd.

Disturbing as it may be to have to deal with, a pile of shit also makes for a good story. And as much as extreme filth gives rise to the affect of disgust, it also has the potential to amuse, excite, fascinate, even arouse. Dirt constitutes what philosopher Julia Kristeva describes as the abject; it is both the source of horror and pleasure: "One does not know it [the abject], one does not desire it, one joys it [*on en jouit*]. Violently and painfully. A passion."[12] Susanna's comparison of toilet contents with an Easter egg hints at the forbidden pleasures of filth.[13]

Indeed, shit opens the space for unrestrained remarks and imagination,[14] often sexual, particularly among the male cleaners. Taking pictures of human excrement to document his work, Marcel says, "I find it hot." Another time he sweeps up a pile whose smell is so foul that even he remarks on it – then he holds the broom out to me.

"Would you lick it for a hundred euros?"

Disgust and laughter go hand in hand. As legal and literary scholar William Ian Miller explains in *The Anatomy of Disgust*, "the whole process of finding pleasure and fascination in the violation of norms that exposes us to disgust enables a good portion of the comic too."[15] Bertha's face creases with disgust, yet also with amusement, when she tells me, "It stinks here, but you should smell the can at my place – that's some stinky shit!"

Her laughter suggests a "sudden discharge of tension."[16] It allows distancing from and coping with a situation.[17] In his study *Laughter*,

---

[12] Kristeva (1982: 9).

[13] In this way, and in a similar vein to Tyler (2011), this chapter moves beyond the predominant focus of the dirty work literature where dirt is solely associated with shame.

[14] Bataille (2012); see also Enzensberger (1968/2011), Countryman (1988), Menninghaus (2003).

[15] Miller (1997: 116), see also Menninghaus (2003).

[16] Menninghaus (2003: 10).   [17] See also e.g. Sanders (2004).

philosopher Henri Bergson writes that "indifference is the natural environment"[18] of laughter. It involves detachment, which facilitates the handling of the disgusting. Through laughter, cleaners' encounter with dirt acquires "social meaning," as Bergson puts it.[19] Laughing together with Bertha over her apartment's stinky toilet provides the basis for sharing an experience, if not forming a collective.[20]

Matthias's shit story points to a further dynamic at play when laughter and disgust intersect: dirt is a vehicle by which cleaners can position themselves as heroic. Rather than succumbing to the affect of disgust, they triumph over it with the instrument of laughter.[21] With such tales, the storytellers not only disgust their audience (Matthias tells his story while others are eating), but simultaneously signal their fortitude and bravery at having faced down the uncanny. Signaling endurance and superior strength, the dirt braggart accrues status and boosts self-worth.

One day, Bertha asks Luisa to clean up a pile of human shit, and Luisa recounts the incident with a jubilant smile.

"A man had" – Luisa mimes the action with a squat. "And it stiiiiinks! Nobody want to remove. It Bertha's side. She say Luisa, you remove? I not."

Luisa's explanation for her capacity to do the job surprises me.

"You see, African woman – no problem."

Handling extreme filth lets Luisa prove herself as the tougher, better cleaner. She attributes her ability to remove disgusting dirt to her ethnic identity and gender, just as some male cleaners embrace the work as an advertisement of their masculinity[22] – a subject we'll return to in Chapter 4.

The intermingling of disgust, laughter and a sense of superiority is most pronounced in the case of Marcel. He revels in tales of his bravado, which are a staple of cleaner lore under Potsdamer Platz. There are the above-mentioned fifteen headless pigeons, whose stench was so overpowering he had to don a mask. Marcel gleefully narrates worse: the time a woman committed suicide by jumping out a window, or the discovery of a corpse in a parking garage in a car, maggots

---

[18] Bergson (1900). [19] Bergson (1900). [20] See also e.g. Collinson (1992).
[21] For a discussion of the so-called superiority thesis of humor, see Lintott (2016).
[22] This shows how endurance is not necessarily only tied to masculine identity, as the existing research suggests, e.g. Ackroyd and Crowdy (1990), Tracy and Scott (2006), Simpson et al. (2014).

crawling through the window. Like any good storyteller, Marcel dwells on the choice detail: he recalls bits of bone and teeth he retrieved from the suicide victim, and a splash of blood on Tom's pants.

What disgusts others makes Marcel laugh and further reinforces his bravery and distinction: he crosses the line between dirt and cleanliness like no other.

"I can do everything, remove everything," he boasts. "There's nothing too gross."

And while others fuss over their soiled uniform, Marcel exults in the mess. "Oh man," he says. "How dirty I look again!"

Some cleaners question the veracity of Marcel's stories, while others respond with awe.

"I wouldn't do it," Christian says. "I couldn't."

While dealing with disgusting dirt as fearlessly and with such verve as Marcel is neither common nor necessarily aspired to by everyone,[23] it is certainly a way to gain respect in the corporate underworld: Marcel enjoys status above those who surrender to the affect of disgust.

"My Hand Is About to Fall Off": The Aches and Pains of Working with Dirt

Working with and against dirt is physically strenuous. Cleaners bear down to scrub sticky substances, they strain, kneel and crawl for out-of-reach targets, they clock significant distances over the course of a shift. During my own stint as a cleaner, it seems as though each shift introduces a new injury. After days of wielding the broom on the streets of the complex, a serious ache reaches from my right hand into my upper arm, a pain all too familiar to Marcel. After working two weeks without time off, it will be two days before he can make a fist again with his right hand.

One shift, Lucas and I spend hours scrubbing glue off a hotel wall. By the end of it, I can barely feel my hand. "Damn it," Lucas complains. "My hand is about to fall off." The glue confronts us like an enemy, and at times it feels like the best we can hope for is a Pyrrhic victory.

---

[23] By contrast, see e.g. Meara (1974), Ackroyd and Crowdy (1990).

Bending repeatedly to clean a series of wall-mounted mirrors, I develop a strange and powerful headache. I wonder if this is a coincidence, but Luisa confirms that it results from all the up and down, at least at first. "First two weeks, I also headache," she tells me.

Cleaners share various techniques to mitigate the strain; I'll leave my fieldwork knowing how to change a mop head without bending down. But the wear and tear take their toll: Ali suffers from backache, Henning's wrist is chronically inflamed, and Michaela can no longer kneel. Cleaners' hands tell the tale, from cuts and blisters to the visible traces of regular detergent exposure.

"You can tell that people work in cleaning," Christian says. "You can see the hard work. They don't have pom-pom hands," a German expression that attributes both physical softness and effeminacy to white-collar labor.

Detergents can do worse to skin than simply roughen it. Alex discovers this when drops of a toilet-cleaning agent land on his face.

"That's really poisonous stuff," he says. "The spot on my face kept getting bigger and bigger. Anton said, it's not a big deal – but it really hurt, and my mom was starting to get worried."

Inhaling fumes can cause headache and vomiting, among other health problems; it can also make cleaners feel high. They describe feeling "completely hammered" after prolonged exposure, "like being on drugs – like Ecstasy."

In the world enclosed under Potsdamer Platz, the fumes may leave cleaners gasping for air.

"I need fresh air, I go fresh air," Alexey puffs. Emerging from the underworld, Alex sighs, "Oh, air, air, air!"

Amid all its other significance, dirt can begin to represent sheer physical pain. Even when excrement isn't the target, the word the cleaners reach for is still *shit*. After kneeling for hours on the roof to scrub deposits from small gauges, Alex complains: "Do you know how shitty it is on the roof? And to kneel the whole time! That's really shit, and now in the heat."

Even as physical disability looms as a threat to cleaners, as with Ali and Alex discussed in the prior chapter, cleaners, especially the male ones, nonetheless cite physical pain to vaunt their hard work. Sometimes they play up their physical suffering to boost their self-image and gain the respect of others. Expressions like "once again, totally demolished," "today we're slogging through it," and, facetiously, "don't strain yourself" highlight the difficulty of the work, a strenuousness that constitutes a badge of honor.

The double-edged nature of such braggadocio is never more apparent than with Marcel. In short order, he pivots from lamenting his sore hand to boasting about the muscles he's developed on the job.

"Look at my arm, look at this muscle!" Marcel has called me over to display an arm that is, in fact, rather thin.

"Yeah, sure," chimes in Paul, miming masturbation. "What a man!"

Marcel laughs. Confident of his status, he is capable of laughing at himself. In any case, he's made his point: even in self-parody, he reminds his audience of the physical demands of the job.

"Working with the Eye": Cutting Corners

Working with dirt can also afford cleaners some liberties. Perhaps they enter a space that has been lightly used, freeing up a pocket of time. Cleaners know how to make a space appear clean without comprehensively cleaning it; they call this "working with the eye." Rather than vacuuming an entire floor, for example, Christian may spot-check it for visible dirt. As aforementioned, a strong detergent smell, Ludwig explains, may give an impression of cleanliness more convincing than the real thing. And since one can never predict what one will encounter in a given shift, the work requires a degree of flexibility.[24] CleanUp therefore grants cleaners some autonomy.

"Cleaners are much less rigorously scheduled than other workers," Ludwig says, "particularly by comparison with other industrial workers."

At Potsdamer Platz, the degree of autonomy varies. Some cleaners work under tight schedules with little leeway. Others decide for themselves how they apportion their work in various locations over a given period. Cleaners use the autonomy to "craft their job,"[25] creating individual regimens governing what, how and how much to clean.[26]

---

[24] Depending on the shift, cleaning can differ from other more routinized service work, such as work in call centers or fast-food restaurants (e.g. Leidner, 1993; Callaghan & Thompson, 2002).

[25] Wrzesniewski and Dutton (2001).

[26] On rules and organization, see also Ortmann (2003), Busby and Iszatt-White (2016).

These rules range from cleaning the glass doors no higher than eye-level, above which is the glass cleaners' responsibility; or wiping down only the easily accessible areas of a floor and not repositioning potentially valuable objects that run the risk of breakage; or the philosophy that what doesn't yield to the first attempt at cleaning, stays.

Some such rules constitute badly kept secrets, at least to the foremen who used to be cleaners themselves.

"On the weekend, you can slack off – even the foremen know this," Christian says. "You let some things slide, you work with your eye. You remind yourself, on Monday it all begins again."

Ultimately, what counts are the clients' impressions, and as long as there are no complaints, it matters little how cleaners conduct their shift.

Cleaners regard their personal rule books as necessary tricks of the trade.[27] Some shifts, for example, are so understaffed that it's impossible to fulfill the contract specifications. With at least implicit management consent, cleaners take some liberties.[28] This represents a degree of autonomy and bolsters a sense of dignity:[29] the cleaner rather than management or client decides how to clean.

By and large, cleaners do not understand such shortcuts as a form of resistance, an unwillingness to work and most certainly don't see it as laziness.[30] Most cleaners maintain and defend a robust work ethic. When Matthias switches from cleaning with Benjamin to cleaning with Christian, for example, he welcomes the resulting boost in productivity.

"We get twice as much done as before," Matthias says. "And this way the time passes much faster. With Benjamin we didn't work too much and then just sat around. That's kind of the shits."

Idleness can accentuate feelings of fatigue, and slow the pace of time; but more importantly, it undermines the cleaners' self-understanding as valuable workers.[31] Bending the rules and working with the eye are

---

[27] See also Gouldner (1954), Blau (1963).
[28] See also Martin et al. (2013), Breslin and Wood (2016).
[29] On the relation between autonomy and dignity, see Meara (1974), Sayer (2007).
[30] On deviance, see Ackroyd and Thompson (1999).
[31] Thus, rather than the boredom of work pushing workers to escape into work breaks and to engage in games, as Roy's (1959) famous "banana time" study

one thing, but outright resistance unbalances a complex calculus of dignity. Cleaners calibrate this balance by embracing the liberties that accompany working with dirt and by simultaneously maintaining their work ethic: they are productive by dint of choice, not powerlessness.

"You Start and It Never Stops": The Endless Fight against Dirt

"It's Sisyphean work," Matthias says about the job. "You start and it never stops." Indeed, while dirtying can happen in manifold ways and more or less of its own accord, the maintenance of cleanliness requires a focused, virtually unceasing effort.[32] Life brings with it dirt that cleaners, in an endless cycle, must sweep up, scrub down, wash out and wipe away. Footsteps on marble, fingerprints on a door handle, hair gel on elevator glass or the motes of dust that flake perpetually from human skin – all of it undoes the cleaners' work. Heavily used areas must be frequently revisited, and often the demand for cleanliness outstrips the possibility of maintaining it.

Outdoors at Potsdamer Platz, Marcel battles the relentless energies of entropy. During the lunch break, office workers eat takeout on a grassy knoll, and every gust of wind distributes their litter over a wider area. Marcel goes from one piece of garbage to the next, each one almost immediately replaced by a new errant paper cup or plastic wrapper. Once I start working with Marcel, I begin to see cigarette butts everywhere I go. "It really is never-ending," Marcel sighs. "They are everywhere."

The more fine-grained the cleaning process, the more cleaners struggle with the endlessness of dirt. As an intermixed and boundary-less matter, dirt can never be eradicated, only barely contained.[33] Assigned to a newly renovated five-star hotel before its reopening, the cleaners find they simply cannot get on top of the dust: the more workers enter the hotel, the more the dust rises. "You just don't get it clean," Christian says. "The dust is everywhere."

The cleaning process is supposed to be traceless, but it, too, can spread dirt or leave detergent streaks. Cleaners develop their own techniques to ensure traceless cleaning. They tinker with the

shows, here the boredom from taking breaks can also make cleaners like Matthias turn to work.
[32] Eriksen (2013: 139).   [33] Karafyllis (2013).

concentration of a cleaner, they wipe the floor in figure-eights, they choreograph the cleaning process as not to leave footprints, backing themselves toward the exit. The quality of the cleaning equipment is of some consequence in this regard. One day, Marcel is left with a punctured dustpan. Whatever he sweeps into it, a portion is left behind.

All this has consequences for the expectations of clients, foremen, account managers and the cleaners themselves. While the cleaning contract between CleanUp and the client spells out objective parameters of what needs to be cleaned, how often and how, the everyday cleaning practice proves to be more complicated. The expectations of cleanliness may be difficult to fulfill even if cleaners follow their contracts to the letter. The struggle with dirt, especially in fine cleaning, can drive cleaners "crazy," as Matthias puts it; their work can feel not just repetitive but futile. And cleaners become frustrated when clients or the CleanUp management doubt their efforts.

"Anton didn't believe us that you can always see footprints at the entrance," Bertha says after a shift in the shopping mall. "But people walk on it. So we did it again with him there, and polished it dry, and then he saw it for himself."

Cleaners are constantly vulnerable to this kind of complaint, which we'll revisit in Chapter 5. The vulnerability and frustration are only compounded when upperworlders dirty spaces they have just cleaned, usually without the slightest consideration for the cleaners' efforts. "I can get so worked up about people who throw stuff everywhere, sometimes directly in front of me," Marcel complains.

The persistence of dirt has one bright side for the cleaners, and it's no small consideration: that persistence constitutes their occupational *raison d'être*. "There will always be jobs," reasons Hermann. Alex agrees (see Chapter 2) as he believes that machines will never be able to do the job as well as a human. Marcel, too, admonishes himself for complaining; cigarette butts are, after all, his bread and butter. They also represent a challenge worthy of yet another distinguished underworlder, Tantalus – a goal always visible and just out of reach: perfection.

Achieving even a temporary state of cleanliness can produce not only aesthetic pleasure, but a sense of accomplishment and gratification. "I just enjoy it when things are clean," Michaela says. Marcel, a self-described "perfectionist," strives to make Potsdamer Platz as clean as possible. It's an all-consuming preoccupation: the cigarette butts and other litter feature prominently in his dreams. And it's the unattainable nature of the goal that sustains Marcel no less than any other perfectionist. Without imperfection, there would be nothing for him to do.

Cleaners welcome dirt as a proof of their value. In this sense, the more dirt, the better. When we work together, Marcel announces a contest: who can collect the most cigarette butts? After a quarter-hour, we compare dustpans and, sure enough, he's the victor. The cleaners regale each other with boastful gripes. The café was "very dirty, coffee, lot of bottles," Luisa reports. The entrance to the apartment house "was ugly," Matthias tells us, "full of spider webs." "Once again, we've worked our asses off," Benjamin announces to the storage room after a shift, pointing to the evidence: a heap of soiled mop heads. Dirt, measured here in mops, proves the cleaners' worth.

Beyond Dirt as a Source of Shame

Dirt plays a pivotal role in cleaners' working lives. Here dirt matters not just symbolically but also in its very materiality.[34] Working with dirt can feel not just cyclical, frustrating and painful, but futile. It may threaten cleaners' health, safety and dignity. Working with dirt can make one feel more like a "bum," as Alex puts it, than a valued member of society. By the same token, the work offers opportunities for earning not only an honest living, but a sense of satisfaction and the respect of others. The accomplishment of cleanliness is both tangible and quantifiable: whether measured in cigarette butts or mop heads, a job well done is its own proof. The job allows for liberties that provide cleaners with a sense of autonomy, and the persistence of dirt translates to janitorial job security.

To treat dirt as merely a source of shame[35] does not do justice to cleaners' lived experience; it elevates the stigma from working with dirt to the predominant factor in cleaners' work lives.[36] How cleaners

---

[34] On the significance of the materiality of dirt, see also Hughes et al. (2016).

[35] This is the dominant assumption of the so-called dirty work literature (e.g. Ashforth & Kreiner, 1999; Kreiner et al., 2006). Here the focus is on how workers cope with the stigma of doing dirty work. In contrast to this, I do not foreground the sense of shame that comes from handling dirt.

[36] Link and Phelan (2001).

regard their work and role depends in part on their background and environment. Depending on the case, depending on a cleaner's socio-economic provenance and situation, pride in work may in fact be the predominant factor.

And as the cleaners show time and again in their relationship to it, there's a flip side to dirt. It's not just a worthy adversary but a fascinating one. The pursuit of it may make work exciting, fun – one might even find it hot. This flies in the face of not only commonly held perceptions but dominant academic assumptions. Sennett and Cobb argue that "the janitor gets little satisfaction from the cleaning."[37] Hughes, who coined the term "dirty work," writes that the "janitor ... does not integrate his dirty work into any deeply satisfying definition of his role that might liquidiate his antagonism to the people whose dirt he handles."[38] Whatever their antagonism to the upperworlders, the cleaners I encounter at Potsdamer Platz, at least intermittently, do in fact glean a sense of satisfaction from their work. To ignore this fact would be to reinforce a stigma and deny what these men and women regularly demonstrate: they approach what they do with both interest and motivation.

Experiences and meaning of dirt vary not only among cleaners but also from moment to moment. Interest and motivation, shame and humiliation, revulsion and eroticism are all in the mix. Dirt plays a significant, even starring role in the cleaners' workplace dramas of dignity, but only one of many.

[37] Sennett and Cobb (1972: 96).   [38] Hughes (1984/2009: 345).

4 | *Separate in the Same Boat*
Others and Allies among the Cleaners

The summer party, hosted by CleanUp and a client, is one of the very few employee events on the company calendar. During my fieldwork, Tom organizes no other get-togethers or team meetings. Perhaps this accounts for some of the excitement leading up to the event. In the prior weeks, the underground corridors are abuzz. The party is fodder for personal gossip – who will dance, or sleep, with whom? – and an opportunity for cleaners to buttonhole managers about assignments and special requests. Not everyone is equally keen on attending. Some dismiss the partygoers as "hypocrites," "losers," "boneheads." Still others can't come, or can only make a brief appearance – Tom hasn't given them the time off. On the whole, however, the party is the topic of the season.

The day starts off with a steamboat ride on Berlin's main river, the Spree (see figure 4.1). The cleaners arrange themselves on the deck, the once-uniformed group suddenly becomes a diverse array of fashion statements. Marcel looks smart in his khaki pants and gray shirt, though he's spilled coffee on it that a motherly colleague didn't quite manage to dab out. Ali sports a Ralph Lauren polo shirt with jeans. Hermann, an ungainly young trainee, arrives in a plain dark T-shirt with black pants; his fellow trainee Lena, decked out in pink from pumps to shades, sniffs that Hermann's outfit probably came from Kik, a discount clothier. Luisa seems out of place in her tight black cocktail dress, high heels, pink pleather bag and pinned-up hair. "Does she think we're partying in a hotel?" Bertha snipes.

Drinks are on the house. An amplified tour guide points out sites along the way. "I don't know any of this, I'm from Bernau," Marcel says ironically. When the boat passes through Kreuzberg, Ali needles xenophobic Marcel: "Look at all my childhood haunts in the hands of the Turks." "What a filthy lot," Marcel responds, playing his part. "All these foreigners."

Figure 4.1 Steamboat ride on the Spree.

For a group that commutes to the city center to labor largely underground, this hour on the water is an opportunity to see Berlin and socialize off the clock. Yet even on this festive deck the party self-segregates. Tom adheres to the client. The male cleaners, including Marcel and Ali, sit out of earshot so they can make off-color jokes – though one says, "Who cares, the client already thinks we're a bunch of lowlifes." The women, including Bertha and Lena, park themselves on the other side of the deck. Only Luisa sits alone. When Lena asks her to join them, she stays put. Perhaps she didn't understand the invitation, or she's more likely keeping her distance. The summer gathering offers only a partial reprieve from workplace pressures. Indeed, it crystallizes the divisions and alliances within the cleaners' world.

This chapter explores the cleaners' relationships and interactions. It examines how these men and women form cliques and establish a status hierarchy, how they create and enforce markers of difference. These markers range from age, gender and ethnicity to fashion, cultural tastes and educational backgrounds. Some are subtle, some as stark as the seating arrangements separating Luisa, the only Black woman on deck, from the rest. But despite these differentiations, a sense of equivalence persists, posing a threat to any sense of specialness. Cleaners wish to believe that their work and their presence are

on some level unique and valued as such, that they are not inter-
changeable and replaceable; and to fortify their sense of worth they
resort to the creation and enforcement of status hierarchies. Such
constructions all too often rest on the most fragile of foundations,
and the risk of collapse plays no small role in cleaners' dramas of
dignity.

"We're No Team!"

At the beginning of my fieldwork, I exhibit a tendency to refer to the
storage room as the "team room." The cleaners quickly break me of
the habit.

"Team room? What team room?" a glass cleaner says, looking
around. "Hey, you – *team room!*"

"Just leave out the team," Benjamin advises. "We're no team."

"Team room," Hans explains, "sounds like some bullshit Tom and
Anton came up with."

For these cleaners, the language of *teams* is part and parcel of the
corporate jargon that comes at them from above and bears scant
relation to their reality or how they want to be perceived.[1] Tom,
indeed, employs the term in telling me how cleaning work requires
collaboration.

"It's necessary for everybody in the team to work together," he says.
"Six or four eyes spot more dirt than two."

He reaches for the term again in explaining his decision not to use
CleanUp's "smiley system," which lets management reward individual
workers with tokens they can exchange for money, vouchers or other
goods.

"I find it better if we collect the smileys and then, as a team, go out to
the Panorama café, or rent go-karts or whatever people want," he says.
"The smiley system only arouses envy."

Conflicts are by no means rare among the cleaners. But unless they
disrupt work, Tom and the foremen leave them to the cleaners to
resolve. Apart from the summer party, Tom's pooling of smileys, and

---

[1] See also Kunda (2006) on cynicism among employees vis-à-vis management
    discourse and practice.

one notable instance of conflict resolution (see his intervention in the conflict between Luisa and Bertha below), I observe few concrete steps by management toward building a sense of workplace community or a shared set of values and experiences. Meanwhile, disparities in contractual arrangements, shift allocations, division of labor and preferential treatment produce and reinforce differences among the staff.[2]

Above and beyond these more managerially driven, structural segregations, a constant striving for differentiation is apparent among the cleaners. The resulting divisions compromise any sense of solidarity.[3] While individual friendships and coalitions emerge at Potsdamer Platz, the cleaners seldom act as a group – as a team. At the beginning and end of a shift, they rarely acknowledge each other. These missing greetings and farewells normally constitute what sociologist Erving Goffman calls "access ritual," greetings signaling openness to and interest in interaction, farewells marking "a state of decreased access."[4] The cleaners, appearing and disappearing without ceremony, signal no such interest or access. Apart from close allies, they prefer to dissociate themselves from the others.

Differentiation can resemble a game that cleaners play against boredom.[5] They zero in on difference as source material for their jokes and gossip: essentially lighthearted, however barbed. But differences are also a wellspring of misunderstanding, prejudice and conflict. Intentionally or not, the spotting of differences sharpens divisions and strengthens alliances as cleaners do "categorical work" to draw lines of demarcation among themselves.[6] Cleaners create inclusions

---

[2] As mentioned in Chapter 2, cleaners like Luisa have only four-hour contracts, while others, like Ali and Marcel, get longer shifts and thus a more substantial income. The latter also benefit from fixed shifts and thus relative autonomy, compared with "floaters" whose shifts vary. Cleaners complain that Tom favors some workers, among them Marcel, and rewards them with perks.

[3] The lack of solidarity may not be surprising given the limited social cohesion as well as segregations of the workforce (Hodson et al., 1993; see also Fantasia, 1988; Cranford, 2012). Yet the divisions among the cleaners go beyond the managerially driven segregations, and social cohesion should not be treated as wholly influenced by external factors: how cleaners construct and practice differences shapes their interactions and self-worth.

[4] Goffman (1971/2017: 79).   [5] See Burawoy (1979), Sherman (2007).

[6] See Tilly (1998) on "categorical work," Lamont (2000) on "boundary work," and also Zerubavel (1993). Note also that social psychology research, especially the work of Tajfel and Turner, shows how categorization lets people form a distinct and positive in-group against a negatively discriminated out-group (see also Ashforth & Mael, 1989; Jenkins, 2008). However, social psychology

and exclusions. They engage in what sociologist Stuart Hall describes as "[s]plitting between that which one is, and that which is the other."[7] The lines they draw are neither fixed nor exclusive; they shift and overlap. What makes the act of categorization so powerful is its capacity to position the "other" as different and inferior and the self as superior. It marks an attempt to create an internal status hierarchy, to engage in so-called "othering."

Underclass within Underworld: The Shame of the Proles

After the boat ride, a barbecue awaits on a parking deck near Potsdamer Platz. Hermann, oddly, ends up sitting with a group of technicians. Susanna overhears one of them ask where Hermann works, to which he responds by building number: B2, B3, B4. "I've never heard of this," the technician replies. The story gets a laugh out of the cleaners. Like his Kik wardrobe, the exchange confirms Hermann's membership in the uneducated "underclass"[8] – a group the cleaners ridicule yet also feel ashamed of. Their sharp "sociological eyes" dissect each others' status in terms of fashion, media consumption, postal code and schooling. Anyone associated with the underclass risks being labeled a "total prole" or a "Hartzer"[9] – a derogatory term for the unemployed.

Hermann's looks are a source of amusement, teasing and concern. Some compare him to Edvard Munch's painting *The Scream*. "Just look at his teeth," Christian says, and indeed Hermann's are variously missing and crooked. Cleaners interpret Hermann's dentition as a sign of his rough family background and years of neglect. Christian urges him to move to a care home, as he did. "They take care of you,"

approaches to diversity tend to neglect issues of inequality and lack contextualization (e.g. DiTomaso et al., 2007). They also employ a static rather than a processual view, which understands identifications as ongoing, contextual and shifting accomplishments (Alvesson et al., 2008). For these reasons, I abstain from drawing on social psychology.

[7] Hall (2000: 147).

[8] Cleaners characterize the underclass "in behavioral terms" (Goldberg, 2000: 166) rather than in purely economic terms.

[9] The expression "Hartzer" derives from the so-called "Hartz reforms," which were labor market and welfare state reforms implemented under the Chancellor Gerhard Schröder (Social Democratic Party) between 2003 and 2005. Peter Hartz was the head of the committee, proposing these reforms, which are therefore named after him.

Christian explains. "You get your teeth done, like me – that's all possible."

The male cleaners, like older brothers, don't just mock Hermann but try to guide him. They push him to work on his appearance, especially if he ever wants to "fuck a woman" (Marcel).

"Women first notice your teeth and nails," Marcel counsels Hermann, whose fingernails are chewed ragged. "You got to take care of them! And your hair – put some gel in it! Oh, how you look!"

Susanna's appearance is another target of derision. One of the older cleaners, with a short round body, her hair dyed dark red, Susanna leaves work one day wearing tattered jeans and a shapeless gray sweater. "What was that?" Christian exclaims. "Did you see how she looked? Yikes – even if she walks around like that in private, it's just sad. I'd rather be seen in work clothes."

Given Susanna's income, acquiring fashionable clothes is probably near the bottom of her list of things to do. Yet even for cleaners like Christian, who struggles financially after years of alcohol abuse, one's appearance is worth investing in no matter what. He, Marcel and others like them have developed styles that distinguish them from the underclass. Clearly, they seek to establish "[s]ymbolic boundaries ... to contest and reframe the meaning of social boundaries."[10] Fashion is a line that they draw between themselves and the underclass with which they are always at risk of being associated.

Media consumption is another line of demarcation. Some cleaners watch *Das Messie Team*, a TV show in which dilapidated, lower-class homes are cleaned and tidied. Cleaners like Benjamin and Matthias call it a "Hartz-IV program" – TV for the unemployed. They likewise dismiss the tabloids, such as *Bild* or *BZ*, often found on the storage room table. "Once again, nothing here," Matthias carps, tossing aside the paper. "There never is," Benjamin replies.

Cleaners particularly denigrate residents of Hellersdorf, a poor, formerly East German district replete with concrete housing blocks known as *Plattenbauten*. Most cleaners live in peripheral districts around Berlin: Bernau, Ahrensfelde, Mahlsdorf, Spandau and Marzahn-Hellersdorf. The eastern districts, such as Marcel's Bernau, are associated with xenophobic Whites, the western districts, such as

---

[10] Lamont and Molnar (2002: 186), see also Newman (2000).

Wedding, where Luisa and Alex live, with immigration and street crime. So Alex is the butt of a running joke that he steals copper from rail lines or construction sites like all the Wedding "gypsies." Cleaners from even marginally more prosperous areas make a point of it. "I live in *South* Mahlsdorf," Matthias says.

Cleaners from Hellersdorf don't bother defending it. "You see people walking around with one or two children, the third one on the way, and they've just turned 19," Susanna says. "All they do is sit around and collect welfare." Predictably, the district's fashion sense comes under fire. "They have such ugly dyed hair and really look like shit," Alex says. Among the cleaners, Hellersdorf is the regional capital of the underclass.

It's also Tom's old district. The cleaners admire him for getting out, for his swift ascent. He stands in stark contrast to Lena, whom Christian pegs as a typical Hellersdorf girl. She dyes her hair in a mélange of black and red with streaks of blond, wears baggy pink and black clothes, has a tongue stud to, as she puts it, "give a better blowjob." It's not just her looks but also her behavior that cleaners pick on; Ali calls it "shameful." She'll drink beer and draw attention to herself on the train, Ali reports, and the others prefer not to be seen with her. They call her a "ghetto loser," a lost case, and make sport of her ignorance, her drinking, her TV tastes, her life. Lena, meanwhile, busies herself pointing out Hermann's flaws and his Kik clothes.

Lena reminds Marcel of other "dumb" people he has encountered at Potsdamer Platz. He recalls a fellow cleaner: "I told him that outside he always has to wear a helmet and he actually did it! You could have told him anything – we laughed our heads off."

When two new female cleaners join, the rumor circulates that one of them is illiterate. In a note to Anton, she misspells the German words for leather and carpet. While the language difficulties of foreigners like Luisa evince frustration and some ridicule, those of native-born Germans spark something approaching outrage, laced with shame. Such difficulties threaten cleaners' dignity as they reinforce the stigma that cleaners are, in Marcel's words, "idiots" and "always replaceable."

For Benjamin, who finished middle school and holds qualifications from other occupations, the educational level of some coworkers is a source of irritation. "Imagine if I were their boss and these were my secretaries and they were supposed to write a letter for me," he says.

"I'd have to check their spelling, check everything." Benjamin expects a level of education appropriate to a bureaucratic occupation – a level he attributes to himself – rather than low-end service work. "To work here, you don't need to have learned anything," he says. "Anybody gets in, you can see that."

If anybody can be a cleaner, even members of the uneducated underclass, Benjamin risks being classed among them. He, Matthias and Marcel try to position themselves as more educated and cultivated vis-à-vis the others – efforts that founder in the presence of a credentialed academic.

"When you write about us at the university, you can invite us and then we will say *euuuuuhh, bleaaaaah*, we are from CleanUp," Benjamin says. He and Matthias pretend to be mentally disabled, smacking themselves on the head. "Knock, knock – *euuuuuhh!*"

The joke sugarcoats some bitterness. It exposes the fragility of their efforts to differentiate: the stigma they attach to others always threatens to adhere to them. For all their efforts, they know the outside world will not differentiate them from the underclass. Their ridicule of Hermann, Lena and Susanna is of a piece with the shame of sharing their origins – and their workplace.

"It's Totally a Male Job": Taking Masculinity to the Cleaners

As the summer barbecue on the parking deck concludes, a pair of boxers arrive. To the blare of rock music, the match begins. The men, including Anton and Tom, approach to watch the fight. After a few rounds, the boxers invite members of the audience to fight them and Tom is the first volunteer. "He's a real boxer, he used to do kickboxing," someone says admiringly. After Tom's round, the crowd shouts for Marcel to go next. "No, no," he demurs. "I'm a pacifist." Others step forward. The challenge appeals to most of the men. It lets them demonstrate their strength and masculinity – qualities Tom values in a cleaner.

When Tom assumed the management of CleanUp's Potsdamer Platz operations, he recruited and replaced people in line with his preferences.

"Since I took over two years ago, I've created a team of 28 glass and building cleaners," Tom tells me. "I've really shaped things up here and switched quite a lot of people. I myself come from glass cleaning and have always searched for people who fit the pattern. It's usually younger guys who can also do glass. But I have nothing against women or older folks, in fact I've told Anton that maybe we should take on a few more now. You want a colorful mix."

In my presence, Tom frequently reiterates CleanUp's emphasis on the value of being "colorful." Yet Tom's recruitment and promotion policies advantage those who match his own profile.[11] "It looks better in front of the client," he says, if his foremen are professional cleaners who are trained, young and male.

Still, women and older people are favored for some opportunities. When the job involves cleaning private homes, women are the foremen's first choice, a preference that may align with client expectations. "Sometimes clients prefer a woman," Anton says. "Women have a knack for it – they have an eye for cleanliness."

Female cleaners, so-called *Tagesdamen*, may also work in public view during business hours, clad in gray suits and white shirts, emptying trash cans and spot-cleaning where needed. Thus, in line with client expectations, Tom and the foremen value the purportedly distinct skill sets of female workers,[12] reinforcing an essentialist understanding of interior cleaning as women's work.[13]

At Potsdamer Platz, the male cleaners largely subscribe to Tom's view that cleaning is a male occupation. "When people think of cleaning, they think of the maid," Alex says. "But this isn't like that. It's totally a male job." The public's association of cleaning with femininity poses a threat to a male cleaner's masculine self-image, and differentiating interior cleaning as women's work is a largely ineffectual attempt to neutralize the threat.[14] And men, too, are assigned interior cleaning when there's insufficient demand for glass and exterior work.

Male cleaners relate to their female coworkers with a mix of chauvinism, derision and concern. Patronizing flirtations, sexual innuendos

---

[11] Kanter (1977) calls this homosocial reproduction. This concept refers to people in powerful positions, especially male managers, promoting candidates who socially resemble themselves in terms of class, ethnicity, values and manner. As a result, people who do not fit the criteria face challenges in rising within the organization (see also Elliott & Smith, 2004).

[12] See also Lorbiecki and Jack (2000), Janssens and Zanoni (2014).

[13] See also West and Zimmermann (1987).

[14] See also Williams (1993), Lupton (2000), Simpson (2004).

and generally the sexualization of female workers are common (also refer to Chapter 1). Though there are also exceptions; Ali only frowns when male cleaners engage in sexual banters. One time during the shift with me, Marcel jokes that the white spots on his pants are "just drops of precum." Clearly, such macho joking attempts to reinforce cleaners' masculine self-image can be taken as a sexual advance, if not harassment.[15] However, such joking seeks to address at least as much the attention of male coworkers as female workers.

Male cleaners often brag about the women they "have" at Potsdamer Platz as a way to gain respect within their male circles. When I ask Hans and Paul – they particularly compete over the female service workers at Potsdamer Platz – what it means to "have" a woman, it turns out that it is more a matter of getting female attention, flirting and perhaps receiving free drinks or food than sexual encounters. Moreover, the exaggerated way in which Marcel and other male cleaners joke about their masculinity can also turn into ridicule, almost inviting emasculating remarks from coworkers, male and female ones alike.

Female workers, on their part, engage in sexual comments too. Yvonne presents herself to Lena and me as sexually insatiable: "I once worked with this guy who was so yummy," she tells us. "Such a tight body. Every time I saw him I felt like a bitch in heat."

Male cleaners also may regard women as too weak for the work. Running up and down stairs, carrying big buckets of water and bags of garbage, lifting heavy grates – "that's not for women," Christian says. It's "physically too difficult," according to Henning. They cite female cleaners who suffer from vertigo, who are quick to complain of blisters on their hands, who can't operate the equipment. "I have never seen a woman who could use a machine," Patrick says. "Me, I can do it on the first try." Cleaners concur with Alex's view that innate differences between the sexes make cleaning an inherently male occupation.

Male cleaners make another argument from the vantage point of chivalrous concern. "This work is germy, really disgusting," Christian says. "It's no job for a woman." Marcel says, "I can't have a woman cleaning up shit and vomit. I wouldn't allow it. That's just wrong."

Indeed, while Marcel is prone to tease me during his shift with repulsive tasks, taking evident pleasure in my smallest sign of disgust,

[15] On humor, sexuality and masculinity, see Collinson (1992).

ultimately he's the one who removes extreme filth. Male cleaners protectively note the dangers for women of cleaning alone late at night or early in the morning. The emphasis on masculinity in these expressions of concern reflects how the men transform negative aspects of the job into badges of honor, or opportunities for occupational gallantry.[16]

But courteousness is selectively applied. Male cleaners routinely speak of women who end up at CleanUp as "stupid" and "ugly," as people without other prospects in life.

"My girlfriend could never work here," Matthias avers. "The women here – just look at them!" Matthias spits. And Benjamin says, "Let's be honest, most of the women here are not very bright."

Nor are most women clamoring for sex-blind assignments. In certain situations, such as public events where customers are likely to be under the influence, some express the need to have male cleaners with them. Nor are many eager to take on Marcel's hardcore rounds. Still, younger trained women are proud to walk around with their glass-cleaning window squeegees, and they jocularly compete with the men on speed and precision. And some of the women, including Luisa, readily take up the challenge of tackling extreme filth: a way to prove themselves.

Female cleaners, especially older ones like Michaela, emphasize their experience and reliability relative to younger, often male, coworkers. They suggest that their blithe junior colleagues speed through rounds in order to make more time for cigarette breaks. In turn, some of the men look down on the older women as slow and inefficient. The oft-ridiculed Hermann boasts, "I work really fast. When I clean the [gynecological] practice I am usually already done at 6. Michaela needs until 7."

The women aren't having it.

"Such a big mouth – my ass he can do everything so much faster!" Michaela exclaims. A trio recalls an incident when a foreman scolded Hermann for a job poorly done. "He can make a big deal about his speed," one says, "but we've all seen the results."

Concern is a two-way street between the sexes. Older women worry that the young men's pace is physically unsustainable, and indeed

---

[16] See Leidner (1991: 208), Tracy and Scott (2006), Slutskaya et al. (2016).

injury is not uncommon among the male cleaners. Older men are a rare breed in this group, partially a reflection of Tom's preference for younger workers. The one or two older men who still work a few shifts are a source of complaints.

"He was just too old," Marcel says of a former colleague. "From three o'clock on, he couldn't do it anymore. He just had to sit down."

How long will Marcel, Hermann and Matthias be able to continue working in a way that supports their masculinist self-image? At what point do they become one of those emasculated older men the younger cleaners ridicule, whom Müller observes "toothlessly wolf-whistling women" and Gustav says "get only piss-poor jobs"?

Differentiations on the basis of age and sex bring about all manner of exclusion, inclusion and identification within the group.[17] Some of the older women, like Michaela, Bertha and Susanna, band together. Marcel half-seriously glorifies the male loyalty, the true brotherhood he finds in his circle with Paul and Christian and the others. They exchange gossip, cell phone videos, reports from their love life, work grievances. They look out for and help one another. On Christian's birthday, Marcel reminds people to congratulate him. After Christian had a relapse with alcohol, Marcel recalls, Tom wanted to dismiss him. But Marcel put a good word in for him and Christian got a reprieve; Tom and Norbert even visited him in the hospital.

Still, workplace solidarity, like gallantry, has its limits. To avoid the booze, Christian skips the summer party. When he invites Marcel and others to a party with his AA group, nobody's interested.

"Too dry for me," Marcel says.

Christian doesn't mention it again.

"No Monkey Cake for Me!": Racism in the Corporate Underworld

Cleaners start to leave the summer party in the early evening. Many have a long commute home, and shifts start at five the next morning. Luisa and Bertha are catching the same train and leave together. This surprises me – especially given the events surrounding Luisa's birthday.

---

[17] See Jenkins (2008) on the relation between categorization and identification.

For days, Luisa had been in a welter of excitement about turning thirty-seven. "I birthday," she told me on our morning shift in the shopping mall. "Bring cake with me – boss said. African cake, the best, with coconut and *condensario*" (condensed milk).

Having gotten wind of Luisa's difficulties with the group, Anton suggested that she bring something to work for her birthday, a German custom. Recognizing that conflicts among the cleaners can interfere with work, management on occasion will try to defuse them. Ludwig, the HR manager, advises his fellow managers to keep an ear to the ground for workplace strife, particularly insofar as it involves prejudice. The company emphatically promotes diversity, or what it terms being "colorful."[18] It positions itself as rising above difference, whether racial, parochial or otherwise.[19]

How management handles diversity in practice largely depends on who is handling it, and various account managers and foremen have distinct approaches. On becoming an account manager, Tom cracked down on certain foreigners. "Before, Russians [i.e. a Russian account manager and Russian foremen] headed the team," Tom says. "Now these Russians are all gone." In their place, Tom hired mostly native German speakers. Some foreign cleaners remained, joined by immigrants like Luisa with cheap four-hour contracts.[20] The trick was helping the foreigners integrate, and Luisa's birthday presented itself as an opportunity – or so Anton thought.

In fact, responses to Luisa's birthday demolished management's notion that it could be the occasion for harmony, racial or otherwise. Alexey, who also cleans in the shopping mall and comes from Kazakhstan, called Luisa's offering a "monkey cake." Bertha waved it dismissively away. "Well then, enjoy," she said – an omen of things to come.

At the end of her shift, at 9 a.m., Luisa set up in the storage room for the celebration. On the table stood her glazed chocolate cake,

---

[18] Here diversity is therefore not made invisible by the management, as it has been noted in industrial contexts (see e.g. Burawoy, 1979; Beynon, 1984).

[19] See also Ailon-Souday and Kunda (2003).

[20] At Potsdamer Platz, German language skills affect workers' status, opportunities and pay (see Acker, 2006), but this is not the case for CleanUp at large. For example, cleaners report how the "team" of another account manager, Dimitrova, from whom Tom took over Potsdamer Platz, is defined by "being Russian."

decorated with red buttercream rosettes and *Happy Birthday Luisa* in sugary script. Beside it, a carton brimmed with Mozambican fried chicken balls. Luisa changed into a celebratory outfit: a dark dress and tight black leggings, her hair pinned to better display long flashy earrings.

The storage room at this hour usually resembles a hive, but not on Luisa's big day. Five cleaners sat around the table. Luisa stood nearby, half-turned away with her shoulders down, hastily eating a piece of cake. A few more pieces were sliced but none taken. With vacant expressions, cleaners quietly sipped their instant coffee and ate their sandwiches.

My arrival broke this tense silence. I took the last remaining chair and Luisa offered me a slice of cake. Everyone expectantly watched.

"Please, I'd love one," I said. "And what are these?"

"These are chicken," Michaela said. "You go first."

"Oh," I said lightly. "Am I your food taster?"

Michaela smiled; in fact she'd already eaten several. "Well, when you keel over," she said, "we'll all know why."

Only Alexey, who had made the monkey slur, ate any more of the cake. No one spoke to Luisa. She stood motionless, her eyes fixed on the floor. A silence lengthened until Benjamin and Matthias entered the room.

"Whose birthday is it?" Benjamin asked.

Someone mumbled that it was Luisa's. "Hey Luisa," Benjamin said. "How do you sing 'Happy Birthday' in African?"

Luisa smiled at Benjamin with her big shy eyes. It became clear that she hadn't understood.

Benjamin began a round of "Happy Birthday" in German, only to abandon it when no one joined in.

Luisa put two pieces of cake on plates, which she handed to Benjamin and Matthias; they refused them. Instead they ate their own sandwiches. Luisa left the plates on the table. She stood there for a few moments as if deliberating what to do next. She made as if to cut more slices, but Michaela intervened.

"No," she said. "Enough is enough."

At this, Luisa quickly wrapped up her almost untouched food and left with a quiet *Tschüss*. As soon as she exited the room, the grievances commenced.

"It's so difficult with her," Benjamin said. "You never know whether she understands you. She doesn't understand a word."

"She doesn't understand anything," Michaela concurred.

The birthday incident hurt Luisa deeply. During our shift the following day, she sighed dejectedly and shook her head, recalling how the others had treated her. She had considered Benjamin one of her few allies, having failed to understand that many of his jokes were in fact at her expense.

"German man say, I not eat from you, not your food," Luisa lamented. Nostalgically she recalled the birthdays she'd celebrated in Mozambique. "In Africa, lots people come to celebrate. Uuhuuhuuu, you must see!"

Luisa's birthday party, an example of what anthropologist Clifford Geertz terms a failed ritual,[21] typifies the aversions and schisms that mark the cleaners' microcosm.[22] At Potsdamer Platz, it is common that German and foreign cleaners alike differentiate among each other based on race and ethnicity.[23] Indeed, racism is not uncommon, despite the company's strict anti-discrimination policy. Racist comments or discriminatory actions by cleaners, foremen or managers can be grounds for reprimand if not dismissal. Cleaners are well aware of this policy.

"If it came out that Marcel was xenophobic, if Tom or the client found out, he'd be gone like that," Ali says. "They don't want people like that here."

In practice, however, the policy is rarely enforced. Evidence is hard to collect and verify, and racist and other discriminatory remarks and

---

[21] Geertz (1957: 33), see also Bell (1992).

[22] Rituals can tell us much about communities. Here we may speak of a "loose coupling" (Goffman, 1983) between rituals and the social structures at play (Turner, 1969; Geertz, 1973; Cheal, 1988). Rituals can both enact social structures as well as produce and transcend them. Rituals are practices of social interaction that carry patterns of meaning. From a functionalist perspective, they serve social integration by creating a shared understanding and common emotional experience – something that is key for holding differentiated social systems together (see Collins, 2004; in the context of organizations, see Trice & Beyer, 1984; Lawrence, 2004; Islam & Zyphur, 2009). Yet not only can rituals exert power by fostering compliance and control, they can also bring about conflicts as well as ambivalence and resistance among the participants (Turner, 1969; Lukes, 1975; in the context of organizations, see also Rosen, 1988; Kunda, 2006; Koschmann & McDonald, 2015).

[23] On racism, stigmatization and discrimination, see also Lamont et al. (2016).

behaviors remain a persistent part of the cleaners' work life. Meanwhile, German and foreign cleaners alike commonly, often lightly trade denigrating remarks about various ethnic and racial groups. They variously refer to Asians as *Feejees*, Black people as *Nigger*, Turks as *Kanake* or *Dreckstürken* (dirty Turks). I hear Jews called "the dirtiest people," and Marcel speaks generally of the "disgusting life" of foreigners.

The cleaners do not necessarily regard themselves as right-wing sympathizers. Even as they give voice to xenophobic and racist attitudes, they often exhibit a conspicuous absence of venom. When Marcel refers to Ali as "our quota Turk," Ali – from Marcel's perspective – is in on the joke. Marcel is what cleaners call a "Hobby Hitler": someone who maintains a bigoted facade while eating Doner kebabs. To invoke the perennial defense and last refuge of the racist, some of his friends at work are immigrants.

But xenophobia and racism are not just an act. Cleaners go to some lengths to justify their resentments and prejudices, denigrating immigrants' work ethic and attitude.[24] These judgments are particularly severe vis-à-vis immigrants like Luisa who struggle with the language.

"People who say they don't understand a word of German – you have to watch out for them," Ali says. "Luisa once cleaned for me, but she left my cleaning cart dirty. Later she said, 'I had to rush to leave, to the church.' But I don't care if you have to go to church – I gave her a clean cart, she should give it back to me that way. You know, such people, who say they don't understand a word – when it's about money and salary, suddenly they can speak just fine."

Michaela is also bothered by coworkers' language problems. "It used to be that only those who spoke German could join CleanUp," she says. "And now everybody is here." Michaela welcomes Tom's stricter line on foreign cleaners and can't understand why some of them, like Luisa, are still around. "They need to be replaced!"

Once again, the occupation's low barriers to entry, supposedly confirmed by the presence of immigrants with poor German skills, threaten cleaners' self-worth. If anyone can do the job, Michaela might turn out to be just another replaceable cog in an indiscriminate machine.

---

[24] See also Lamont (2000: 58).

But as Luisa's failed birthday ritual demonstrate, the language barrier indicates more fundamental cultural clashes brewing under Potsdamer Platz. The racist treatment she experiences is no isolated case. When Christian encounters another African cleaner working to "really loud African music, totally without any melody," that, too, becomes the source of umbrage and ridicule.

"What is she even doing here?" Christian demands. "What is that, some kind of chieftain's dance? If clients came into the office with this kind of music playing, they'd probably call in sick."

As the story gains currency, the ridicule piles on, with parodies of African dance around make-believe voodoo dolls. The joke provides for a shared experience and bonding opportunity among not just the White German cleaners, but some of the immigrants as well.[25] Philosopher Slavoy Žižek writes that what often rankles

about the "other" is the peculiar way he [sic] organizes his enjoyment ... : the smell of "their" food, "their" noisy songs and dances, "their" strange manners, "their" attitude to work. To the racist, the "other" is either a workaholic stealing our jobs or an idler living on our labor, and it is quite amusing to notice the haste with which one passes from reproaching the other with a refusal to work to reproaching him for the theft of work.[26]

At Potsdamer Platz, the music is implicated in the African cleaner's alleged inability to coexist with her colleagues. "That" – the music – "is why she works by herself upstairs," Laura says. "You cannot work with her. And can you imagine, something like that in my house?"

In Laura's formulation, a foreign worker in the workplace becomes an intruder, a disturbing "noise,"[27] a "something" to be avoided. In denigrating the "other," Laura seeks to raise her own status above that of someone at the same altitude on the organizational chart: the notion that the African cleaner is *in Laura's house* symbolically negates that threatening hierarchical equivalence. Along the same lines, a new cleaner balks when assigned parts of Luisa's shift. "That's slave work," this young man says. "I'm doing nigger work here." The slur is an attempt to confirm a dominant social position that is manifestly under

---

[25] See also Collins (2004).   [26] Žižek (2000: 596).   [27] Rancière (2010).

threat, if not ridiculous, in this context, as he has been hired to do precisely the same work as the woman he calls slave.[28]

This racially charged tension between differentiation and equivalence sheds light on Bertha's interactions with Luisa and Alexey. She constantly scolds them and orders them around, her raised voice echoing through the mall, to the extent that I initially mistake her for their bullying boss.[29]

"Just look at her," Bertha says. "She really takes her time. She looks like she's about to fall asleep."

The threat of equivalence, once again, is at the root of the resentment. "They take everyone here," I overhear Bertha complain to Hans. "Why do they do that? Deaf, blind, mute – whatever!"

"Even the disabled," Hans concurs. He indicates Luisa. "But who cares, she only works four hours."

"Yes," Bertha impatiently allows. "But you know, she earns as much [per hour] as I do!"

The racism and xenophobia are felt; they take their toll. People "don't say hello, they just look at you," Ali says. Alexey laments how coworkers' hostility, particularly in response to language mistakes, makes it difficult to practice German, thus compounding the difficulty of integration.

The foreign-born cleaners are more receptive than some of their colleagues to Tom's emphasis on teamwork.

"Bertha always so *my side, your side*," Alexey complains. "Not team. Foreigners not like that. Germans like that."

Sometimes the immigrants find ways of pushing back, for example when Luisa exults in spotting dirt that Bertha has missed.

"Look, her side," Luisa says triumphantly in one such instance. "Looks shit! Germans so dirty, so dirty."

At times, Alexey and Luisa purposefully speed their work so that Bertha can't keep up – something that's difficult for her to stomach. The next day Bertha will work even faster so she can resume hurrying and harrying the two of them. This particular manifestation of the conflict doesn't interfere with the company's productivity goals, but rather spurs competition.

---

[28] See also Rosette et al. (2013).
[29] On bullying, see also Soylu and Sheehy-Skeffington (2015).

Foreign cleaners also respond by building coalitions. Although Luisa and Viola, a *Tagesdame*, seldom see each other at work – Viola works during business hours – they frequently exchange messages and sometimes meet up in their free time. The friendship with Viola – whom Anton calls the "kind soul" – becomes a "safe space"[30] for Luisa. Although both face the "multiple jeopardy"[31] of being both Black and female, Viola is much better integrated and never, at least in my presence, the target of racist comments and excluding behaviors. The dividing lines are not fixed, and even categorically comparable experiences admit variation.[32] Categories of difference seem to matter less than the maintenance of internal status hierarchies and jockeying within them.

Bertha finds herself on the receiving end of ridicule when the others discover her Turkish surname. "Aydin," pronounces Benjamin. "That says it all." He and Matthias joke about organizing a party: "Luisa can bring her antelope cake," Benjamin says. "And Aydin brings a giant doner kebab for everyone."

When they call her "Aydin," Bertha grins and bears it – mute, for once.

She also finds herself the recipient of an informal reprimand from management for her treatment of Luisa. When Luisa's birthday party fails to improve her standing, Tom has a talk with Bertha about her continuing waspish remarks. Bertha pushes back, Tom tells me; she claims that management always tries to work against her.

"And I said to her, my numbers are only as good as you all are down there," Tom recounts. "And when you're not doing your job, then after about six months I might as well just pack it in up here. I think she got the message."

Tom's use of "down there" and "up here" reflects the importance he places on the status hierarchy. His message from above succeeds, he believes, in renewing Bertha's sense that he recognizes and relies on her for her work. And after the talk, things do indeed improve between Bertha and Luisa. Instead of fighting, Anton observes, they begin to "work much better together – a big relief" for the management.

Luisa also notes how Tom keeps an eye on the situation, going from her to Bertha, asking each whether "all is good." After some time,

---

[30] Janssens and Steyaert (2019).   [31] King (1988).
[32] See also Lamphere et al. (1993).

Bertha even tells me, with a managerial tone, that "work-wise, I can't complain about Luisa."

Still later, when Anton relocates Luisa, Bertha is unhappy.

"It never fails," she laments. "They always take the good ones."

Dramas of Dignity in the Cleaners' Microcosm

The Potsdamer Platz underworld does not constitute a so-called melting pot in which differences do not matter. Cleaners show little interest in defining themselves as one group or in articulating common interests.[33] The stigmatization that cleaning and cleaners face by no means "facilitates the development of strong occupational or work-group cultures."[34] On the contrary, cleaners constantly seek to differentiate among themselves. While such efforts spur the formation of cliques, friendships and coalitions, and solidarity within these,[35] it also leads to workplace division and strife. Here it is not so much "physical isolation, high turnover and interpersonal competition for rewards,"[36] or the presence of a piecework system of production[37] that undermines an overarching solidarity. Rather, the lack of entry barriers to cleaning makes cleaners feel devalued and easily replaceable: "anyone," even the uneducated and unskilled, can do it. Against such negative equivalence of belonging to a group of "anyones," cleaners scale what hierarchy they can through acts of differentiation.

Cleaners don't merely encounter a set of differences in the workplace but actively create, mobilize and practice them in their interactions.[38] While these interactions partially reflect and draw inspiration from management's preference for German-speaking, trained, younger and male cleaners at Potsdamer Platz, cleaners' differentiation efforts also go beyond it.[39] Cleaners categorize "others" to establish their own superiority.[40] They mobilize general stereotypes, discriminatory labels and cultural prejudices, if not outright racism, and link them to moral

---

[33] See Thompson's (1966) understanding of class.
[34] Ashforth and Kreiner (1999: 419).　　[35] See also di Leonardo (1984).
[36] Ashforth and Kreiner (1999: 420).　　[37] Burawoy (1979).
[38] This illustrates the need to not only study different markers of difference (e.g. Holvino, 2010; Rodriguez et al., 2016) but also to take an emic approach to diversity (Tatli & Özbilgin, 2012).
[39] This shows the need to study "othering" not only between management and employees (e.g. Nisim & Benjamin, 2010) but also among employees.
[40] See also Janssens and Steyaert (2019).

judgments about work.[41] As Hughes explains in his essay *The Social Drama of Work*, "about the worst thing you can say about others is that they are lazy and have poor work habits. 'They' don't have our concept of work. This judgment about working quality makes up a large bulk of our moral judgments."[42]

Judgments about work easily become entangled with moral arguments. As documented in Chapter 2, cleaners valorize work precisely because they come from the social underworld. In drawing on more widely held categories and referring to moral judgments about work, cleaners seek to justify the status hierarchy they help establish. This in turn enables cleaners to avoid seeing themselves as racist, misogynist and so forth.[43] At the same time, the valorization of work raises the stakes for perceptions of their own job performance and work ethic. A poor review or a reprimand risks undermining cleaners' self-worth.

No single status hierarchy governs the workplace beneath Potsdamer Platz. No stable and dominant group achieves a wholesale "social closure" – Weber's term when one group gains privileged access to resources and power by excluding another.[44] The categories cleaners draw on to differentiate one another may shift, overlap and clash. So, too, may the lines of demarcation, along with the alliances and divisions they map. So, too, may the relative importance of the categories.[45] A cleaner who engages in othering on Friday afternoon may on Monday morning find herself its target.

Cleaners so "othered" are not passive victims; they may resist. They may make fun of their persecutors and point out their deficiencies, their differences. They may also fraternize with them, be in on the joke or otherwise reconcile; they may ultimately, like Bertha and Luisa, catch a common train. This is not to minimize real harm to the dignity of cleaners who find their difference targeted. The discrimination and harassment they face take at minimum an emotional toll, particularly in the absence of robust management support.

Cleaners who engage in othering to enhance their sense of worth run into trouble if the status hierarchies they attempt to produce and

---

[41] This confirms Lamont's (2000: 82) criticism of social psychology research, which fails to sufficiently account for the specific categories people employ in certain contexts. My research shows how people also employ the categories in strategic and dynamic ways.

[42] Hughes (1976: 7).   [43] See also Lamont (2000).   [44] Weber (1978).

[45] See also Adib and Guerrier (2003).

enforce are contested within the group or discounted externally.[46] A cleaner may advertise his masculinity in an attempt to overcome the stigma attached to his occupation, but success is likely to evade him.[47] When cleaners face the upperworld, particularly people of higher status, internal status hierarchies are prone to collapse. The categorization may suddenly turn against them as they find themselves treated as precisely the uneducated, rough people they have sought to dissociate themselves from. The other's "spoiled"[48] features perpetually threaten to spoil oneself, and the consequences for dignity may be grave. In this way do the cleaners find themselves in the same boat, yet apart.

---

[46] See also Jenkins (2008).
[47] My findings therefore differ in this regard from Tracy and Scott (2006) and Slutskaya et al. (2016).
[48] Goffman (1963/1990).

5 | *When Worlds Collide*
Cleaners at Work in the Upperworld

Working as a cleaner at Potsdamer Platz changes my perspective on the upperworld. It lets me experience what it means to access the upperworld from the underworld. I share cleaners' excitement when entering rich people's apartments, catching glimpses of private, pampered lives. In my cleaning uniform, I get a taste of the precariousness of cleaners' standing aboveground. It requires a thick skin to be so regularly ignored, treated like a disturbance, condescended and complained to. I come to understand why a simple "hello" or "good morning" from an upperworlder can mean so much to a cleaner.

None of this is to suggest that I could actually feel what cleaners feel in the upperworld. Even when the upperworlders fail to recognize me as such, I remain one of them. The office worker's complaint about coffee stains on the conference table doesn't upset me as it does the cleaners, whose sense of worth is bound up with the job of keeping it clean. My impersonation of a service worker is neither permanent nor uniformly convincing. When foreign tourists ask me in broken English where to find the toilet, they do a double take when I answer them fluently. My sister, an attorney who works at Potsdamer Platz, meets me at a café in the complex and our waiter is baffled by the pairing – business suit and cleaning uniform, a disturbance of the social order. I take his confusion as a reminder that it's less of a uniform on me than a disguise.

The disguise lays bare how differently people are treated on either side of the corporate divide. In the upperworld, cleaners constantly confront questions of their worth; the world aboveground sets the stage for innumerable dramas of dignity.

Client as King

At CleanUp, it's no secret that client encounters are difficult for cleaners, foremen and account managers alike. Since such encounters bring together people of different backgrounds, cultures and status, the human resources department trains account managers and foremen in what Ludwig calls "interaction knowledge." But cleaners, who interact more seldom with clients, get no such training.

Interaction knowledge calls to mind Goffman's notion that people seek to manage impressions in front of others by the way they present themselves in interaction.[1] Ludwig, similarly, explains to account managers and foremen that interaction knowledge will help them "assume the right role in front of clients." The "right role" is one that strikes a professional balance between catering to client needs and preventing clients from dictating the terms of the interaction, for example by talking cleaners into taking on unpaid "extras." The training workshops teach account managers and foremen impression management skills, showing them how to avoid appearing insecure and defensive and instead project a knowledgeable and respectable presence.

At one such workshop, participants perform role-plays to practice responding to customer complaints and extra-contractual requests. In one of these, Margot, an external trainer, asks Nadine, a CleanUp account manager, to show how she responds to a pushy client who calls her at 10 p.m. with complaints and a threat to cancel the contract. Margot plays a tough customer, and Nadine's emotions get the better of her – she weeps.

Margot is a tough coach. "Stand up for yourself, say no!" she shouts at Nadine. "You are not helpless! Let's do it again – this time do it for your children, for your life!"

The room is silent. People look away from the fraught scene, perhaps remembering similar encounters on the job. Their response combines shame and exasperation: Margot's approach seems unrealistic to some, given the pressures they face in such situations.

The workshop frames the problem of client interaction largely as an issue of individual self-presentation, but it is no less one of inequality. The interactions take place within, produce and reinforce "asymmetric relations."[2] Given both the socioeconomic gulf and the status disparity separating CleanUp employees and clients, CleanUp employees often lack what sociologist Arlie Hochschild, in *The Managed Heart*, termed

[1] Goffman (1959/1990).   [2] Goffman (1956: 481).

a "status shield."[3] The idea is that status can protect people from "the displaced feelings of others."[4] It can function as a shield against rude, humiliating and abusive client treatment.

The very idea of service implies asymmetry, and the notion of "customer sovereignty"[5] is manifest in the common expression, often heard at CleanUp, that "the client is king." Such an approach is not only fallacious – there are necessarily limits to the service[6] – but it also puts the service provider in a position of subservience, expected to display what Goffman terms "deference":

that component of activity which functions as a symbolic means by which appreciation is regularly conveyed *to* a recipient *of* this recipient, or of something of which this recipient is taken as a symbol, extension, or agent.[7]

In service work, the "marks of devotion"[8] can take the form of, among other things, "encouraging smiles ... attentive listening ... appreciative laughter ... comments of affirmation, admiration or concern."[9] Hochschild famously coined the notion of "emotional labor" to capture how workers have to "induce or suppress feeling in order to sustain the outward countenance that produces the proper state of mind in others."[10] In her study of household workers, sociologist Judith Rollins shows how employers thrive on the servitude of employees – usually black women – as a way to reinforce their higher status and frame the employment relationship as one of maternalism.[11] Inequality is simultaneously built into service interactions and normalized by them.[12]

Though Ludwig campaigns at the training workshops against the idea that the client is king, employees face a different reality in practice. Under pressure to acquire and retain clients, account managers bend over backward to please them, a dynamic that trickles down through the company hierarchy.

One hears the occasional story of a friendly client, but managers and foremen mostly describe undignified treatment and textbook examples of asymmetric relations.

[3] Hochschild (1983/2003: 163).
[4] Hochschild (1983/2003: 163); see also Kolb (2014).
[5] Korczynski (2009), Korczynski and Evans (2013).   [6] Korczynski (2009).
[7] Goffman (1956: 477); emphasis in original.   [8] Goffman (1956: 477).
[9] Hochschild (1983/2003: 84).   [10] Hochschild (1983/2003: 7).
[11] Rollins (1985).   [12] Sherman (2007), Hanser (2012).

"The client talks to me like, 'I am God and you are shit,'" says Slavoy, an account manager. "At times, they treat you like you're nobody," says Norbert, a foreman. "The first thing you learn here is to keep your mouth shut," says Tim, another foreman. "You cannot talk back."

If account managers and foremen feel this way, how do cleaners experience and approach interactions with clients? In contrast to interactive service workers, cleaners are neither trained for such interactions nor equipped with company scripts and routines. They are not practicing role-plays. Company scripts may threaten a worker's sense of autonomy and authenticity, yet may afford "some protection from assaults on their selves" – a tension that sociologist Robin Leidner captures in her study of McDonald's workers and insurance agents.[13] Face-to-face interactions between cleaners and clients at Potsdamer Platz are limited; cleaners are spatially and temporally made invisible by building design,[14] working hours and various rules, such as the one requiring them to use underground tunnels instead of the more direct surface routes. Yet, from time to time, cleaners may encounter clients, and they inevitably encounter upperworlders.

Cleaners do not always clearly distinguish between clients and the other upperworlders who work, reside or spend money at Potsdamer Platz. All benefit from cleaners' work and belong to a different world. Cleaners tend to treat people of high status as equal to clients in importance, perhaps assuming that they are influential and could complain about them. But before exploring face-to-face encounters with upperworld denizens, let's look at how cleaners approach the upperworld itself.

Cleaners in the Upperworld: Exclusivity under Fire

As soon as we arrive at our destination in an exclusive apartment complex, Susanna, Michaela and I start to conjecture: Who is Frau Kaiser, whose flat we are cleaning? What does she look like? What kind of life does she lead? How rich must she be to afford this flat? Anton thinks the rent is at least €1,300, until recently an astronomical sum in Berlin. We fan out like detectives, each starting in a different room, amassing clues.

[13] Leidner (1993: 14).   [14] See also Brody (2016).

"Look at the kitchen," Susanna calls. "There's only dust, no grease – she doesn't cook."

"Yeah, it's not too bad here," Michaela says, "especially compared to Dr. Berger. Maybe it's a second home she doesn't really use – or she has so much money, she eats out."

A bit later, Michaela announces from the bathroom, "She must have long, black hair – it's everywhere."

The Buddha statue provokes smirks, as does the quasi-medicinal tea inventory.

"Ooh, tea for relaxation – how lovely!" Susanna says. "We could use some of this."

Cleaners' sharp "sociological eyes" zero in on evidence relating to lifestyle, taste and especially affluence (also refer to Chapter 3 for a discussion on cleaners as dirt detectives).[15] They particularly target distinctions between the upperworld – with its aura of exclusivity, fame and prestige – and their own environment. That aura doesn't emanate uniformly from upperworld locations – for example, the Potsdamer Platz McDonald's – and what particularly catches cleaners' attention are those spots where status differences are the most pronounced: five-star hotels, professional-services offices and luxury homes and "million-euro cars," that is, a "Bugatti or some other ridiculous automobile." Cleaners relate to the upperworld by annexing, debunking and resenting its status hallmarks.

"Entering Everywhere": *Annexing Exclusivity*

Attuned to the luxury they see on the job, cleaners take pictures of luxury cars and other status symbols,[16] scan ads for home prices and make note of eye-popping pay stubs glimpsed on a desk. It's a high-value perk to enter the lair of a famous soccer player or a movie star in town for the Berlinale. Stories circulate about a "sheik from Dubai" whose flat is replete with gold – "what der Führer," Marcel ironically claims, "could only dream of." At the sheik's behest, €20,000 worth of pebbles surround the trees in the vicinity of his building – an irritant to

---

[15] Bourdieu (1984/2010); see also Llewellyn and Hindmarsh (2013).
[16] See Sauder (2005).

Marcel, who is responsible for keeping them off the sidewalk. But he is nonetheless fascinated by the sheik, by the influence and wealth he both wields and represents.

Cleaners enjoy their access to the upperworld; it allows them to annex some of the exclusivity. During the film festival, fans crowd and clamor to glimpse a film star, while the cleaners, Marcel says, "can enter everywhere and see all sorts of stars." Even the access bought with a cleaner's uniform is preferable to none; even low-status privilege buys them bragging rights.

Ali walks through "his building," "his territory," with a ring full of keys. He's greeted by name by both the guy with a mop and the woman with a corner office. When people praise the building's architecture, Ali thanks them. Pointing to a long queue of people waiting to ascend to the rooftop cafe, Ali lets it be known that his access and connections afford him free tickets and skip-the-line privileges – perks he gladly shares with his CleanUp coworkers. Whatever his status in the larger social order, his share of exclusive access in this corner of the upperworld lets him stake a claim to specialness.[17]

"Not That Great": Debunking the Upperworld

Even as the upperworld fascinates them, cleaners nonetheless take pleasure in tearing it down. Access to a hidden world can do much to tarnish its mystique, as well as confront cleaners with uncomfortable truths about their own status in it and their self-worth.

The apartment of a famous soccer coach is "actually nothing special," Susanna reports. "It's so small." In any case, she wouldn't want to live at Potsdamer Platz. "It's nice to look at, but it's too crowded."

Cleaning the renovated five-star hotel before its reopening, cleaners notice spots where the imported Italian plaster, installed by specialists, looks unfinished. "Is this supposed to be art?" a cleaner asks. Another drily responds: "Five-star art."

In the rooms designed according to ancient Chinese principles of good energy flow, every time a cleaner moves so much as a wastepaper basket someone shouts: "Oh shit! There goes our feng shui!" The simmering contents of a stockpot in a restaurant kitchen give an

---

[17] See also Bearman (2005).

impression of stewed birds, prompting one cleaner to say: "I thought I noticed fewer pigeons out there!" The mockery results in part from a clash of tastes and lifestyles.[18] But it also lets cleaners distance themselves from the upperworld and challenge something more fundamental: its value system.

The debunking of the upperworld constitutes a defense against exclusive status that might otherwise inspire feelings of inferiority.[19] Whatever special access they might enjoy, none of the cleaners will be reserving a table at the hotel restaurant. They may look and touch, but they may not keep or stay. (The Potsdamer Platz establishments they can afford – McDonald's, snack bars, shops, theaters – are not debunked.) To debunk is to invert a hierarchy, to pity privilege, to see through a facade that tourists, consumers and the clueless rich fall for. Cleaners may have low status, goes this line of thought, but at least they won't be fed a plate of stewed pigeons.

Resenting the "Fancy-schmancy"

When I discover a layer of mold in Frau Kaiser's refrigerator, Susanna and Michaela drop what they're doing to examine it.

"Champagne and Chanel nail polish in the fridge and then *this*," Susanna says with disdain.

Cleaners on their rounds uncover the "true" character of the upperworld, the filth behind the facade.

Rollins explains in her study of household workers how "*ressentiment* is more than hostility. It is a long-term, seething, deep-rooted negative feeling toward those whom one feels unjustly have power or an advantage over one's life."[20]

At Potsdamer Platz, such ressentiment takes the form of pointing out upperworlders' moral and social deficiencies.[21] Cleaners have their own derisive taxonomy for those they clean up after: the "suits," "snotty people," "the fancy-schmancy" and the "persnickety," the arrogant noses in the air. They criticize them as ill-mannered, shameless, needy and, worst of all, dirty. Thus, cleaners reverse the common

---

[18] Bourdieu (1984/2010).   [19] See also Rollins (1985).
[20] Rollins (1985: 227).   [21] See also Sherman (2007).

association of the working class with impurity and moral weakness, and the bourgeoisie with cleanliness and virtue,[22] associations deeply ingrained in the German culture since the nineteenth century.[23] The richer and more arrogant, cleaners contend, the dirtier people are.[24] Benjamin and Matthias skewer Potsdamer Platz's tagline, "the Platz to be"; instead, it is "the Platz to flee." Other cleaners note how the "fancy-schmancy" women with suits and manicures "behave like pigs"; the "shit millionaires" are "really disgusting" with their dirty fridges. "Here you have such rich people," one cleaner says, "but then you see how dirty it looks, and how bad it smells!"

Alex and Ali frequently mention dirt and filth in the same breath with rich people.

"They walk around so posh, so piss-elegant, but when sitting on the toilet the truth comes out!"

In the *History of Shit*, psychoanalyst Dominique Laporte notes how to "touch, even lightly, on the relationship of a subject to his shit, is to modify not only that subject's relationship to the totality of his body, but his very relationship to the world and to those representations that he constructs of his situation in society."[25] It is precisely the "representation" of luxury, glamor and thus superiority that cleaners seek to undermine by relating the upperworlders with defecation. Linking wealth and money with shit is a common trope: filthy lucre. Freud developed how the interest in money connects to infants' first possessions – their excrement.[26]

For cleaners, the connection between wealth and shit exposes the immorality of the upperworld. As Laporte notes, there is "the poor man's law, which suspects corruption within luxury and wealth at the source of stench."[27]

"Clients who are particularly fussy are always the dirtiest in the toilet," Hans says. "These people really have no decency."

Service recipients are regarded as weak and powerless, dependent on cleaners, without whom they would "perish in their own crap," Susanna remarks.

Saying that the upperworlders not only shit, but that they do so in an unhygienic manner, turns the social hierarchy upside down.

---

[22] Elias (1939/1996).   [23] Reagin (2007).
[24] There have also been suggestions that wealthy clients might treat service workers better (e.g. Sherman, 2007).
[25] Laporte (2002: 29).   [26] Freud (1908).   [27] Laporte (2002: 40).

"They're human beings just like anybody else, and they have to shit," Ali says. "And I have seen it – they are really disgusting! Like leaving a nice load of diarrhea without flushing. I believe they're dirtier than us. And without us, they would be nothing. They need people to clean up after their filth."

Beneath Ali's rapport with clients, his habitual politeness and deference, runs this undercurrent of resentment. To maintain a sense of worth, cleaners engage in "condemning the condemners."[28] They ascribe not just dirtiness, but worse dirtiness, to a class they think looks down on them.

Personal Encounters with the Upperworld

For cleaners, interacting with upperworlders may seem like a no-win situation. Cleaners report being ignored, spoken down to, treated as a disturbance. Upperworlders rarely welcome the cleaners' presence, if they even acknowledge it they show appreciation for their work even more rarely.

"We Are the Invisibles": Cleaners as Non-persons

To clean another person's space entails occupying and temporarily taking charge of it. In contrast to service work, which takes place in a defined space belonging to the service provider,[29] the space to be cleaned belongs to the recipient. This can make it difficult for cleaners to do their work. In the early mornings, the lights in the shopping mall are sometimes still off. "No light and then we are supposed to see everything and clean – that's impossible," Michaela complains.

In the presence of clients, cleaners may be not only hindered in their work but rudely treated. At Potsdamer Platz, people will cross the cleaning barriers, step over mops and tread on wet floors, dirtying them.

Anecdotes about encounters with office workers are also a staple of cleaners' complaints: the guy who spills coffee on the freshly cleaned

---

[28] Ashforth and Kreiner (1999).
[29] E.g. Hochschild's (1983/2003) flight attendants are trained to consider the cabin a "home."

stairs, then acts as if nothing has happened, or those who obstruct the cleaners' work, then complain about it.

"The problem is when you clean an office during the day, and people are on their computer," Tanja says. "You ask, could I get in here for a second? Would I be bothering you? And they almost always ignore you or they just say, not now! You ask three days in a row and then on the fourth day, they see dust and complain – *why wasn't my space cleaned?* And then you have a problem."

Working in the client's presence, the cleaners are damned if they do, damned if they don't: their presence is unwelcome, their absence reprimanded.

Upperworlders may decline to make the slightest accommodation for cleaners' work.

"I sometimes get really annoyed when people use the toilets I'm cleaning, even when there are four other toilets," one cleaner says. "They would just have to walk a little ways down, not even 25 meters." Marcel tells how once he "wiped all the dirt into one heap. Then two women came and stood directly on it. I kept getting closer and closer and tried to make eye contact with them, but they just stood there."

My own experience underscores this point. In the shopping mall, my task is to wipe benches and the surrounding area. Just as I start my work, a woman sits down on the bench. She goes only so far as to lift her legs so I can wipe the floor beneath her.

So it's no surprise if cleaners feel they are treated as non-existent, as figures beyond perception – as what Goffman calls a "non-person."[30] As such, cleaners "are present during the interaction but in some respects do not take the role either of performer or of audience, nor do they ... pretend to be what they are not."[31] Their basic person-hood – their existence – is denied, and such treatment can be even more humiliating than outright stigma. As Rollins puts it, after Frantz Fanon, "A feeling of inferiority? No, a feeling of nonexistence."[32]

Upperworlders may ignore cleaners almost naturally, with no intention to insult. To ignore is an expression of the "ability to annihilate the humanness and even, at times, the very existence"[33] of service workers. One morning, as the shopping mall fills with people on their

---

[30] Goffman (1959/1990).   [31] Goffman (1959/1990: 150).
[32] In Rollins (1985: 210).   [33] Rollins (1985: 209).

way to work, a woman bumps into Luisa and sends her cart rolling away. In such instances, perhaps an apology is muttered, but more likely it is not.

Elevator rides offer stark examples of upperworlders treating cleaners as non-persons.[34] One morning Christian and I board an elevator occupied by an office worker whose office and desk we clean on a daily basis. When we enter, the worker looks away.

"I hate that," Christian says later. "Not even to say hello – and on top of that picking his nose!"

Various reasons might explain why the office worker doesn't greet us. Perhaps the encounter, or guilt about his privilege, makes him feel uncomfortable; perhaps he suspects that we cleaners despise him for his status and prefer not to engage with him; or perhaps he simply doesn't greet anyone in elevators, irrespective of status, just as the cleaners often fail to acknowledge each other's comings and goings underground. Whatever the actual reason or reasons, cleaners take it personally; they *hate that*. To be treated as a non-person is an attack on one's dignity.

For Goffman, servants are typical examples of non-persons, and the dynamic is as old as service and servitude. In *The Theory of the Leisure Class*, economist and sociologist Thorstein Veblen describes how servants' presence is unwelcomed, yet tolerated by their employers.

"Personal contact with the hired persons whose aid is called in to fulfill the routine of decency is commonly distasteful to the occupants of the house, but their presence is endured and paid for," Veblen writes. "The presence of domestic servants, and of the special class of body servants in an eminent degree, is a concession of physical comfort to the moral need of pecuniary decency."[35]

That today's service workers are still treated as "socially dead" might be related to their proximity, their access to the client's intimate spaces. By approaching them as non-persons, their knowledge is rendered "of no use in social life."[36] Indeed, some cleaners suspect that upperworlders ignore them precisely because they are privy to the dirty laundry. Cleaners' access to the upperworld's backstage areas allows them to unmask that world and penetrate its exclusivity –

---

[34] For a discussion of social encounters during elevator rides, see Hirschhauer (1999).

[35] Veblen (1899/2003: 46).   [36] Bearman (2005: 7).

something that provides them with "the makings of a kind of magical power over"[37] the upperworlders. Treating cleaners as non-persons neutralizes that power.

"It's like we are not there," an account manager says at a workshop. "We don't see anything, we don't hear anything. We are the invisibles."

Cleaners may challenge such treatment by directly addressing upperworlders. As Hans and I mop the lobby, a woman passes directly in front of us without acknowledging our presence. "Good morning!" Hans exclaims. The woman turns and reciprocates the greeting with a friendly smile. Whether she has ignored us out of contempt or habit, Hans takes it as a slight, and doesn't let it stand.

Top Down: Cleaners as Inferiors

Cleaners regularly contend with rude and high-handed treatment. One morning, I'm cleaning outside around the fountain when an office worker calls me over. I approach and without a word she throws packaging waste into my shovel. A garbage can stands not two meters away. Another time, Mr. Schmidt, a high-ranked manager at a client company, approaches Ali, who has just changed his schedule.

"Ah, you're leaving already?" Mr. Schmidt says.

"Yes," Ali replies. "I've been here since 5:30."

Mr. Schmidt is not satisfied. "I will look into this," he says.

Ali keeps his cool, but the encounter is nonetheless a blow to his pride in being his "own boss." It is humiliating. Humiliation "happens only *in relation*. It is a transitive, interpersonal process. One is humiliated only in other people's minds, according to other people's lights."[38] The client's questioning not only signals distrust, but indicates on what shaky ground even Ali stands with his long service and personal relationships with both management and client.

Cleaners are often spoken to with the familiar pronoun *Du*, whereas they use the formal address *Sie*. Following Goffman, salutations are "ceremonial activities" that belong to "status rituals."[39] The interrelation of conversation, deferential behavior and status is manifest in the

---

[37] Hughes (1958/2012: 51).   [38] Koestenbaum (2011: 11; emphasis in original).
[39] Goffman (1956: 478).

implicit expectation that cleaners yield control over a conversation's start and length.[40]

At the end of a shift, Christian approaches an office worker and asks, "Last Friday – was everything OK?"

She answers abruptly, apparently annoyed: "Yes."

On leaving, he asks, "Door open, closed? Lights on or off?"

"Just leave it!" she exclaims – her patience is at an end.

Merely initiating a conversation may cross a line of deference. When Henning tells the foreman Michael that he spoke to a client, Michael reacts with irritation. Henning has failed to observe what Goffman terms "avoidance rituals." These refer "to those forms of deference which lead the actor to keep at a distance from the recipient," reflecting the "sociological distance" between them.[41] Whereas subordinates are expected to engage in avoidance rituals when interacting with superiors, the latter can treat the former in more familiar ways, for example by addressing them as *Du* rather than *Sie*.

At Potsdamer Platz, the elevator is a hot spot for avoidance rituals. Ali grants upperworlders first access to an elevator and refrains from entering with his cart and equipment if they risk crowding the car. Carts can also delay rides if they have to wheel out and back in at each stop to make way for riders. Signaling his courtesy and attentiveness, Ali will call the elevator when he spots a client in the lobby. In this partly ceremonial act of deferential service, he will then extend his arm to prevent the door from closing while the client enters the elevator and Ali yields it.

Such deferential displays don't necessarily indicate that cleaners accept their inferior position. They may perform deference without feeling any genuine respect or regard, allowing them "a kind of inner autonomy, holding off the ceremonial order by the very act of upholding it."[42] Ali will yield an elevator, but he will not hesitate to express resentment toward the same people he treats with such solicitous politesse. In this drama of dignity, one act plays out in front of the audience, while backstage the actor gives voice to his grievances and protects his self-esteem.

[40] See Rollins (1985).   [41] Goffman (1956: 481).   [42] Goffman (1956: 478).

At times, cleaners "insinuate all kinds of disregard by carefully modifying intonation, pronunciation, pacing"[43] in what may seem to be deferential behavior. When Benjamin and Matthias encounter an upperworlder in the elevator, they greet her with exaggerated solicitude, which pivots to lewd malice the moment she – they call her "that old bitch" – exits.

Other cleaners refrain altogether from deferential behavior. When Hans and I are assigned to clean Ali's building, I mention Ali's elevator routine and Hans isn't impressed. "Nah," he says. "We'll never get anything done." As a result, we find ourselves several times crammed into elevators with visibly irritated businesspeople.

In resisting the inferior position inherent in deferential behavior, cleaners protect their dignity. Hans doesn't hesitate to take a smoking break in front of the client. Strutting through the lobby of the building we're there to clean, he greets the client with a smile and smokes as if he owned the place.

"I'm not going to let people take this from me," Hans says. "I know my rights and a break is part of it."

In fact, cigarette breaks are not recognized under the law as legitimate time off during work hours.[44] But Hans smiles confidently to those he meets, and walks around Potsdamer Platz with his head held high.

Face-to-Face Confrontations

Cleaners take great pride in the praise they receive. An approving note, comment or the rare phone call means a lot to them. By the same token, complaints can be devastating.

Regardless of its substance, cleaners tend to immediately reject a complaint as unfair. Either they have cleaned the object as required or the contract allocated too few resources for the job.[45]

"URGENT!!!" reads a note of complaint sent about Christian. "The tables in the conference rooms are not properly wiped and fingerprints are still on the coffee mugs – something he needs to take care of."

---

[43] Goffman (1956: 478).

[44] For a critical discussion of smoking regulations at work, see Brewis and Grey (2008).

[45] That cleaners fiddle with standards does not necessarily represent resistance, as Lundberg and Karlsson (2011) suggest. Such fiddling might also be necessary as too few resources are allocated to a shift.

Christian is furious. Cleaners can feel virtually powerless to defend themselves against complaints. No matter how good a job they've done, any shred of paper or drop of water could provoke one. "They can always find something," cleaners lament.

After Henning vacuums the long red carpet in the renovated hotel lobby, a group of construction workers tromps through, leaving muddy tracks. The hotel manager asks Henning to vacuum everything again, and his tone suggests that Henning might not have done the job properly the first time.

"You're on your knees to get it clean and five minutes later everything is filthy again," Henning sighs.

Cleaners struggle to achieve the respect they think their work has earned them, and every client complaint may seem like an attack, a confirmation of the assumption that cleaners are lazy and uncommitted.

"They think we're the bottom of the barrel," Lars says. "They treat us like bums who don't know anything. They find one thing wrong and they come down so hard on us."

Sometimes, clients appear to think they know the cleaners' job better than they themselves do.

"People who clean at home, they think they know how it's done," Michaela says. "But of course it's not the same."

During the breakfast break, Michaela tells the others about the new manager of the shop she cleans. "He told me I should first wipe the whole place and then vacuum it, so that I don't raise all the dust. But I told him this doesn't make sense."

Despite CleanUp's efforts to cast its cleaners as professionals, clients rarely approach them this way. One day Mr. Gregor, the manager of the apartment complex, enters the lobby as Christian and I are cleaning it and cries, "It's been moved again!" The glass plate of the front desk rests on little rubber magnets that tend to shift over time. The client reproaches Christian, addressing him as *Du*.

"Do you always move them when you clean?" Mr. Gregor demands. "It just doesn't look good. These are the kinds of details that matter!"

"No, we only clean the top," Christian quietly responds, and moves to help the manager lift the plate.

"Do you always touch it like that with your hands?" Mr. Gregor barks.

Mr. Gregor is leaving fingerprints on the glass from below. I'm attempting to wipe them off before they put the plate down when my cloth inadvertently catches a magnet.

"You are moving them!" Mr. Gregor cries. "Yes!"

I apologize. Mr. Gregor is incensed. Putting the plate down, he nearly catches our fingers. "Hands off!"

Everyone needs a time-out after this. Leaning against the wall in an inner courtyard, Christian smokes furiously. "That was absolutely unacceptable, how he talked to us." Christian mimics the manager. "Well, these details matter!" He smokes and rants. "I can't handle these people! He is such an ass. I can't suck up to him, I can't do it anymore. Look at me, I'm shaking."

These kinds of confrontations bring to the fore how difficult it is for cleaners to maintain their dignity while interacting with clients. They feel unfairly targeted, and no matter what they do or say, their guilt is assumed. If you talk back, you risk your job.

"I wouldn't care if they had fired me," Christian says. "But whatever – I don't want people talking to me like that."

But Christian didn't talk back; he feared his anger might get out of hand. Instead he is left to indulge in fantasies of revenge. "I'd love to throw him to the fans of FC Union" (a Berlin soccer team) "and make him shout, 'I hate the FC Union.' He wouldn't get out of there alive."

Apart from work, cleaners like Christian interact little, if at all, with people outside their socioeconomic class (refer to Chapter 2). As CleanUp doesn't train cleaners how to interact with clients, they face these encounters unprepared. They are not in a position to make "verbal claims."[46] They do not seem to have what philosopher Jacques Rancière terms "voice" in the upperworld; they largely remain "noise," in the words of Rancière, to those who encounter them there.[47]

Compounding the problem is a perceived lack of management support. Cleaners feel they are "systematically left on their own, isolated from the abusive customer and from management, who place them in the position of putting up with the abuse."[48] Along these lines,

---

[46] Sauder (2005).   [47] Rancière (2010).   [48] Korczynski (2003: 75).

Benjamin and Matthias complain that Tom responds subserviently to client complaints. "He's panic-stricken," Benjamin says. "It never fails. That pisses me off so much."

So Benjamin and Matthias are the more amazed when they witness Tom pushing back against a client. Tom has them mop the floor in front of the client to prove that the stains in question require a more expensive polishing.

Matthias and Benjamin laugh recalling the bewildered complainer: finally, a client put in his place.

Tom also comes to Marcel's defense. Faced with a series of complaints about his outdoor territory, Tom suggests that, as a proof of his work, Marcel takes before and after pictures (see figure 5.1). Marcel likes the idea; he looks forward to showing the client a "nice picture of shit where you can still see pieces of corn in it."

Marcel also takes matters into his own hands, frequently going up to people who have littered and telling them to dispose of their garbage properly.

"Hey, is this your stuff?" he asks a group of teens who have just left the detritus of their McDonald's picnic on the square. "Pick it up!"

And they do. As Ali later explains, "People are actually afraid of Marcel. You don't fuck with that guy."

Like Hans smoking on company time, Marcel exercises privilege that is not universally distributed among the cleaners. Even if her language skills didn't get in the way, even if she had Marcel's intimidating physical presence, Luisa on her fixed-term contract could much less afford to risk upsetting even a group of teens. Confrontation is exceptional; cleaners mostly feel they must hold their peace.

Even Marcel's privilege has its limits. After reprimanding a man who has been spitting and throwing his cigarette butts on the pavement, Marcel suddenly finds himself confronting three more men, all of them spitting in front of him to demonstrate the limits of his authority. Marcel beats a hasty retreat.

Cleaners also turn to one another for support. After the incident with Mr. Gregor, Christian tells the story to whoever will listen. In the evening, he calls Marcel, who tries to calm him down. The incident has compounded the strain on Christian's already fragile self-worth, and Marcel worries it could trigger a relapse with alcohol.

Figure 5.1 Picture after having removed human feces.

"Good That You Are Here!": Appreciative Encounters

Cleaners welcome any sign of recognition or appreciation. When upperworlders greet cleaners, thank them or exchange a few words in passing, it goes a long way; it may be worth bragging points.

A client praises Marcel – "Good that you're here. You can tell the difference!" – and Marcel proudly shares the compliment with the other cleaners, perhaps conscious that the implied comparison may reflect poorly on them.

When a group of young people sees me on cigarette butt patrol, they politely inquire where they can leave theirs so that I don't wind up picking up after them. Another time, I'm cleaning in the shopping mall next to a man who's standing there talking on the phone. He interrupts his conversation in order to catch my attention and thank me.

A woman working in a shop in the mall greets Bertha every morning. When Bertha returns from her summer vacation, the woman says approvingly, "One can see that you are back!"

Score one for Bertha in her competition with Luisa. Luisa, for her part, beams after a customer approaches her in the mall a couple of times, handing over a banknote with the benediction, "I like African people!"

Luisa finds these exchanges all the more fortifying to the extent she feels ostracized by her coworkers.

Cleaners do not necessarily find gifts condescending,[49] though they may confirm their status as both servant and, as in Luisa's case, immigrant/outsider. Perhaps they perceive them more like tips, something that cleaners more typically receive from hotel guests. In his famous study on the symbolic significance of gifts, anthropologist and sociologist Marcel Mauss argues that gifts one does not "reciprocate" signal that "one is ... unequal."[50] "To give is to show one's superiority, to be more, to be higher in rank, *magister*," Mauss writes. "To accept without giving in return, or without giving more back, is to become client and servant, to become small, to fall lower (*minister*)."[51]

The kind of inequality Mauss attaches to one-way gifts doesn't seem to matter to cleaners.[52] On the contrary, they disapprove of gifts that entail expectations of exchange, namely in the form of extra work. One time, a young man, presumably the manager of a café, asks me to pick up cigarette butts in front of his business.

"I'm not sure that's our area to clean," I tell him.

He insists that it is. As I'm picking up the cigarette butts, he offers me a coffee on the house.

When I describe the incident to Marcel, he warns me against accepting freebies.

"Don't get taken in," he says. "When I started here, I always did all sorts of extra things for everyone, and got lots of free coffee. But in the

---

[49] In this way, my findings differ from Rollins (1985).
[50] Mauss (1950/1990: 53).   [51] Mauss (1950/1990: 95, emphasis in original).
[52] See also Sherman (2007).

end you're like this," and Marcel trembles as though overdosing on caffeine. "I can buy my own coffee."

But when the beautiful blonde Starbucks barista approaches Marcel with a complimentary coffee after he's power-washed the sidewalk in front of the café, he is willing to make an exception.

Sometimes clients treat cleaners as though they were invisible – and sometimes cleaners wish that they would. Some upperworlders, once they start talking to service personnel, may forget to stop. Every time Matthias and Benjamin encounter Mrs. Dietrich, an older woman who lives in one of the apartment complexes, she pulls them over for a chat. They have heard her life story, they know about her very rich husband and their inability to have children, about her ongoing struggle with cancer. They know her opinions on the state of the world.

"Today people do not really talk to one another anymore," Mrs. Dietrich laments. "What with the mobile phone and emails ..."

Matthias and Benjamin like Mrs. Dietrich, though they mock her risible attempts to bridge the status divide. "My husband wanted to buy me a Porsche," Matthias says in a lacerating impersonation. "But I preferred to take the public train."

"I could see going out with her for coffee and cake," Benjamin says, adding mordantly: "But we probably won't be hooking up after."

Even as upperworlders like Mrs. Dietrich try to establish a more intimate relationship with service workers, the status gulf persists, perhaps even reinforced by their encounters. During an elevator ride, Hans and I experience how even a friendly conversation can bring status differences to the fore. Sharing the marble-lined elevator in the Kollhoff building with a well-dressed office worker, I am puzzled that the elevator goes up though I've pressed the ground-floor button.

The woman smiles. "Looks like we're going up first," she says.

"It doesn't matter," I reply. "We'll enjoy this beautiful elevator a little longer."

The woman looks at me, astonished. "Beautiful!" she exclaims. "It's shabby and it's not going to improve. They're not renovating anything."

Hans and I exchange glances.

"Well," he says after the attorney has exited at her floor. "Imagine what she's used to."

All this shows how it does not require "antagonistic attitudes" toward clients, as sociologist Peter Bearman in his study *Doormen* suggests, for cleaners to experience and "see social class."[53] On the contrary, even seemingly friendly and appreciative encounters can reinforce status differences. Rather than elevating cleaners' sense of worth, they may make cleaners feel alienated, if not degraded.

Only Ali among this group has managed to establish a special position for himself. Years of serving the client in a professional and deferential manner have earned him a degree of independence from CleanUp. In addition, the client has given Ali an "office": a small, windowless space on the minus-two basement level that is accessed through a machine room. Apart from the cleaning materials he safeguards there (for "his" building only the cleanest mops and cloths will do), he has a small desk and a few salvaged chairs. At his desk, Ali takes care of paperwork and adds detail to his map of the building's sprawling staircases. The map lets him pinpoint where a step or railing needs repair, and the client likes to follow its progress.

"You see, I am an architect," Ali says. "This is not cleaning. The work gets done based on what I write down here."

Ali cannot "cast [himself] as powerful" and "equal to" the clients "by establishing meaningful relationships with them on the basis of a standard of reciprocal treatment."[54] His interactions with clients, like his subterranean office, reinforce the status differences they may be intended to smooth over. Still, his status remains elevated vis-à-vis his fellow cleaners.

Does that status make Ali the envy of his peers? Not necessarily: many are unwilling to pay the price he pays in deference and engagement. Alex can't understand why Ali would work so hard, indeed take on extra work, in order to ingratiate himself with the higher-ups. To Alex and others, closer relationships with clients are a mixed blessing. Familiar clients might be more forgiving if the cleaner screws something up. But they might also exploit a personal connection by demanding more work. For most cleaners, the path of least resistance is that of least interaction.

---

[53] Bearman (2005: 169).   [54] Sherman (2007: 17).

"We Don't Want to See Them!": The Invisible Cleaner

For Goffman, "maintenance of face" – the positive self-image a person projects when in contact with another – "is a condition of interaction, not its objective."[55] This may explain why some cleaners wish to avoid encounters with upperworlders altogether. The perceived threat to their self-worth looms too large. Potsdamer Platz is designed to minimize such encounters, as are the cleaners' contracts and schedules. Cleaners and other service workers at Potsdamer Platz are meant to be as invisible as possible, and many of them prefer it that way.

"I'd rather go back to train station cleaning," Christian says after the incident with Mr. Gregor. "Nobody talks to you, you are simply left alone."

Goffman maintains that "[i]t would seem that the role of non-person usually carries with it some subordination and disrespect, but we must not underestimate the degree to which the person who is given or who takes such a role can use it as a defence."[56] Cleaners are relieved when working in the absence of clients – among other reasons, they feel less surveilled (also refer to Chapter 6). "I really hate it," Michaela says, "if someone is always looking over my shoulder."

Cleaners actively make themselves invisible. As soon as a client appears in the space, the cleaner shifts gears, working as fast as possible to minimize the potential for interaction. Ignoring the other goes both ways across the Potsdamer Platz divide. This doesn't represent a gesture of politeness in the form of what Goffman terms "civil inattention," but instead marks a defense against status confrontations.

"We don't want to see them," Anton says. "And they don't want to see us either."

Invisibility is also a means of examining, perhaps questioning, inequality. It lets service workers collect data on the wealthy people they serve, on the employer, the client, the contract and even what Marx calls the surplus value – CleanUp's profit.

Christian sees a folder with the CleanUp contract on a client's desk and can't resist opening it. When he sees what CleanUp charges, he calculates the hourly rate and CleanUp's profit. "You have to subtract

---

[55] Goffman (1967: 12).   [56] Goffman (1959/1990: 151–152).

for supplies, but with the hours, they are definitely doing good business," Christian says. Much of that good business, he notes, relies on cleaners covering more ground in less time, or on cheaper labor. "Here they save on one cleaner by sending Hermann," who, as a trainee, is paid less.

What clients pay and what CleanUp makes constitute a regular subject of conversation among the cleaners, engendering resentment.

"CleanUp makes so much money here," Alex says in Ali's building. "They make like eight thousand euros a month, and we do this for nothing."

Beyond CleanUp's wages and fees, basic income inequality stokes resentment as well. After seeing a wage slip on the desk of a client, Alex sounds out a cost-benefit comparison of white-collar and blue-collar experience.

"We destroy ourselves physically, and they do it mentally," he reasons. "But with them everything is good when they look at their bank balance at the end of the month."

Alex insists that he doesn't envy the professionals of the upper-world – he has no desire to spend his life sitting at a desk pushing paper. But to be paid so little for work that "destroys" his body – that he considers unjust.

Neither knowledge of the surplus value of their work nor daily reminders of income inequality have led cleaners to collectively mobilize and demand better working conditions and pay, at least not yet. Faced with questions about their worth against this backdrop of wealth and privilege, they are more apt to turn their anger and sense of injustice against fellow cleaners, as the interpersonal dramas discussed in Chapter 4 demonstrate.

Driven Apart: Encounters between the Worlds

Benjamin and Matthias are eager to show me a secret hang-out, an apartment building rooftop with a beautiful view. After parking the cleaning cart out of sight, we climb a flight of stairs to the rooftop, where we sit and take in the vast vista: up close the glassy spectacle of Potsdamer Platz, and beyond it the city skyline.

"Look at that place, what an awesome terrace," Matthias says. "It's perfect for barbecues. There's a vacant unit – hey Benjamin, you want to share a flat?"

Meanwhile, I've noticed that only a low railing stands between me and an eight-story drop. Struck with vertigo, I ask Benjamin for more room.

"Well," he says, "we face the abyss everyday."

The subject has changed; the mood turns.

"Look at what kind of shit work we have to do," Benjamin says. Potsdamer Platz is a "prestige object" for CleanUp, but that prestige accentuates by contrast the cleaners' lack of it. Much as they may enjoy their access to this world, such access makes them all too aware of the socioeconomic inequality that consigns them to their role.

Forays into the upperworld thus constitute both blessing and curse. Through access, cleaners may gain insight, and stories, even satisfying social interactions. But they are left working for people they deem, on the whole, arrogant and demanding. The upperworld's exclusivity and society may in some instances rub off to some degree, granting someone like Ali special status among his peers. More often than not, however, the opposite is true.[57] The more exposure cleaners get to the upperworld, the more they come face-to-face with an inflexible status hierarchy that poses a serious ongoing threat to their dignity. Whatever the upperworlders' intentions, their interactions with the cleaners too often leave the latter feeling as they've been treated as non-persons: inferior, incompetent, lazy; disturbances in the environment. The issue is not just stigmatization and abuse by customers,[58] but denial of the cleaners' personhood.

This doesn't mean that cleaners are passive victims.[59] On the contrary, cleaners frame their situation and debunk their environment in ways that provide them with a defensive superiority. To varying degrees, they confront upperworlders, sometimes just by making them-

---

[57] At Potsdamer Platz, the tendency is therefore different than in Sherman's luxury hotels, where "at all levels of relationships, guests tended to exhibit reciprocal behavior toward workers, by recognizing both their basis personhood and their effort" (Sherman, 2007: 186; see also Bearman, 2005). One could speculate that this difference has something to do with the overall status of cleaning work as well as the closer personal relation and guest dependency inherent in luxury hotel service.

[58] These tend to be commonly studied in customer service work (e.g. Van Maanen, 1991; Korczynski, 2009).

[59] See also Hochschild (1983/2003), Leidner (1993), Korczynski (2009).

selves seen and heard.[60] Cleaners like Marcel even show attempts at "changing the behaviors"[61] they find unacceptable in those they serve.[62] But the confrontational cleaner cannot be confident of management support, and those working under fixed-term contracts can ill afford to risk upsetting either clients or their employer.

Call it the Potsdamer Platz paradox: encounters between those who work and live in the complex and those who labor there out of sight tend to drive the worlds further apart. The upperworld, failing to recognize these workers or their contribution, proves a crowded arena for dramas of dignity.[63] And the rift between the worlds is both the wellspring of these dramas and the means of escape from them. For cleaners, the invisible underworld can be a refuge from a landscape of indignities.

---

[60] Thus, their "resistance" does not need to be "silent" (Star & Strauss, 1999: 18), but on the contrary can involve speaking up.

[61] Rollins (1985: 232).

[62] In this way, the cleaners' behavior differs from Rollins's domestic workers.

[63] In contrast to Bearman's (2005) doormen and Sherman's (2007) luxury hotel service workers, cleaners in the upperworld therefore experience difficulties arranging themselves with the status differential involved and finding ways to elevate status.

6 | *"Back to the Dark Side"*
Cleaners' Tactics against Surveillance

Indulging in a McFlurry is a much longed-for reward after a day of mopping sunless hallways, and sometimes it can't wait until after hours. Today, it's Benjamin's idea to take a McFlurry break during our shift with Matthias.

"Matthias needs this, otherwise he's such a miserable son of a bitch," Benjamin says. "It's the low blood sugar," he explains.

Benjamin, Matthias and I sit in the dark in one of the many marble apartment building lobbies. They all look the same: a Rothko reproduction on the wall, a dried-out plant, a couple of basket chairs, often lacking cushions, a side table. In order to evade detection by the motion sensor, we move as little as possible. Our eyes and ears remain vigilant. Benjamin and Matthias constantly look up from their phones in case a foreman, manager, client or a security guard passes by. Several noises test our reflexes.

"Shhhh, quiet – quick!" Benjamin exclaims.

We leap to our feet, grabbing cleaning cloths and hiding the McFlurrys among the detergents on our cleaning cart. We're energetically wiping down the nearest surface when we realize it's a false alarm and return to our melting snacks.

On another occasion, we aren't so lucky.

"We're waiting for our boss," Benjamin tells the security guard who has caught us lounging.

"Here?" the guard asks. "Again?"

We retreat, humiliated. Matthias is incensed.

"I told you! Next time we don't sit here," he says. "This security guard – he thinks he's the enforcer!"

Taking a break during the shift entails the thrill of hide-and-seek, adding not only a touch of excitement to the workday but also a sense of autonomy and superiority. Here the authority tables are turned. Cleaners can usually outwit the CleanUp management, the clients and guards. They are one step ahead in their knowledge of Potsdamer Platz's spatial and temporal order, using it to determine what pathways, terraces, lobbies and general spaces are good bets and during which hours.

Yet given Potsdamer Platz's high density, the profligate use of glass as a building material, and a proliferation of security cameras, escaping the corporate gaze is an uphill battle.

"Potsdamer Platz, everybody knows this, is really shit," says Lucas, a CleanUp employee temporarily assigned to the complex. "You are monitored everywhere."

Absent an intimate knowledge of the property, along with acute antennas for the presence of management, clients, security guards and cameras, a heightened sense can prevail of being watched and thus controlled. Several times when I think I've found a quiet and unobserved spot to enter field notes into my phone, a coworker suddenly appears from around a corner or from the balcony of the opposite building to wave hello, or a foreman unexpectedly materializes.

"You've got to really watch out here," Matthias says. "Everyone can see you. In fact you don't always know who the people passing by you are."

For this reason, cleaners gravitate to the minus areas, to the dark and out-of-the-way spaces hidden from the upperworld.

"Dear friends of the sun," Matthias archly rhapsodizes after we sneak out with Benjamin to buy coffee during our shift, "now back to the dark side we go."

This time we opt to sit on a minus-level staircase. We sit in the dark, but at least we don't have to be constantly mindful of surveillance. Benjamin and Matthias tease me with the football song they've made into one about CleanUp and myself. To a catchy tune, they chant, "Our love! Our club! F.C. football club! CleanUp! CleanUp! F.C. *Jana!*" With a little coffee, some sugar or cigarettes or some combination, the cleaners' inventive energies find an outlet, even underground.

"They Watch You Closely": Surveillance at Potsdamer Platz

Surveillance consists of "the systematic monitoring of people or groups in order to regulate or govern their behavior."[1] In today's workplaces,

---

[1] Monahan (2011: 498; emphasis taken out).

surveillance takes on various shapes and forms, such as direct managerial supervision, security cameras, offline and online inspections as well as ever more sophisticated digital tracking systems.[2] All these are designed to monitor workers, whether mobile or fixed to a certain workspace, anywhere and at all times, creating *panoptic*, if not *post-panoptic* working conditions.[3]

At Potsdamer Platz, clients and upperworlders, the security guards and the security cameras, the CleanUp management, the foremen, and at times even coworkers can provide cleaners with the sensation of being surveilled. As we saw in the previous chapter, clients, and upperworlders more generally, tend to ignore cleaners and treat them as nonpersons; still, the feeling persists of being surveilled.

Cleaning a lobby with Ali and Alex, I notice how office workers observe me, sometimes almost staring. Asked to make sense of this, Alex says, "They watch you like a hawk. They want to see how you work, and whether you do it right. These motherfuckers – they think they're better."

In a passing moment, can upperworlders know whether I'm doing it right, and would they even care? Whatever the motivation, upperworlders' glances seem unfriendly and leave me feeling not only surveilled but even humiliated. Alex's response shows how cleaners interpret surveillance as distrust in their motivation and ability to work, thus undermining their sense of worth.

Alex also points out how surveillance manifests hierarchy. Indeed, inherent to the idea of surveillance is watching – *veillance* – from above – *sur*. As the etymology makes clear, the watcher is in an elevated position.

---

[2] Lyon (2001), Staples (2014). For instance, in the service industries, such as call centers, dense networks of surveillance exist (e.g. Taylor & Bain, 1999; see also Lloyd, 2016). For a recent discussion of surveillance in organization studies, see Albu (2020). Note that it is important not to assume that new technologies necessarily imply fuller and greater surveillance (Ball et al., 2005).

[3] Foucault (1977) famously adopted the idea of the panopticon from Bentham's prison study to capture the workings of disciplinary power, whereby the very sense of being potentially watched makes people discipline themselves. Post-panopticon refers to the idea that surveillance does not need to be confined to particular spaces and enclosed institutions and the gaze may not target individuals but their representations (see e.g. Deleuze, 1992; Bauman, 2000; Haggerty & Ericson, 2000; for an overview on surveillance theories, see Galič et al., 2016).

Cleaners are also suspicious of the security guards and the security cameras in the elevators, lobbies and other spaces at Potsdamer Platz. Security guards can, indeed, collect all kinds of information on the cleaners. Not only do the guards operate the cameras[4] and patrol the complex, but cleaners also call them to gain access to certain doors and gateways to which they are not given the key.[5] Cleaners don't trust them, as they work for CleanUp's main competitor.

"You have to be on your guard," Michaela says. "They are not from CleanUp but from Shining, and they monitor us sometimes."

Cleaners suspect that security guards give information to the client. Indeed, security guards observe cleaners and talk down to them.

"One time I was standing by the container over here, and you were just hanging out while you were on the clock," a security guard contemptuously remarks to a group of cleaners. "Not just one of you, all of you!"

Even the potential for surveillance has an effect. When cleaners enter a space, they check for cameras. When Hermann puts his legs up on a chair in a lobby, Christian scolds him.

"Hey, what are you doing, sitting like that?" Christian gestures to a camera. "You're being watched!"

In addition to the security cameras, cleaners regard company-supplied technology with suspicion. The *Tagesdamen* – the female cleaners in the shopping mall – all receive a mobile phone from CleanUp so that they are reachable at all times. At one point, Tom hands out walkie-talkies to the foremen, Marcel and some glass cleaners.

"Why do you have these walkie-talkies now?" I ask.

"It's all about control, that's clear," Paul says. "It's exactly the same thing with the mobile phones. And it's nonsense. They could just call us."

Much communication among the cleaners, the foremen and Tom does indeed take place via personal mobile phones. Potsdamer Platz is just too large of a space for CleanUp management to keep a direct eye on everyone all the time; it therefore relies on technology.[6]

---

[4] On electronic surveillance in service work, see e.g. Poster (2011), Ball and Margulis (2011).
[5] On surveillance and access codes, see e.g. Lyon (2003).
[6] On surveillance, technology and work, see e.g. Brown and Korczynski (2010), Sewell and Taskin (2015), Elliott and Long (2016), Newlands (2020).

Cleaners also face more direct behavioral supervision along with quality control procedures. There are regular inspection rounds at Potsdamer Platz when the client, Tom and foremen walk from object to object, check the cleanliness and see whether the items listed on the contract are fulfilled to the client's satisfaction. Cleaners often learn about the inspection round the day of, news that causes a stir among them. Not only do they clean more carefully, but they also take more care not to be seen slacking off. Nobody wants to be the cause of a client's complaint or the object of a manager's ire.

Inspection rounds are not isolated incidents, but an ever-present phenomenon. As Anton puts it, "Inspection is always on."

On an everyday basis, CleanUp foremen walk through the different objects, corridors and hallways of Potsdamer Platz, scanning for any irregularity. Running a finger under a railing, looking into garbage bins and opening doors to hallways, they search for dirt cleaners have failed to catch: dust not wiped away, garbage not picked up, floors not scrubbed.

Foremen regard it as part of their job to spot cleaners who are slacking off.

"What are you doing here?" Anton shouts to cleaners smoking on a balcony where they mistakenly think that they can't be seen.

From the cleaners' perspective, the foremen's surveillance oscillates between care and coercion. As sociologist David Lyon points out in *Surveillance Society*, surveillance may serve to protect yet also to inspect the other and enforce discipline.[7] When the foremen point out cameras to cleaners, make them aware of the clients' presence and warn them not to be caught sitting down, they do indeed seem to have the cleaners' interests in mind, at least in part: such care aims to save cleaners, and ultimately also CleanUp, from getting into trouble.

Foremen are held responsible for maintaining order, which helps explain why foremen's surveillance can easily shift from care to control. Cleaners observe a change in Anton's behavior toward them after Tom's return from vacation, during which Anton assumed his responsibilities. As soon as Tom is back, cleaners complain that Anton becomes stricter, as though to prove in front of Tom that he has everything under control.

---

[7] Lyon (2001); see also Sewell and Barker (2006).

"Anton is really cracking the whip," Lena says. "He's checking absolutely everything."

Surveillance also influences how cleaners relate to one another.[8] Ali goes so far as to monitor the recordings of security cameras installed in his building. When he sees how, in his absence, some of the cleaners fail to follow his instructions and properly clean the café in the morning, he tells Anton to no longer allocate them to his building.

Cleaners monitor each other even when they don't have "their own" object to consider. Spotting each other's mistakes and infractions inflames conflicts, and can give those who watch the other a sense of power. Competition plays a role here, as does lack of trust, if not outright animosity (refer to Chapter 4).

When Benjamin, Matthias and I pass the McDonald's café en route to our next assignment and catch sight of Marcel sitting there with a girl, Benjamin rubs his hands together.

"Ah ha!" he exclaims. "Look who's once again hanging out with a chick on company time! And this after he tells us he only goes to McDonald's once a day and that we're not allowed to!"

Benjamin suggests that we needle Marcel on our way past him. "Don't even say anything, just stare as we walk by." As we pass, Marcel calls to Benjamin using his surname: "Yo, Friedrichs! What's your problem?" Benjamin cackles with pleasure in holding this over Marcel's head.

Sometimes cleaners keep an eye on each other to protect themselves, since clients' or managers' complaints can have adverse consequences for everyone.[9] In one instance, Alexey advises me to perk up my demeanor.

"You have to be careful, how you stand around," he says, making a vacant face, slouching with his hands in his pockets. This is especially the case, he explains, since we can't always know who the client is.

"To clean like that does not look good for client," he says. "Boss from client comes by here. We sometimes don't know, how looks like, but then we have to look like we have fun and work fast."

Even as such interventions by coworkers can have a disciplinary effect – after Alexey's correction, I make an effort to stand up straight – there is also an element of care and solidarity at play here.

[8] On peer surveillance in the context of teamwork and worker empowerment programs, see Sewell (1998).
[9] See also Ball (2010).

Sometimes the ways in which cleaners warn each other seem like a game. They use it to startle each other, perhaps to signal cleverness, that one is a step ahead in being conscious of surveillance. Indeed, surveillance manifests a hierarchy, topped not only by the one who surveils but also, or instead, by the one with knowledge of surveillance.

One time, as I use my mobile phone in the shopping mall, Marcel startles me shouting "Caught!" The exclamation is both serious and playful: he clearly enjoys having managed to scare me, but it's also a warning.

"It's not good when the client sees you like that," he says. "He doesn't know if you're taking your break."

In the game of provoking surveillance anxiety, players develop both offensive and defensive skills.

"Have you already seen Mr. Schmidt today?" Marcel asks Paul, referring to the client boss.

"No," Paul answers.

"But he has seen you!" Marcel menacingly replies.

"Yes, he always follows me around," Paul says. "Even when I go home. I open the door and there he is, ready to haul me away."

Paul, all too familiar with Marcel and his jests, doesn't fall for the trap: to worry that Mr. Schmidt actually saw him that day would place him in the role of not only the joke's rube but the panopticon's victim, twice at the bottom of the surveillance hierarchy. Instead he plays along, and takes it up a notch, signaling anything but fear and preserving his dignity. And yet, for all the jokes and teasing and bravado, the banter bears a kernel of truth. Surveillance is a real issue for the cleaners.

Taken together, the sense of being watched shapes cleaners' everyday work experience. While there are moments when surveillance can produce a sense of care, being watched, especially by clients, security guards and CleanUp management, largely constitutes an attack on cleaners' sense of worth. It stands for distrust in their work ability and efforts, and the resulting need to control them. Through surveillance, cleaners feel, people seek to assert authority over them by positioning themselves above them – something that also happens within the group of cleaners. But as much as cleaners take surveillance seriously and regard it as a threat, even an insult to their dignity, they also use it to playfully tease and test each other. Indeed, it is one thing to be surveilled; it is quite another how one responds to surveillance.

Against, Off and Away: Three Confrontations with Surveillance

Surveillance constitutes an interactive process, whereby the "strategic actions of both watchers and the watched can be thought of as moves in a game, although unlike traditional games, the rules may not be equally binding on all players."[10] At Potsdamer Platz, I observe something like a game between the cleaners and those watching them. In *The Practice of Everyday Life*, philosopher Michel de Certeau maintains that a tactic "must vigilantly make use of the cracks that particular conjunctions open in the surveillance of the proprietary powers."[11] Cleaners engage in various tactics ranging from what I term *turning off* and *away* from surveillance to *turning against* those who watch them. For cleaners, the urge to counter surveillance in order to retain a sense of dignity – no matter how fragile and short-lived – can surpass the fear of getting into trouble.

"I Don't Care!": Turning against Surveillance

For surveillance to work, people need to care about being surveilled.[12] This may be the case, among other reasons, because people search for recognition from those watching them,[13] or are afraid of sanctions that would result from non-compliance. One way to upset surveillance, therefore, is by refusing to care about it, that is, to accept and follow the implicit hierarchy inherent in surveillance between those watching and those being watched. This can take the form of ignoring being watched,[14] or even directly confronting those watching.

In a few instances, I observed how cleaners turn against and explicitly resist the gaze, or, to be more precise, its disciplinary effects. When faced with yet another security camera in a lobby, Matthias grabs his crotch and aims a pelvic thrust in its direction.

"Here I am!" he calls. "Always nice to have the security! Why not say hello?"

This refusal to let the gaze of security guards and security cameras intimidate him is also a refusal to let them exercise authority over him.

---

[10] Marx (2003: 374).
[11] de Certeau (1988: 37); on tactics, see also May (1999).   [12] Marx (2003).
[13] To use the famous example of philosopher Louis Althusser, people turn to the policeman, as they believe the policeman's hailing addresses them.
[14] Marx (2003).

Instead, he turns the tables and stares back. His sexual gesture upends the figure of the self-disciplined worker daunted by the shame inherent in being surveilled.

Lucas, the CleanUp employee just temporarily posted to Potsdamer Platz, recounts a comparable incident of refusing surveillance intimidation. Taking a short break from the minus area to get some fresh air, he finds himself approached.

"Some guy in a suit says to me, what are you doing standing around here?" he recalls. "And I was like, you know what? I don't care. I need some fresh air now."

Such a refusal entails a direct and overt confrontation with the watchers.[15] Rather than positioning themselves as deferential underlings who accept the authority of those surveilling them, cleaners in such confrontations summon a more assertive and dignified self. To contest surveillance they mobilize their masculinity, if not their sexuality, and stand up for their physical needs. Such rebelliousness can be risky; the confrontation might not be without consequence. It's one thing to lob a vulgar gesture at the surveillance camera, or to take a coffee break in the light of day, and quite another to contest the authority of one's immediate superior.

Dead Zones and Crashing Phones: Turning Off Surveillance

For surveillance to work, people not only need to care about being watched, they also need to be visible to those watching them. This in turn means that invisibility can serve to finesse, if not contest, surveillance.

One tactic related to invisibility involves turning off one's mobile phone or other devices to make oneself unreachable by management with its and clients' urgent and frequent demands.

"One has to learn not to pick up all the time when the foremen call," Henning says.

"My mobile phone always crashes," Lucas says ironically. "Or it just has no reception."

Henning smiles recalling the time that Michael, a foreman, called him at the end of his shift to ask that he work late. "Just then, my battery died."

---

[15] Thus do the Potsdamer Platz cleaners not only try to get "the better of monitoring" (Ball, 2010: 94) but actively challenge it.

The following day, Michael approached Henning to ask why he hadn't picked up. Upon hearing Henning's excuse, Michael responded with a look of disbelief. Indeed, cleaners often offer their excuses in ways that indicate that the foremen are supposed to know they're lying.

"Once a foreman spit back, funny how your phone always crashes on a Friday," Lucas recalls. "To which I responded, no, this can happen any day of the week."

In addition to the malfunctioning phone, cleaners invent further excuses for being inaccessible.

"At nine I take a break no matter what," Gustav says. "The other day I'm on my break and Anton calls. I pick up and tell him, 'I'm taking a shit!' and hang up."

Of course, cleaners have to take care not to overuse their excuses, and the foremen's responses indicate their skepticism. Nevertheless, turning off communication channels provides cleaners with moments of breaking free from the managerial grip.

Even cleaners who are equipped with walkie-talkies from CleanUp employ this tactic. The quality of the audio is so bad to begin with that Marcel sometimes can't understand Anton and his instructions, but beyond this cleaners actively turn the devices off.[16] The system transmits every conversation to every device, creating a staticky and garbled din throughout the day.

"Yesterday I walked around with it the whole day," Paul says. "Finally I had to turn it off, I couldn't listen to it anymore. Later on Anton called me: 'I can't find you!'"

But it's not just cleaners who make themselves technologically invisible and inaccessible. Foremen, too, sometimes fail to respond to queries from the cleaners. At times, foremen turn off their own phones to have a break.

In the storage room, especially if the door is closed against the smell of the adjacent garbage room, reception frequently cuts out. But connectivity dead spots are to be found throughout Potsdamer Platz's underworld, making cleaners periodically unreachable. Only after an hour has passed, one afternoon does Christian's phone show that

---

[16] See also Winiecki and Wigman (2007: 126) on call center agents using the mute button so that customers cannot hear them.

Anton, the foreman, tried reaching him earlier. Such an hour can save cleaners from being summoned to assume unpleasant responsibilities.

Benjamin takes it a step further. He refuses to give out his number to either management or his coworkers, thus making no effort to "mask" the fact that he is "blocking"[17] access to communication. Benjamin openly engages in turning off.

"Why don't you give your number to Anton?" I ask him. "Or share it with me?" Benjamin has called me several times from a blocked number.

"No, no, no, no!" Benjamin exclaims. "Are you crazy? That's a total secret. Once Tom called me at 10 p.m. I was in bed! I'm not having it – this is my private number."

As a result, management has to call his coworker Matthias if it wants to reach Benjamin. For Benjamin, his personal phone number is part and parcel of private life, a zone that should be protected from managerial intrusion. He is not obliged to share it, and the very act of keeping it secret affords him a sense of separation between work and private life, along with a degree of freedom from control by management.[18]

Turning off is about interrupting communication channels, making oneself virtually and physically invisible and thereby carving out spaces and periods of autonomy. Compared with turning against, turning off lets the worker withdraw from rather than directly confront managerial surveillance. In the former case, cleaners openly resist the gaze. In the latter, by contrast, cleaners mainly use technology, its malfunction or absence as an excuse for their invisibility, while still – with the exception of Benjamin – holding up the "front-stage performance"[19] of the disciplined and compliant worker vis-à-vis CleanUp management, even if only in an ironical, even cheeky way.[20]

Cleaners do not even seek to construct a watertight "masking" of the fact that they engage in blocking. The whimsical ways in which cleaners like Lucas or Henning report the malfunctioning of their phone insinuate to the foremen that the excuse is fraudulent, but also incontestable. Cleaners seem to gain a sense of dignity from not only turning off but also signaling to the management their own duplicity

---

[17] Marx (2003).
[18] On secrecy in organizational life, see also Costas and Grey (2016).
[19] Goffman (1959/1990).   [20] See also Collinson (2003).

and proudly broadcasting it to coworkers. In these instances, it is they who manage surveillance rather than the other way around.

While turning off provides cleaners with momentary respites, it's not a sustainable tactic. Cleaners enjoy using a mobile phone during the workday. They frequently send each other messages, show each other videos and pictures, listen to music and make private calls. The cleaners' mobile-phone use is so heavy that Ali suggests that, if he were a foreman, he would introduce a ban. Turning off can only last as long as cleaners can abstain from entertaining themselves with their phones and using them to interact with each other. Indeed, Benjamin's refusal to engage virtually with other cleaners is the rare exception, one that marks his self-chosen outsider status.

Stepping into the Shadows: Turning Away from Surveillance

Most frequently, cleaners opt for a third tactic that plays with invisibility: turning away. Cleaners sidestep into spaces invisible to management, clients, security guards and the public.[21] To discover these shadow places, cleaners need to closely monitor those they have reason to believe are watching them; to avoid being watched, they must watch the watchers.[22]

To decide where, when and how to hide, the cleaners assemble detailed profiles of those whose surveillance they evade. A vital skill is the ability to detect the appearance of the clients, CleanUp managers or security guards. Cleaners therefore activate their senses to detect the others' voices, faces and other physical characteristics, at times even their odor.[23]

One day Lena plunks herself down at a table in the storage room, then freezes.

"Was Anton here?" she asks. "It smells like his cologne."

She shuttles off to the other side of the room.

Cleaners also track movement patterns of the corporate gaze. What paths do the foreman or client follow, and when? What spaces do they avoid? Cleaners keep tabs on who is where, for how long and on what

[21] See also Marx (2003) on avoidance moves.
[22] See also Marx (2003) on "counter-surveillance" and Mann et al. (2003) on "sousveillance."
[23] On scent and organizations, see Corbett (2006), Śliwa and Riach (2012), Riach and Warren (2015).

day. Bertha figures out that "at 8 o'clock on the dot, Tom always walks down here, because all the bosses meet in front over there and go to McDonald's." It is therefore better not to take her cigarette break at this end of the building at that hour. Similarly, Benjamin observes that "the client only does the inspection until 1 o'clock, and after that he's busy with other things." This gives Matthias, Benjamin and me clearance to freely walk outside the building, which is not permitted at this hour.

Some of the reverse surveillance extends even to management's home lives, if those coincide with the workplace.

"The boss lives upstairs," Benjamin tells me when we hang out in the lobby. "We have to be careful when the elevator goes up to the seventh floor."

The better attuned they are to these schedules, the more the cleaners notice any irregularity. Why is Tom's gray Ford still missing from its parking place at this hour? Or isn't it strange, Benjamin muses, that Anton walks through the shopping mall, rather than down the side street by McDonald's?

Cleaners share warning signs that they've detected. "The top CleanUp boss is visiting today," Ali informs Paul, Marcel and others during the breakfast break.

If the client, CleanUp manager or security guard comes into view during an unsanctioned break, cleaners learn to quickly pretend as if they're working.[24] This may require some preparedness: standing instead of sitting down, for example, or maintaining a cleaning rag in one hand while drinking coffee with the other.

It also helps to have an excuse prepared: one might be waiting for the boss, or making up a missed break. If they're discovered, cleaners have to think on their feet. Traveling through a usually management-free underground tunnel to fetch a coffee from McDonald's during his shift, Hans runs into Anton. He takes the offensive, exclaiming, "Good that I found you! I wanted to ask you something ..."

Successfully turning away hinges on knowing the lay of the land. Cleaners identify obscure spaces: the darker corners, the streets at the edges of the complex, scaffolding, out-of-the-way balconies, less-trafficked lobbies and hallways, underground tunnels and various

---

[24] See Ackroyd (2012) on "business" and Collinson and Collinson's (1997) analysis of workers pretending to work late hours.

other underworld nooks and crannies. Importantly, the spots cleaners turn to are not necessarily "backstage" or "transient" spaces[25] (also refer to Chapter 1). Instead, they often also belong to the cleaners' work territory, such as the apartment lobbies they clean or the area in front of McDonald's. Temporarily inhabiting these spaces for leisure is thus easier to disguise and defend.

The spaces vary from cleaner to cleaner, shift to shift, opportunity to opportunity. When I work with Hans in Ali's building for a week, we hang out with Paul in a space below ground level waiting for the workday to end. For twenty minutes or so we play catch with balled-up cleaning rags. Such underground spaces are the safest. Reception is spotty and one is less likely to run into a boss or guard. These places may lack fresh air and a window on the world going by, but rather than being closed off from life, they can perhaps paradoxically give cleaners a sense of being in the thick of things.

As in the case of turning off, the tactic of turning away works through invisibility. Cleaners actively search for, create and find times and spaces outside the watchers' field of vision. They strategically exploit the invisibility their work brings with it.[26] Compared with turning against, turning away does not require that cleaners overtly resist surveillance. They covertly outwit it. Here the focus is not on interrupting communication channels but on using the spaces in alternative, heterogeneous – "differential"[27] – ways.

The tactic of turning away involves the constant potentiality of having to engage in "impression management"[28] in case a client appears or one encounters CleanUp superiors. Cleaners therefore have a repertory of impression-management techniques at the ready. While in the case of turning off, cleaners may insinuate to their interlocutors the very fact that they purposefully engage in turning off in order to outwit the gaze, turning away is about keeping under the radar as much as possible. Cleaners can derive a sense of dignity from outwitting surveillance in the pursuit of autonomy – dignity that can, however, easily be undermined if the cleaner gets caught.

In contrast to turning off, turning away requires cleaners to be highly attuned to the profiles, preferences and movement patterns of

[25] See Shortt (2015), Courpasson et al. (2017).
[26] See also Otis and Zhao (2016).   [27] Lefebvre (1974/1991: 408).
[28] Goffman (1959/1990).

those watching them. Turning away therefore involves a "heightened self-consciousness" whereby people become "skilled manipulators of self," a quality organization theorist David Collinson has attributed to employees who respond to surveillance through "dramaturgical selves."[29] In addition, it may require a heightened consciousness of those potentially watching them.

Cleaners who are new to Potsdamer Platz and its spatial and temporal order, and to the movement patterns, preferences and profiles of those watching them, cannot easily turn away from surveillance. Similarly, turning away requires cleaners to have some autonomy in the first place. The more cleaners are fixed to a certain workspace at a certain time and the more they work in visible, public areas aboveground – as is the case for those working in the shopping mall – the less opportunity they have to turn away undetected.

Still, even the shopping mall cleaners like Bertha find ways to turn away at times, for example in the early hours when CleanUp management and the client are not often present. But, on the whole, those who work in hidden spaces like the underworld's hallways and garbage rooms are less exposed to surveillance.

Working outside is a mixed blessing with respect to surveillance and turning away. While Marcel feels that "everyone can always see" him during his shift outside, he nonetheless enjoys the autonomy of being able to choose which street to clean and when – something that brings with it opportunities to engage in turning away. Importantly, no matter the nature or location of the shift, a cleaner's position in the workplace hierarchy is a crucial factor. Cleaners like Alexey or Luisa with more precarious status may not risk it.[30]

All in all, the tactics of turning against, off and away show that cleaners search for, find and create ways to overtly or covertly resist, withdraw from and outwit the gaze. The extent to which cleaners challenge surveillance differs. In the case of turning away, they develop workarounds, but in front of management and clients they may hide the ways in which they engage in this tactic. Turning off is more complex in that cleaners fabricate excuses, yet may insinuate the truth of the matter to management. Only turning against opposes surveillance in more direct ways. The tactics of turning away and off show how cleaners not only "make use ... of the cracks" in surveillance, as

[29] Collinson (2003).   [30] See also Portillo (2012).

de Certeau puts it;[31] they actively generate "spatio-temporal gaps between watcher and watched"[32] by exploiting their invisibility in the corporate underworld.

But if cleaners put so much effort into outwitting and resisting surveillance, does this imply that they also resist work? Put differently, how does cleaners' engagement in such tactics go hand in hand with the ways in which their self-worth is bound up with their work?

Resistant to Surveillance and Ready to Work

In many ways, cleaners' tactics are reminiscent of classic examples of resistance whereby workers engage in oppositional workplace practices.[33] Despite parallels between resistance to surveillance and resistance to work, it is important not to conflate them. Cleaners may outwit surveillance in order to preserve their ability to continue working, for example when they step outside to get fresh air.

The thirty-minute break allocated to cleaners at 9 a.m. often doesn't suffice to fulfill their needs. During the break, cleaners change the water, throw dirty mops and rags into the washing machines, and fill the cleaning carts with fresh materials and equipment. The break is a time to prepare for what comes next as well as take a pause after work already performed. For the cleaners, it's an indispensable part of their work life. But too many activities are crammed into it. Besides work-related duties and preparations, personal needs have to be met in those thirty minutes: buying and consuming food, making coffee, going to the toilet, sitting down, moisturizing chapped hands, reapplying deodorant, dozing off, getting a breath of fresh air, smoking a cigarette and, importantly, interacting socially with coworkers, sending texts and making private calls. So it's unsurprising that cleaners try to outwit surveillance during work hours in order to supplement their break time. These improvised pauses can help them rejuvenate and even help them do their job in the first place.

During my time in the field, it puzzles me at first how cleaners seek to depict themselves as hard working and diligent while simultaneously spending so much time and effort engaging in tactics against

---

[31] de Certeau (1988: 37).   [32] Ball (2005: 102); see also Ball (2002).
[33] E.g. Jermier et al. (1994), Ackroyd and Thompson (1999), Collinson and Ackroyd (2005), Mumby (2005).

surveillance, apparently in order to resist or evade work. Indeed, from a client or manager's point of view, the cleaner who takes coffee breaks during working hours may seem to confirm the stigmatized image of the cleaner as lazy and unmotivated – the kind of worker who justifies the need for even further surveillance.[34]

But from the cleaners' perspective, the importance of resistance to surveillance lies in gaining autonomy and therefore dignity; it does not lie in shirking work responsibilities. On the contrary, cleaners frown upon and socially sanction those who slack off, for example Bertha's complaints stated in Chapter 4 about Luisa's alleged idleness.

At the same time, Bertha herself steps out to obscure corners around the shopping mall to smoke cigarettes and make numerous phone calls over the course of her shift. Her practice of using work time for purposes other than work – what de Certeau refers to as "la perruque"[35] – could be regarded as subversive.[36] For Bertha, there is no contradiction between her complaint about Luisa, her embrace of a work ethic and her own behavior during the shift. Indeed, she engages with private matters only to the point that she can still finish her cleaning. She ends one call saying, "I've got to hang up now or I'm not going to get anything done."

A porous line separates outwitting surveillance and resisting work. Outwitting the gaze provides cleaners with an important sense of autonomy, yet not working violates their work ethic. This shows the complex calculus of dignity at play here (also refer to Chapter 3): cleaners want to feel that they have chosen to work hard of their own accord, not because they have been coerced; and that is the sense of coercion that surveillance manifests.

---

[34] Anteby and Chan (2018) suggest that this striving toward resisting surveillance may result in potential self-fulfilling cycles of coercive surveillance, as the very resistance may spur management to engage in and justify further surveillance. However, whether this implication needs to be interpreted as the "darker side" (Anteby & Chan, 2018: 260) of resistance depends on how one approaches the newly introduced surveillance. In their *Editorial: Doing Surveillance Studies*, Ball, Haggerty and Whitson (2005: 136) warn researchers not to believe in an "'ever more surveillance' narrative ... [as] it relies upon a highly questionable assumption of institutional competence or even perfection".

[35] De Certeau (1988: 24).

[36] See Paulsen's critique (2015) of the common assumption that work time necessarily implies that people work, and that such "empty labor" must thus be subversive.

Christian, for example, rants against cleaners who leave their work unfinished. "That kind of work ethic is really the shits," he says. One day we encounter Patrick, apparently under the influence on the job, walking unsteadily and slurring his speech.

"Hey!" he shouts to us, entering the lobby where Christian and I are mopping the floor. He implores us to join him on his cigarette break. "I am so, so alone!" he wails. Patrick works by himself. "In my head I am singing the whole time, I hate this house so much, I hate it!"

All this unfolds in front of a receptionist, now shaking her head. Christian hurries Patrick out of the lobby, ashamed of him and his blatant resistance to work. Patrick's performance conforms with precisely the stigmatized image that cleaners like Christian combat.

This isn't to say that Christian doesn't take cigarette breaks on the clock. His preferred location in the early morning is a balcony where he can observe the complex coming to life: office workers greeting one another, the streets slowly filling with tourists and consumers. The balcony allows him to watch others while preventing others from watching him. He keeps his turning away from surveillance under the radar. He wouldn't want the receptionist or the inhabitants of the apartment complex to see his illicit cigarette break. And Christian makes sure to fulfill his work duties, alternating between intense periods of work and short breaks.

All this suggests that cleaners may resist surveillance and still live up to a work ethic that remains vital to their sense of worth given their backgrounds in the social underworld (refer to Chapter 2).[37] At the same time, this does not make them into docile rule-followers. Autonomy, being their "own boss," which cleaners like Marcel define as being able to decide for oneself when and where to "stop for a break," means a lot to them as it serves to overcome the feeling of being powerless and dependent: "[t]o be dignified or have dignity is first to be in control of oneself, competently and appropriately exercising one's powers."[38] Their sense of dignity, rather than surveillance,

---

[37] This suggests that resistance in itself may not necessarily boost a sense of dignity (see Hodson, 2001), but the specific resistance to surveillance. Moreover, here it is not the piecework system that makes cleaners seek to fulfill their work shift (see Burawoy, 1979) but the ways in which their sense of worth is entangled with being valuable workers due to their particular backgrounds.

[38] Sayer (2007: 568).

seems to make cleaners work hard and refrain from resisting work. Surveillance, particularly its coercive nature, undermines both cleaners' sense of autonomy and their self-esteem, driving them to resist it.

Out of Sight, Out of Mind: The Corporate Underworld as Vexed Refuge from Surveillance

Dressed in the cleaning uniform, my visibility and invisibility change. Just as I become invisible in the upperworld, often ignored or over-looked by people who would normally notice me, I become visible in the cleaners' world. However, there is another visibility that I fail to notice right away: the visibility related to being surveilled. With a certain naivety or ignorant bliss, I walk through the streets, squares and buildings of Potsdamer Platz, phoning colleagues from the univer-sity, typing in field notes, taking pictures. Perhaps because of my preoccupation with observing cleaners,[39] I fail to see how I am being watched myself. But cleaners quickly make me aware of the presence of surveillance. They almost seem to enjoy the warning, scaring and teasing me that some client or they themselves have witnessed me doing something I shouldn't have. It is a moment of asserting their superiority as it shows how they are one step ahead both of those engaging in surveillance and those being surveilled.

All this underscores how cleaners' invisibility is only half the prob-lem. Invisibility implies that cleaners cannot be seen or are not noticed – that there is a lack of eyes directed toward them. Yet the opposite is equally true. As a cleaner, one can feel more visible as clients, security guards, CleanUp management, foremen, coworkers and upper-worlders give one the sense of being watched. Indeed, the client and CleanUp mandate that cleaners wear their cleaning uniform at all times. In the heat of summer, Alexey has to do his outdoor rounds sweating under his CleanUp thermal jacket, as CleanUp hasn't pro-vided him with a company t-shirt.

The visibility that comes with the cleaning uniform in the upper-world can make one feel monitored, inspected, judged and controlled rather than recognized and respected. Indeed, recognition is one thing,

---

[39] Note the difference between observation and surveillance. As I develop in the Appendix, I was careful about the findings I reported to management. My field observations did not aim at surveilling cleaners in order to regulate or govern them.

surveillance, another. It is therefore not surprising that cleaners engage in tactics of turning against, off and away from surveillance. They turn to the "dark side," the corporate underworld, as this can constitute a refuge from surveillance, opening avenues for autonomy and ultimately dignity. Cleaners thus embrace invisibility when their visibility to clients, the public, and management threatens their sense of autonomy.[40] Rather than perceiving their invisibility as problematic, they exploit it to resist surveillance.

For cleaners, surveillance can come with a degree of thrill and excitement in the hunt for ways to outwit and resist it. It can also summon feelings of degradation and indignity. Making themselves invisible by turning to the corporate underworld can provide cleaners with the sense of being able to outwit those surveilling them as they have superior temporal and spatial knowledge. However, that sense of superiority may not survive an unexpected encounter with a client or CleanUp supervisor. Getting caught and having to explain and excuse themselves pushes cleaners into a dignity-threatening position of inferiority. Turning off and away provides cleaners with more freedom, but hidden spaces in the minus area force tradeoffs in terms of their lack of connectivity, air and light. Aboveground retreats are riskier but allow cleaners to watch the hustle and bustle of Potsdamer Platz. But no matter how strenuously cleaners resist surveillance, it does not follow that they resist work too. Indeed, for cleaners, maintaining dignity requires a balancing act of outwitting surveillance, finding autonomy and working hard enough to uphold a work ethic and related sense of self-worth.

---

[40] Thus, my study adds to research interested in the question of "[u]nder what conditions is visibility or invisibility problematic" (Poster et al., 2016: 287) by pointing out how the sense of dignity matters for how workers make sense of visibility or invisibility. Visibility can be problematic when it is associated with surveillance rather than recognition, whereas invisibility can serve to protect from surveillance, yet manifest and reinforce the lack of recognition.

Leaving the Minus Area Behind

When the alarm rings at 4 a.m. the morning of my last day in the field, I rouse myself easily. Starting tomorrow I can sleep in. It's autumn, and I need a jacket for my bike ride to Potsdamer Platz, just as in the spring when I began. A kind of anticipatory nostalgia is already coloring my experience of physical labor in offices and hotels, malls and tunnels and on the streets of the complex. That labor was my passport to a microcosm whose faces and voices and conflicts and friendships constitute a world I will miss.

New opportunities, new worlds await me: a research fellowship in Copenhagen, the pressure to publish and find a tenured position. Cleaners respond to the demands and privileges of my academic life with a mix of envy, compassion, curiosity and some judgment. When I commiserate with Luisa about the unlikeliness of my finding work in Berlin, she advises me to pray and to bring all my papers – which papers I fail to clarify – to her church for help.

The older Polish cleaner Maria reprimands me for setting the wrong priorities.

"What? Thirty years old and no man?" Maria exclaims. "Wrong what you do. Must find husband with lots of money."

Hearing about my move to Copenhagen, Marcel says goodbye with one of his signature provocations: "Long-distance relationships are shit."

Ali texts me later that day, "Oh, Jana, what a nice life you have."

"Ali, how do you mean that?" I respond. "Because I'm leaving?"

After an unusually long pause, he texts, "Well ... yes."

Yes: with cautious optimism, I expect to rise in the upperworld. The cleaners are likely to continue making their way where they are. As starkly as any disparity of privilege on display at Potsdamer Platz, my departure highlights the chasm of class, race, education and opportunity that separates the two worlds.

Dramas of Dignity in the Corporate Underworld

Over the course of my time at Potsdamer Platz, I found myself not just in a workplace Tartarus but also at times in something touched by Elysium: lighter, more humorous, joyful, social. Below Potsdamer Platz, frustration and enjoyment, pride and shame, coalition and conflict, disgust and fascination, hope for a better life and despair of change are all intertwined.

The corporate underworld is a labyrinthine, dark and stinking place, alternately stifling and cold. It is the "minus area" of society where people are paid to deal with the filth and excess of upperworld life. This underworld amounts to infrastructure designed to make cleaners and other workers invisible so that they do not disturb the exclusive and sparkling aura of the world aboveground.

But for the cleaners, the corporate underworld can stand for more than invisibility, inequality and dirt. They also regard it as a place to meet and greet and escape the indignities experienced in the upperworld. Most importantly, it marks their place of work. For people who come from the margins of society, from a world of unemployment, immigration, drug addiction and criminal records, working as a cleaner carries the hope of attaining a dignified and deserved place in society. Despite the occasional exception like Tom who rises through the ranks to a managerial position, most cleaners have no expectation of scaling a career ladder into the upperworld. Perhaps in spite of, perhaps because of its terminal nature, they strongly attach moral value to the work, which allows them to dissociate themselves from the unemployed and others of the social underworld.

For cleaners, their work is not just "dirty work," or work that deals with the "physically disgusting."[1] Cleaners report and I can confirm that dealing with dirt can also be enjoyable: varied, fun, even exciting. Cleaning comes with certain liberties, and having cleaned a space can provide one with a sense of accomplishment. Cleaners also gain exclusive access to the spaces if not the substance of upperworld life.

None of this is to deny that the opposite can hold true: the work can be repetitive, boring, disgusting, humiliating and painful. But the assumption is faulty that this line of work is inherently unpleasant

---

[1] Hughes (1984/2009: 344); see also e.g. Ashforth and Kreiner (1999), Ashforth et al. (2007).

because dirt must necessarily repel. It does not allow for the possibility that cleaners experience their work differently, and risks fueling the stigma that cleaners must necessarily lack in motivation and engagement. Most of the cleaners I worked with in the field were indisputably motivated and engaged. They worked hard in large part because the job is their ticket to an earned place in society. This, however, is where the trouble with dignity begins.

Cleaners turn to their work to find dignity, yet it is here where their dignity is easily undermined. Others are all too ready to deny them the place in society they seek to attain. Cleaners' dignity is constantly at stake when interacting with other workers, CleanUp management, clients and upperworlders. The cleaners' story is neither one of unmitigated failure nor of total success; they do dignify their work and role even as that dignity is perpetually challenged. This tension gives rise to what I have termed *dramas of dignity*.

Cleaners can derive a sense of worth through developing relationships with and receiving support from people up and down the corporate hierarchy. Working independently, being their "own boss," can be a cause for pride, as can compliments and signs of appreciation for their efforts. By the same token, a critical or offensive comment from another cleaner, a jaundiced look from a manager, a single client complaint or an unreciprocated greeting from an upperworlder may represent a hurtful challenge to a cleaner's dignity and threaten that sense of worth.

Cleaning constitutes a catch basin for diverse groups of people. They do not share an occupational culture, and CleanUp's professionalization efforts matter little in terms of how cleaners define themselves. Instead of uniting the cleaners as a group, their dramas of dignity risk catalyzing division and conflict. Above and beyond more managerially driven, structural segregations, cleaners constantly strive to differentiate themselves from one another. They stigmatize coworkers, and the corporate underworld below Potsdamer Platz is all too fertile ground for racist, misogynist and generally discriminatory attitudes and behaviors. For some cleaners, the way fellow workers talk and relate to them causes more pain than how clients, upperworlders or CleanUp management does.

That cleaners engage in "othering" toward each other is not unrelated to their experiences in the upperworld; the disrespect they exhibit reflects the disrespect they receive.[2] Whether accusing coworkers of laziness and incompetence or surveilling or failing to greet one another, these behaviors parallel how their superiors in the corporate and societal hierarchy behave toward them. Cleaners do not regard the lack of respect they receive as personal failure.[3] Rather than blaming themselves, they blame the other: the foreigner or German, the woman or man, the elder or youth, the uneducated or the denizen of a worse neighborhood than theirs. The other is a bad worker who spoils the occupation, its image and ultimately the cleaners' status.

In otherness, there is mobility: today's snubbed workplace slacker can become tomorrow's ally, and vice versa. But whatever internal status hierarchy cleaners establish, it is eclipsed in confrontation with upperworlders, for whom cleaners all remain nobodies: uneducated people conducting unpleasant work that anyone could do and that nobody with any wit or wherewithal would choose.

Dramas of dignity may drive cleaners apart or help forge coalitions and friendships. Cleaners can find support in one another, confidants and counselors to help them navigate and cope with workplace turbulence. Notwithstanding the significance of these friendships and coalitions for the individual, cleaners do not form a workplace community. Their efforts to set themselves apart undermine community building and reinforce workplace inequality both internally and with respect to the world outside the workplace. Preoccupied with their own individual dramas of dignity, cleaners refrain from joining forces to fight for recognition, share insights on the surplus value they provide and demand higher wages and better working conditions. Whereas cleaners may be part of a new invisible "service proletariat,"[4] they do not engage in efforts to articulate, as the historian E. P. Thompson famously studied, "the identity of their interests as between themselves, and as against other men whose interests are different from (and usually opposed to) theirs."[5] Cleaners do not work toward the making of a class – in fact, they actively work against it.

Cleaners also address their dramas of dignity by debunking and resenting the upperworld. Rather than accepting it when upperworlders ignore them, cleaners can make their presence unignorable, for example by confronting litterers. Such individual acts

[2] Hodson (2001).   [3] See Sennett and Cobb (1972).
[4] Bernardi and Garrido (2008), Staab (2014).   [5] Thompson (1966: 9).

notwithstanding, upperworlders routinely pass over cleaners without acknowledging them, and CleanUp management rarely supports Potsdamer Platz cleaners in their efforts to achieve a more dignified position vis-à-vis the upperworld. On the contrary, the very working conditions, the limited manpower and hours allocated to shifts, can make it difficult for cleaners to properly fulfill their shifts, leaving them subject to client complaints. Fixed-term contracts and limited hours can also discourage cleaners from speaking up in front of clients and upperworlders, more generally.

The withdrawal to the corporate underworld constitutes a further way in which cleaners deal with their dramas of dignity. Given that interactions with clients, the CleanUp management and the broader upperworld can so easily undermine their dignity, they actively seek out minus-level invisibility. It allows them to avoid being treated like a non-person or an inferior. To the extent they trigger these flights underground, encounters between the under- and upperworlds can drive them further apart.

Compounding cleaners' lack of recognition in the upperworld is the sense of being watched by clients, security guards, CleanUp management and even coworkers. Cleaners face a strange combination of feeling both treated as though invisible yet also monitored, inspected and judged. Apart from a few incidents of care, cleaners interpret surveillance as coercive, a sign of distrust in their ability and motivation. Surveillance therefore directly attacks cleaners' dignity. But cleaners also exploit their invisibility to confront surveillance, engaging in tactics such as turning against, off and away. Finding ways to outwit the watchers can bring about excitement, thrill and even a sense of superiority, though all this can easily collapse when cleaners get caught.

Such dramas do not push cleaners to the point of resisting work altogether, which would threaten not only their income and stability, but their dignity. In the cleaners' world, shoddy work is disapproved of in moral terms, and socially sanctioned. Within friendships, cleaners can make fun of each other's ways of working, but outside of closer circles such remarks are received as serious insults.

This is not to say that cleaners docilely play the role CleanUp and clients expect of them. Cleaners may ask foremen for more hours, better contracts or different shift allocations. Few show any interest in following CleanUp's particular emphasis on professionalism.

Deferential behavior runs counter to their dignity. Cleaners may bend the rules on the job, for instance by "working with the eye," not merely helping them get through understaffed shifts on time but also constituting an important way to assert autonomy.

In the corporate underworld, a complex calculus of dignity plays out. Cleaners take certain liberties in order to feel autonomous rather than powerless, they may refrain from showing the deferential behavior clients or the CleanUp management expects of them, and they may also resist surveillance. The cleaners nonetheless maintain their work ethic. The liberties cleaners take, their acts of disobedience or even resistance may be better understood as attempts to navigate the landscape of indignity than as rejections of work per se. Such minor rebellions may in fact constitute a valid defense of a cleaner's sense of worth.

Invisible Service Workers in the Corporate Underworld: Return of the Servant Society?

Cleaners are, of course, not the only workers facing the kinds of work-related dramas of dignity this book has focused on. They stand for various low-end invisible service workers who find themselves in some corporate underworld, for example the tailors, kitchen workers and garbage men who are also deep below the ground of Potsdamer Platz. The verticalization of cities, and with it the construction of minus areas for service workers below seemingly exclusive and glamorous upperworlds, catering to consumers, residents, professionals and tourists, can be detected all over the world.[6]

The spatial divide of "up" and "down" and the presence of large numbers of service workers are not historically unprecedented. Potsdamer Platz's underworld may remind one of the early twentieth-century "downstairs" depicted in popular British TV series, such as *Upstairs, Downstairs* and *Downton Abbey* or in George Orwell's *Down and Out in Paris and London*. Of course, there are differences between the invisible service workers of today and the past when it comes to workers' rights and minimum wages, and, with the advent of outsourcing, service workers like cleaners are often no longer directly employed by the service recipients. These differences aside, the literary

---

[6] Graham (2016).

and dramatic depiction of past invisible service workers remind us how for all the talk about newness, the future, and the "city for the twenty-first century," places like Potsdamer Platz mark a return or perhaps continuation of a past that we may have thought to have left behind. It stands for a society that relegates service workers to a presence from below – a society where segregation is kept invisible even as it takes place in the midst of city life.

The presence of invisible service work at the lower end of the labor market hierarchy in terms of pay and status is also likely to remain, if not rise, unless the trend toward market deregulation and the outsourcing of services from companies and private households reverses.[7] Moreover, it is likely that these kinds of jobs continue to function as a catch basin for a variety of people, especially as migration to Europe and within it continues. So far, there is little that suggests that digitalization will decrease the need for invisible service work.

Take the typical day of Potsdamer Platz office workers. The white shirts they put on in the morning were collected, cleaned and delivered by a twenty-four-hour dry cleaning service, the electric scooters they use to commute have been charged overnight by the "juicers," the office buildings where they work are monitored and inspected day and night by patrolling security guards, desks have been wiped clean at dawn, to-go lunch sandwiches prepared in the early morning, and the Amazon packages that await them at home packed by warehouse workers. This shows how what Christoph Bartmann has termed the "new middle classes"[8] increasingly rely, alongside digital technology,[9] on the work of various "servants" to manage their social and work life, bringing about inequalities in our society.

Lady Liberty and Harold Lloyd: Minus-level Images of Aspiration and Desperation

One morning, on my way to the garbage collection point on the minus-four level, I encountered two iconic American images taped to the wall

---

[7] Interestingly, though there are online platforms through which individuals sell cleaning services directly to private households, in Germany and the United States a return to companies with employed cleaners has been noted due to legal and quality-related issues of self-employed platform workers (Schmidt, 2017).

[8] Bartmann (2016).

[9] See Krajewski (2018) on the history of servanthood and the rise of technology.

Figure C.1 The Statue of Liberty in Potsdamer Platz's underworld.

of the long corridor: the Statue of Liberty and Harold Lloyd dangling from the hands of a clock atop a skyscraper (see figures C.1 and C.2).[10] Asked about these images, cleaners drew a blank. One speculated that they were meant to hang in an upperworld lobby, were instead discarded, and wound up here after being salvaged from the trash.

This explanation, the very images, and their out-of-place status in the minus area puzzled me. The Statue of Liberty stands for the hope of a better future, for freedom, for a new world and home for people from all over the world seeking refuge and opportunity.[11] It is the iconic symbol for the promise of the American Dream whereby, in exchange for hard work, people can ascend the social ladder. Harold Lloyd's famous image from the silent comedy *Safety Last!* represents the dark flip-side of the American Dream. Lloyd hides his lack of success and money from the girlfriend he wants to marry, and gets by as a salesclerk in a department store. His hopes and aspirations to make it to the top end with him dangling over the abyss.

---

[10] See also Costas and Kunda (2015).

[11] In fact, my Greek grandfather with his brothers probably also arrived on Ellis Island in early twentieth century. Upon arrival he mentioned his Greek surname *Kostakis* and the Americans turned it into *Costas*. That's where my name, which is usually a first name in Greece, comes from.

Figure C.2 Harold Lloyd in Potsdamer Platz's underworld.

That these images do not find their place in Potsdamer Platz's upper-world may be indicative of how little significance they carry there. Upperworlders who have made it to the top need neither to be reminded of their freedoms and privileges nor to preoccupy themselves with the fears of holding on for dear life at a dizzying height.

The Statue of Liberty may speak more to the underworld to the extent that the occupations found here, like cleaning, constitute a catch basin for people from different walks of life and parts of the world. The corporate underworld comes with the hope of arriving, finding a place and possibly (re-)integrating into society in exchange for hard work. However, most service workers do not expect to make it to the top or even to the other side of the corporate divide; nobody would confuse the cleaners' experience with a German version of the American Dream. The reality they face makes it too clear to them that they are at the bottom of the labor market hierarchy and are likely to stay there. In contrast to Harold Lloyd, cleaners are not even aspiring to achieve upperworld success – yet still they dangle over an abyss.

Cleaners' lack of hopes and aspirations beyond the corporate under-world, however, shouldn't be taken to mean that they placidly accept their position in society. They are rather too aware of the inequality at hand to believe in the meanings conveyed by the utopian image of the Statue of Liberty, and as a result get caught up in its dystopian flip-side, symbolized by Harold Lloyd's image. Cleaners do struggle and fight for their place in society, for recognition and dignity. It is a fight that plays out in our midst but, like the cleaners themselves, largely remains invisible.

Postscript

In Germany, during the coronavirus lockdown in spring 2020, the government introduced the classification of *Systemrelevante Berufe*, or system-relevant occupations. Responsible for the provision of basic supplies and services, these occupations were deemed essential for the functioning of the society and economy and must be carried out at all times. For people in these jobs, working from home and maintaining social distance has not been an option. Those who kept their jobs continued to work on site, braving acute shortages of protective equipment at the beginning of the crisis. System-relevant occupations include doctors, nurses, grocery store employees, package deliverers – and cleaners.

But even as the crisis has highlighted how much our lives rely on the work of people in system-relevant occupations, these nonetheless remain among the most precarious and – doctors aside – low-paid jobs. Bouquets, thank you notes and applause for these workers have provided them with moments of appreciation and recognition, yet they remain at the bottom of the labor hierarchy in terms of status and compensation. It is precisely this tension between the inherent value of the work, along with the sense of worth workers derive from it and its negligible status that continues to catalyze dramas of dignity among cleaners and workers like them.

While cleaners working in critical businesses and institutions like hospitals and subway systems continued working or saw their workload increase with the onset of the pandemic, others faced straitened demand for their services. Offices, schools, shops, restaurants and entertainment centers either closed or dramatically reduced their operations, reducing the need for cleaners. Conversely, the homes where workers now worked and children stayed home may have needed cleaning more than ever, but social distancing practices have discouraged people from hiring cleaners. Before the pandemic, cleaners were expected to be invisible workers whose labor we benefited from

157

without having to face them in person. Amid a viral health crisis, many former and potential employers saw even their unseen presence as an unacceptable risk.

Some months before the coronavirus outbreak, I decided to get back in touch with the cleaners at Potsdamer Platz. I was curious to find out how their lives developed. Enough time had passed that my contact information was out of date. So, for the first time since leaving the field, I visited one of the buildings at Potsdamer Platz where Ali had worked, and left my number for him with the receptionist.

A few hours later, Ali's familiar and friendly voice greeted me on the phone, and we made a date to get together. Over coffee, which Ali insisted on paying for, he caught me up on Potsdamer Platz news. CleanUp had lost the contract to a competitor. Ali had a new uniform, new colleagues and foremen, but continued to do the same shifts in "his building." He seemed content, proud of his independence at work and his children's achievements in school and at university.

After a foray into hotel cleaning, Luisa returned to Potsdamer Platz. Ali put her in touch with the new cleaning company, which assigned her to the shopping mall shift she and I had worked together. We spoke by phone and her update was sunny. The new company gave her a permanent, full-time contract, so now she had a stable income that she didn't need to supplement with part-time work. The foremen and her coworkers were mostly foreigners and "very nice." Her dream of running her own business had yet to be fulfilled, but her situation at work, where significant deficits of stability and respect had narrowed if not closed, represented a dramatic turnaround with respect to her dignity.

Other cleaners moved on from Potsdamer Platz. Ali reported that Alex had left Berlin with his Palestinian girlfriend before her family could intervene in what Alex feared would be a violent intervention on behalf of the family's honor. He left without a trace, and nobody, including Ali, knew where he was or what he was doing – something that Ali labored to convince the girlfriend's family of when they appeared unannounced at Potsdamer Platz to squeeze him for information.

Shortly after my departure from Potsdamer Platz, Marcel was promoted to foreman. Not every cleaner was happy about the promotion; some, especially foreign cleaners, felt he discriminated against them. When CleanUp's contract ended, Marcel, suffering from a knee injury, managed to move out of cleaning into building maintenance. He was lucky to get the job, said Ali, who thought Marcel's success in landing it said more about his connections than his skills or qualifications.

But Marcel is the exception among this group, most of whom remained cleaners and even still work for CleanUp, or moved into similar jobs. The ways in which the work-lives of the cleaners developed in recent years show to some extent how cleaning can turn out to be, after all, what I have termed a catch basin. It is an occupation where people can find work, and which can thus keep them from falling out of the labor market (back) into unemployment – contingent, of course, on economic prosperity. At the same time, those who remained within cleaning, one could argue, are caught up in it – the second meaning I attributed to the notion of the catch basin. But even those cleaners have succeeded in bettering their situation. Moreover, not everyone gets caught in the basin, as Marcel's trajectory demonstrates.

Whether cleaners remained in the occupation or moved on, their stories demonstrate the extent to which networks shape prospects. Whether it's Ali's relationship with the client, Marcel's with management, or the cleaners' friendships with one another, relationships formed and cultivated on the job can pave the path of a certain occupational mobility and advancement. This suggests that as much as invisibility, internal conflicts and a rift with the upperworld characterize their workplace, cleaners in the corporate underworld are neither completely isolated nor without any opportunities to develop networks. These networks can offer an important safety net, point of contact and portal to a work-life, possibly even extending beyond the underworld.

After the coronavirus outbreak, I once again got in touch with the cleaners to find out how the crisis and the lockdown were affecting them. Salaried cleaners had weathered the storm well. Ali's employer made sure that he still worked full-time, assigning him to other objects when the café was shuttered and restoring him to that shift when it reopened.

Luisa and others stayed home for a couple of months before resuming their normal shifts when stores and offices reopened. In the interim, they had benefitted from the short-term working allowances with which the government paid part of employees' salaries to help prevent layoffs. For them, the time of not working was nevertheless tough.

Apart from the uncertainty about the future, they missed the daily rhythm of getting up and going to work, of being active.

Although worried about catching the virus, Luisa was glad to start cleaning again. After all, she, like so many of the other cleaners I encountered at Potsdamer Platz, sees in her work more than just a way to make money. It also gives her a sense of purpose, meaning, and ultimately, dignity.

Appendix

The aim of my ethnography was to get into the thick of things instead of observing cleaners from a distance, from above. From the outset of my fieldwork, I was transparent about my role. While not denying my upperworld background, I did not emphasize it, as this would have brought to the fore the status differences that come with "studying down."[1] Instead, I stressed to the cleaners that I was there to learn from them as a kind of apprentice. I did so in hopes of mitigating the status differential and honoring cleaners with some degree of recognition for their skills, work and selves.

By wearing the CleanUp uniform alongside the cleaners, I learned more than I could otherwise have hoped about the job, the workplace, its culture and the landscape of Potsdamer Platz above and below street level. Becoming a cleaner, however temporarily, also enabled me to observe at close range the social interactions within their microcosm, engage in small talk with cleaners[2] and develop personal relationships with them. These relationships continued even after working hours, for example via text messages, on a couple of visits to Luisa's home, at lunch with Ali. I accepted invitations to the summer party and the Christmas party. By the end of my fieldwork, I had become a familiar face, someone who participated in the daily life of the cleaners, who could be asked if not counted on to pick up a shift if someone needed a substitute.

This approach to fieldwork allowed me gain the trust of cleaners and therefore more effectively draw out their own insights into their respective worlds at work and beyond,[3] their perspectives on "how

---

[1] On studying down, see Schwartzman (1993), Hannerz (2006), Stryker and González (2014).

[2] On the significance of small talk in ethnographic research, see Driessen and Jansen (2013).

[3] As Van Maanen (2011a: 228) explains, "seeing the world as others do is the only way of being in that world for any length of time with these other people."

things work"[4] or do not work. Still, my ethnography was not without its problems and tensions. At the outset of field research, I thought I should carry a small notebook so I could jot down catchwords to be elaborated on later on that day in detailed field notes.[5] I quickly saw this could not work. Notebooks and pens are alien objects in cleaners' work lives. Apart from reporting their hours, or perhaps responding to a note from a client, cleaners barely write down anything over the course of a workday. Indeed, it almost seemed as though cleaners had unpleasant associations with documents, as though they were something official that could be used against them. After I had already entered the field, Ludwig, the HR manager, confirmed that workers "do not like to write things down. They prefer to communicate by speech. Perhaps they do not dare. It is also a question of cultural background."

Therefore it seemed inappropriate to take out a notebook in front of cleaners. The times I could go to the toilet to take field notes in private were also limited. For this reason, I bought my first smartphone. Cleaners frequently use their smartphones, so I didn't attract so much attention when keying in a few catchwords on the job, capturing native terms and expressions (see figure A.1).[6] Still, after a while, cleaners started making fun of me as being addicted to my phone, asking whether my boyfriend was on my case and thus I had to text him all the time. I also became known for taking very long toilet breaks.

The importance of field notes was underscored by my decision not to conduct any formal interviews with cleaners. An interview situation would have been too unfamiliar and uncomfortable for them, and would have reinforced the status gap between us. My ethnography thus largely builds on informal, ethnographic interviews I conducted in the field.[7] Ethnographic interviewing is conducive to "shedding light on the personal experiences, interpersonal dynamics and cultural meanings of participants in their social worlds."[8] For me, it proved to be beneficial as I could ask cleaners about their views on and reactions to situations as they were unfolding. The interviews could take place in unexpected moments, for instance while waiting for the foreman or the client, in between or during shifts. Since I stayed long enough in the field and shared shifts with the same cleaner for long

[4] Watson (2011).   [5] On ethnographic field notes, see Emerson et al. (1995).
[6] See Spradley (1980a).   [7] See Spradley (1980b).   [8] Heyl (2001: 372).

Figure A.1 Taking field notes.

periods of time, I also had plenty of opportunities to engage in informal interviews that focused on the cleaners' life history, and to raise questions about things they said or did that I had trouble making sense of – particularly, as with Luisa, when confronting a language barrier.

Being a "participant as observer,"[9] participating in the field more than observing it, was crucial for better understanding what it means

[9] Gold (1958).

to work as a cleaner, and for developing trust-based relationships. I was not a full-time participant: I didn't have to work six days a week, and could change shifts every two to three weeks. In this way, I could travel through the corporate underworld and visit its various sights and spaces, learning about diverse kinds of cleaning work.[10] Importantly, my mobility in the workplace enabled me to get to know more of the staff.

Each switch from one shift to another, from one cleaner to another, required me to adjust to new situations and people. I always had to make sure that cleaners were granting me access within the access. This was particularly important, as the cleaners themselves did not have a say in whether I joined them or not – a manifestation of the power dynamic inherent in "studying down." The foremen allocated shifts, and I could ask them to place me at a particular object. As a result of their lack of choice, I felt it incumbent upon me to demonstrate to the cleaners that I was not there to control them but to learn from them by working at their side. I also emphasized to them that I was not paid by CleanUp and not taking away their hours, which some of them so badly needed.

From the start, the agreement with CleanUp was that I would work alongside the cleaners and assist them rather than take over their shifts. When it came out that, in my shift with Christian, a newly hired foreman mistakenly allocated fewer hours to Christian because of me, Anton and I intervened, making sure Christian was paid as much as usual. Apart from a week working for Ali so he could go on vacation, I joined the shifts as an apprentice rather than as a staff cleaner for whom CleanUp charged the client.

This apprentice role turned out to be productive. It legitimized my asking so many questions, and also legitimized for cleaners the labor of answering them. To the extent that I could share the burden of their cleaning duties, they benefitted from my presence. In front of other workers at Potsdamer Platz, cleaners seemed to enjoy introducing me as their intern or assistant, perhaps as a way to elevate their status.

Over the course of my fieldwork, I developed close relationships with some of the cleaners I assisted. At times, they seemed to treat me as a confidant. They welcomed my presence; I was someone to talk to who was keenly interested in listening to what they had to say. At

---

[10] On the traveler metaphor in relation to interviewing, see Kvale (1996).

one point, Benjamin described me as a "social worker" because, as he explained, I lent an ear. Luisa mentioned several times how happy she was to have me on her side as so few others bothered engaging with her. Cleaners shared with me their opinions, for example about coworkers, their worries and secrets; Marcel showed me where he hid his cleaning equipment.

Naturally, some of my relationships at CleanUp were closer than others. I became one of Luisa's few allies. Ali connected to me, among other reasons, because of my Southern-European and thus partially non-German cultural background. Some of the male cleaners, for example Marcel and Benjamin, enjoyed flirting with me, as they do with other female workers at Potsdamer Platz. As much as their interest was productive in terms of their opening up to me, it also required me to set boundaries, for example by emphasizing that I have a boyfriend and responding professionally – coolly – to flirtatious text messages.

There were also cleaners with whom I found it more difficult to find a common ground and a basis for connection. Some, especially those with whom I didn't share a shift, joked that I am an "undercover boss." These cleaners remained suspicious of the purpose of my stay and role at Potsdamer Platz. From time to time, even cleaners I did share shifts and develop closer relationships with made remarks about my connections to the CleanUp management. They noticed that I arrived at work with a CleanUp uniform that is of higher quality than what cleaners usually receive; that I knew Norbert, the foreman, with whom I'd done CleanUp training workshops before arriving at Potsdamer Platz; and that the foremen and Tom treated me differently. My presence as a researcher from the university was also alluded to in conversation, sometimes just to make fun of my incapacities, for example my inability to put the mop on the stick without bending down. While my status as an outsider and someone with connections to CleanUp management popped up on occasion, it usually faded into the background, the more so the longer I assisted cleaners in their shifts.

The role I took in the field entailed its share of difficulties. I felt significant pressure to do a good job, as any mistakes I made could reflect poorly on cleaners and get them into trouble (refer to Chapter 5 which cites an incident of the client's ire after I mistakenly shifted a rubber magnet). My exertions on the job – from cultivating relationships to cleaning toilets – took their toll on my health. At one point, I suffered such extreme exhaustion that I experienced acute hearing loss. My doctor told me I should abandon my fieldwork, that the environment must be very hostile and thus too stressful for me. While her assumptions about the workplace may reveal more about an upperworlder's perspective than my actual situation – in which I felt more camaraderie than hostility – I nonetheless followed her advice and took two weeks off to recover. This made me realize that the more deeply I immersed myself in the field, the more I needed to find ways to distance myself from it so that I would not wind up again becoming incapacitated.

One reason my participation in the field was so exhausting was that I inevitably got involved in the conflicts within the cleaners' microcosm. The voices I captured in the field were frequently in dispute. The often racist hostilities against Luisa left me more than troubled. The birthday cake incident (discussed in Chapter 4) made painfully apparent to me the degree to which I had been sitting, complicit, on the fence with respect to the ongoing conflict. By eating the cake, I signaled my support for Luisa, taking an active stance. Already I had been one of the few people who made an effort to talk to Luisa during the workday and had met up with her after work. But it made me uneasy that I didn't intervene even more assertively during the birthday incident, for instance, by objecting to the "monkey" or "antelope" comments as racist. Nor was I comfortable with the fact that I refrained from telling other cleaners, especially those hostile toward Luisa, about my visits to her home. I felt torn whether I did enough in terms of "taking a more active responsibility for contributing to a more just world and trying to reconcile antagonisms in power configurations," as Sierk Ybema and colleagues have called on organizational ethnographers to do.[11]

By the same token, had I intervened more, I would have risked taking a paternalistic stance that framed Luisa as a victim and me as something akin to judge – a risk that can come with "studying down." In addition, such an intervention would have risked discouraging her antagonists from openly engaging with me, making it difficult, if not impossible, to accurately discern their points of view.[12]

[11] Ybema et al. (2009: 247).
[12] Since the rise of the right-wing party Alternative for Germany, there is much debate in Germany whether and how to talk and interact with people who hold extreme positions (see Leo et al., 2017).

When engaging with cleaners, I often had to abstain from revealing much about who I am and what I believe. While I didn't lie to the cleaners, I did not openly share with them information about my life and views. A certain withholding of information, for instance that my sister worked as an attorney at Potsdamer Platz, and some vagueness about myself, helped me avoid reinforcing the status difference between them and me. It nonetheless created an asymmetry of information that made me feel uncomfortable, especially when cleaners asked direct questions about my life, my income, my interest in men, my background and so on. Given Marcel's hostility to foreigners, I opted not to mention to him my Greek background. After finding out about it from someone else, Marcel told me with apparent seriousness that I was disinvited from joining him and others on a break. "We only want to be among Germans here, not Greeks," he said.

But then Marcel started laughing, and called me over. It was merely one of his jokes.

I entered the field with a genuine interest in what it means to work and live as a cleaner. I did not have in mind a specific research question beyond that. This openness allowed me to pursue diverse interests, freely following the action in the field. It also meant that I gathered a great deal of data on different topics,[13] and took more time to develop my overarching framing of dignity.

I took various approaches to interpret my data, from systematic to more creative ones. I read through my field notes several times, and coded them according to various emerging topics, such as dirt, space and surveillance. I constructed detailed profiles of different cleaners. I wrote up in narrative form the most memorable incidents, like Luisa's birthday and Christian's encounter with Mr. Gregor. I wrote more freewheeling meditations on some themes, such as dirt, the underworld labyrinth and elevators.[14] Parallel to this, relevant literature, both academic and non-academic, along with conversations with colleagues and friends, aided my interpretation of what I encountered at Potsdamer Platz. Approaching my data in these various ways allowed me to develop a focus, discern various connections and associations within my data, and find how the "[s]mall facts speak to large issues,"

[13] As Hammersley and Atkinson (2007: 37) point out, "all ethnographers have to resist the very ready temptation to try to see, hear, and participate in everything that goes on."

[14] See also Kunda (2013).

as Geertz has put the ethnographer's move from the more detailed to the general.[15]

In hindsight, it might not be surprising that dignity emerged as a central theme in my ethnography. Dignity is a fundamental concern for cleaners, particularly when they interact with the upperworld, and my very presence as an upperworlder among them might have helped bring the matter to the fore. Undoubtedly, my way of being shaped my findings, the data I generated (how people related to me, what they chose to speak about and how they framed it) and how I interpreted it. However, I don't believe that this lessens the importance of my findings. Moreover, while I clearly had an influence on the field, I stayed long enough at Potsdamer Platz to be able to gain insights into how people talk and interact in their usual everyday work life. In any case, all this shows the importance of putting my findings into their specific context, pointing out my role in the field, and distinguishing between first-order, emic (what participants in the field say and do) and second-order, etic perspectives (how I interpret those words and actions).[16]

Writing up an ethnography is no small task. As Gideon Kunda has suggested, "the more conscientious one is as a fieldworker, the more impossible one has demonstrated one's task [of writing it up] to be."[17] In addition to the sheer quantity of the data, I found that the closeness of relationships I had developed with certain cleaners also complicated the work. Twice after I left the field, I got a phone call from Luisa while sitting at my desk and analyzing data that concerned her. This closeness felt like interference, like something that threatened a sufficiently critical remove. Indeed, the more time that passed and the more distance I had from my experiences in the field, the easier it was to write.

In writing up my ethnography, I experimented with different writing styles, drawing on John Van Maanen's classification of realist, confessional and impressionist approaches.[18] I didn't want the book to focus on my experience at the expense of the cleaners'. But nor did I want to leave it out. Ultimately, acting as a cleaner embedded with the staff helped illuminate critical dynamics in the relation between the under- and upperworld that might otherwise have remained obscure.

---

[15] Geertz (1973: 23).   [16] See Van Maanen (1979), Fetterman (2010).
[17] Kunda (2006: 246).   [18] Van Maanen (2011b).

I gave significant thought to ethical considerations with respect to protecting the privacy of the participants in the study, and let my writing be guided by the principle that it should not cause them harm.[19] Indeed, apart from my academic interest in the field, I had and retain an interest in the implications of my research for those involved in my fieldwork.[20]

In the last days before I left the field at Potsdamer Platz, I told the cleaners that I was going to meet with the HR manager and other CleanUp managers. I would be sharing my preliminary findings with them, but assured the cleaners that I wouldn't share any information that could be traced to a particular person.

Perhaps naively, I thought that this meeting with management and my closing presentation could be an opportunity for making suggestions on things that could improve cleaners' work lives, and I asked cleaners what they would like me to suggest to management. The response was varied. Perhaps predictably, Marcel opted not to take the offer seriously and asked if management would consider instituting weekly visits to a brothel. Others put in requests for better equipment, especially better gloves. Still others rejected my offer to be their intermediary: whatever they said would "come to nothing," at best. A request to management, I was told, "will always result in the opposite."

The closing presentation took place at CleanUp's Berlin headquarters, a few kilometers east of Potsdamer Platz. It was attended by Ludwig, the HR manager; the managing director of CleanUp Berlin and his assistant; and, to my surprise, Tom. My presentation focused on the different ways cleaners related to their work and role, to CleanUp's emphasis on professionalism, and to the training programs and career prospects within CleanUp. I presented the tensions between the external image of cleaning and cleaners, and their understandings of themselves and their work. I pointed to the ways in which occupational indeterminacy – the idea that anyone can become a cleaner – could undermine cleaners' sense of worth and foster conflicts among the staff. I also noted how professionalism meant little to cleaners, especially if they lacked professional equipment, such as gloves, and how cleaners found it difficult to assume a more confident stance

[19] See Bell and Bryman (2007).   [20] See Silverman (2000).

toward demanding clients if they didn't feel supported by the management.

The CleanUp higher-ups listened to my presentation with curiosity. Given the hierarchy involved, it is difficult for them as managers to access cleaners' points of view. Some of my points were controversial: Ludwig defended both occupational indeterminacy and CleanUp's emphasis on professionalism as means of boosting the status of cleaning and cleaners while remaining open to a diverse range of potential employees. The management nonetheless said they took my findings and point of view as a thought-provoking stimulus, and the managing director's assistant was going to look into the issue with the gloves.

Before leaving the field, I contemplated returning to Potsdamer Platz from time to time – as a cleaner – to keep up with my onetime colleagues. CleanUp's management had no objections. I soon realized, however, how this idea was less productive than it was a revelation of my attachment to the cleaners, of the difficulty of letting go. After my fieldwork, I started a fellowship in Copenhagen, and had neither the time nor the energy to reassemble a mop and return to the corporate underworld.

Some months after my departure, the management of CleanUp Berlin invited me to their annual Christmas party. I drove there with Luisa and was reunited with many of the cleaners from Potsdamer Platz. It was a jolly gathering, but tensions between the cleaners once again came to the fore, and I felt caught in the middle. As the evening wore on, people were getting drunk, and I decided to duck out early. The experience felt like a return to the past, to a place where I no longer belonged. I let my contact with the cleaners trail off to a few messages or phone calls, until those, too, ceased. Apart from writing about it and meeting with my sister for the occasional lunch date, Potsdamer Platz has become a place I pass by on my way through the city – a site of memory and a closed portal to another world.

References

Abbott, A. (1988) *The System of Professions: An Essay on the Division of Expert Labor*. Chicago: University of Chicago Press.

Acker, J. (2006) "Inequality Regimes: Gender, Class, and Race in Organizations." *Gender & Society*, 20 (4): 441–464.

Ackroyd, S. (2012) "Even More Misbehavior: What Has Happened in the Last Twenty Years?" In Barnes, A., & Taksa, L. (Eds.) *Rethinking Misbehavior and Resistance in Organizations*. Bingley: Emerald, 1–28.

Ackroyd, S., & Crowdy, P. (1990) "Can Culture Be Managed? Working with Raw Material: The Case of the English Slaughterhouse Workers." *Personnel Review*, 19 (5): 3–14.

Ackroyd, S., & Thompson, P. (1999) *Organisational Misbehaviour*. London: Sage.

Adib, A., & Guerrier, Y. (2003) "The Interlocking of Gender with Nationality, Race, Ethnicity and Class: The Narratives of Women in Hotel Work." *Gender, Work & Organization*, 10 (4): 413–432.

Adorno, T. W., & Horkheimer, M. (1944/1997) *Dialectic of Enlightenment*. London: Verso.

Aguiar, L. M., & Herod, A. (Eds.) (2006) *Dirty Work of Neoliberalism: Cleaners in the Global Economy*. Hoboken: John Wiley & Sons.

Ailon-Souday, G., & Kunda, G. (2003) "The Local Selves of Global Workers: The Social Construction of National Identity in the Face of Organizational Globalization." *Organization Studies*, 24 (7): 1073–1096.

Albu, O. (2020) "Their Eyes on Me: (Im)Possibilities of Anonymous Work in Civil Society Organizations." Paper presented at the *6th Global Transparency Conference*, Copenhagen, May 19–21, 2020.

Alvesson, M., Ashcraft, K. L., & Thomas, R. (2008) "Identity Matters: Reflections on the Construction of Identity Scholarship in Organization Studies." *Organization*, 15 (1): 5–28.

AMJ Editors (2010) "Moving Forward by Looking Back: Reclaiming Unconventional Research Contexts and Samples in Organizational Scholarship." *Academy of Management Journal*, 53 (4): 665–671.

Anteby, M., & Chan, C. K. (2018) "A Self-Fulfilling Cycle of Coercive Surveillance: Workers' Invisibility Practices and Managerial Justification." *Organization Science*, 29 (2): 247–263.

Anteby, M., Chan, C. K., & DiBenigno., J. (2016) "Three Lenses on Occupations and Professions in Organizations: Becoming, Doing, and Relating." *Academy of Management Annals*, 10 (1): 183–244.

ArbeitGestalten (2017) *Branchenreport Gebäudereinigung: Arbeitszeiten und Arbeitsverhältnisse*. www.arbeitgestaltengmbh.de/assets/projekte/Joboption-Berlin/Broschuere-Branchenreport-GebRein.pdf (accessed April 2018).

Ashcraft, K. L. (2013) "The Glass Slipper: 'Incorporating' Occupational Identity in Management Studies." *Academy of Management Review*, 38 (1): 6–31.

Ashforth, B. E., & Kreiner, G. E. (1999) "'How Can You Do It?': Dirty Work and the Challenge of Constructing a Positive Identity." *Academy of Management Review*, 24 (3): 413–434.

Ashforth, B. E., Kreiner, G. E., Clark, M. A., & Fugate, M. (2007) "Normalizing Dirty Work: Managerial Tactics for Countering Occupational Taint." *Academy of Management Journal*, 50 (1): 149–174.

Ashforth, B. E., & Mael, F. (1989) "Social Identity Theory and the Organization." *Academy of Management Review*, 14 (1): 20–39.

Augé, M. (1995) *Non-places: Introduction to an Anthropology of Supermodernity*. Howe, J. (trans.). London: Verso.

Baier, H. (1991) *Schmutz: Über Abfälle in der Zivilisation Europas*. Konstanz: Universitätsverlag.

Ball, K. S. (2002) "Elements of Surveillance: A New Framework and Future Research Directions." *Information, Communication and Society*, 5 (4): 573–590.

(2005) "Organization, Surveillance and the Body." *Organization*, 12 (1): 89–108.

(2010) "Workplace Surveillance: An Overview." *Labor History*, 51 (1): 87–106.

Ball, K. S., Haggerty, K. D., & Whitson, J. (2005) "Doing Surveillance Studies." *Surveillance & Society*, 3 (2/3): 129–138.

Ball, K. S., & Margulis, S. T. (2011) "Electronic Monitoring and Surveillance in Call Centres: A Framework for Investigation." *New Technology, Work and Employment*, 26 (2): 113–126.

Baran, B. E., Rogelberg, S. G., Lopina, E. C., Allen, J. A., Spitzmüller, C., & Bergman, M. (2012) "Shouldering a Silent Burden: The Toll of Dirty Tasks." *Human Relations*, 65 (5): 597–626.

Bartmann, C. (2016) *Die Rückkehr der Diener: Das neue Bürgertum und sein Personal*. München: Hanser Verlag.

Bataille, G. (2012) *The Story of the Eye*. London: Penguin Books.

Bauman, Z. (2000) *Liquid Modernity*. Malden: Blackwell.

Bearman, P. (2005) *Doormen*. Chicago: University of Chicago Press.

Bell, C. (1992) *Ritual Theory, Ritual Practice*. Oxford: Oxford University Press.

Bell, E., & Bryman, A. (2007) "The Ethics of Management Research: An Exploratory Content Analysis." *British Journal of Management*, 18 (1): 63–77.

Bergson, H. (1900) *Laughter: An Essay on the Meaning of the Comic*. http://eremita.di.uminho.pt/gutenberg/4/3/5/4352/4352-h/4352-h.htm (accessed September 2020).

Berliner Zeitung (2017) "Coworking-Space am Potsdamer Platz: US-Anbieter WeWork mietet 14 Etagen des Debis-Turms." www.berliner-zeitung.de/berlin/coworking-am-potsdamer-platz-us-anbieter-mietet-14-etagen-des-ehemaligen-debis-turms-29023780 (accessed February 2018).

Bernardi, F., & Garrido, L. (2008) "Is There a New Service Proletariat? Post-industrial Employment Growth and Social Inequality in Spain." *European Sociological Review*, 24 (3): 299–313.

Best, K., & Hindmarsh, J. (2019) "Embodied Spatial Practices and Everyday Organization: The Work of Tour Guides and Their Audiences." *Human Relations*, 72 (2): 248–271.

Beyes, T. (2019) "Uncanny Matters: Kafka's Burrow, the Unhomely and the Study of Organizational Space." *Ephemera: Theory & Politics in Organization*, 19 (1): 179–192.

Beyes, T., & De Cock, C. (2017) "Adorno's Grey, Taussig's Blue: Colour, Organization and Critical Affect." *Organization*, 24 (1): 59–78.

Beynon, H. (1984) *Working for Ford: Men, Masculinity, Mass Production and Militancy*. London: Allen Lane.

Blau, P. M. (1963) *The Dynamics of Bureaucracy: A Study of Interpersonal Relations in Two Government Agencies*. Chicago: University of Chicago Press.

Bolton, S. C. (2005) "Women's Work, Dirty Work: The Gynaecology Nurse as 'Other'." *Gender, Work & Society*, 12 (2): 169–186.

Bosch, G., Kalina, T., Kern, C., Neuffer, S., Schwarzkopf, M., & Weinkopf, C. (2011) "Evaluation bestehender gesetzlicher Mindestlohnregelungen – Branche: Gebäudereinigung. Abschlussbericht." www.bmas.de/SharedDocs/Downloads/DE/PDF-Meldungen/evaluation-mindestlohn-gebaedereinigung.pdf?__blob=publicationFile (accessed March 2018).

Bosch, G., Kalina, T., & Weinkopf, C. (2012) "Wirkungen der Mindestlohnregelungen in der Gebäudereining." *Journal for Labour Market Research*, 45 (3/4): 209–231.

Bosch, G., & Weinkopf, C. (Eds.) (2008) *Low-Wage Work in Germany*. New York: Russell Sage Foundation.

Bourdieu, P. (1984/2010) *Distinction: A Social Critique of the Judgement of Taste*. London: Routledge.

Breslin, D., & Wood, G. (2016) "Rule Breaking in Social Care: Hierarchy, Contentiousness and Informal Rules." *Work, Employment and Society*, 30 (5): 750–765.

Brewis, J., & Grey, C. (2008) "The Regulation of Smoking at Work." *Human Relations*, 61 (7): 965–987.

Brody, D. (2016) *Housekeeping by Design: Hotels and Labor*. Chicago: University of Chicago Press.

Brown, K., & Korczynski, M. (2010) "When Caring and Surveillance Technology Meet: Organizational Commitment and Discretionary Effort in Home Care Work." *Work and Occupations*, 37 (3): 404–432.

Bublitz, H., & Spreen, D. (2004) "Architektur einer Geschlechterkonstruktion. Der Potsdamer Platz aus der Perspektive der Gender Studies." In Fischer, M., & Makropoulos, M. (Eds.) *Potsdamer Platz: Soziologische Theorien zu einem Ort der Moderne*. München: Wilhelm Fink Verlag, 139–158.

Burawoy, M. (1979) *Manufacturing Consent*. Chicago: University of Chicago Press.

Busby, J. S., & Iszatt-White, M. (2016) "Rationalizing Violation: Ordered Accounts of Intentionality in the Breaking of Safety Rules." *Organization Studies*, 37 (1): 35–53.

Callaghan, G., & Thompson, P. (2002) "'We Recruit Attitude': The Selection and Shaping of Routine Call Centre Labour." *Journal of Management Studies*, 39 (2): 233–254.

Cheal, D. (1988) "The Postmodern Origin of Ritual." *Journal for the Theory of Social Behaviour*, 18 (3): 269–290.

Clifford, J., & Marcus, G. E. (Eds.) (1986) *Writing Culture: The Poetics and Politics of Ethnography*. Berkeley: University of California Press.

Collins, R. (2000) "Situational Stratification: A Micro-Macro Theory of Inequality." *Sociological Theory*, 18 (1): 17–43.

(2004) *Interaction Ritual Chains*. Princeton: Princeton University Press.

Collinson, D. L. (1992) *Managing the Shopfloor: Subjectivity, Masculinity and Workplace Culture*. Berlin: De Gruyter.

(2003) "Identities and Insecurities: Selves at Work." *Organization*, 10 (3): 527–547.

Collinson, D. L., & Ackroyd, S. (2005) "Resistance. Misbehaviour and Dissent." In Ackroyd, S., Thompson, P., Tolbert, P., & Batt, P. (Eds.) *The Oxford Handbook of Work and Organizations*. Oxford: Oxford University Press, 305–326.

Collinson, D. L., & Collinson, M. (1997) "Delayering Managers, Time-Space Surveillance and Its Gendered Effects." *Organization*, 4 (3): 373–405.

Colomb, C. (2011) *Staging the New Berlin: Place Marketing and the Politics of Urban Reinvention Post-1989*. London and New York: Routledge.

Corbett, M. J. (2006) "Scents of Identity: Organisation Studies and the Cultural Conundrum of the Nose." *Culture and Organization*, 12 (3): 221–232.

Costas, J., & Grey, C. (2016) *Secrecy at Work: The Hidden Architecture of Organizational Life*. Stanford: Stanford University Press.

Costas, J., & Kunda, G. (2015) The Future of Work: Worlds Apart. *Pacific Standard*. www.psmag.com/business-economics/the-future-of-work-worlds-apart (accessed July 2020).

Countryman, L. W. (1988) *Dirt, Greed and Sex: Sexual Ethics in the New Testament*. Minneapolis: Fortress Press.

Courpasson, D., Dany, F., & Delbridge, R. (2017) "Politics of Place: The Meaningfulness of Resisting Places." *Human Relations*, 70 (2): 237–259.

Crain, M., Poster, W., & Cherry, M. (2016) *Invisible Labor: Hidden Work in the Contemporary World*. Oakland: University of California Press.

Cranford, C. (2012) "Gendered Projects of Solidarity: Workplace Organizing among Immigrant Women and Men." *Gender, Work and Organization*, 19 (2): 142–164.

Cresswell, T. (2004) *Place: A Short Introduction*. Oxford: Blackwell Publishing.

Dale, K., & Burrell, G. (2008) *The Spaces of Organization and the Organization of Space: Power, Identity and Materiality at Work*. Basingstoke: Palgrave Macmillan.

De Certeau, M. (1988) *The Practice of Everyday Life*. Randall, S. F. (trans.). Berkeley: University of California Press.

Deleuze, G. (1992) "Postscript on the Societies of Control." *October*, 59 (Winter): 3–7.

Di Leonardo, M. (1984) *The Varieties of Ethnic Experience: Kinship, Class, and Gender among California Italian-Americans*. Ithaca: Cornell University Press.

DiTomaso, N., Post, C., & Parks-Yancy, R. (2007) "Workforce Diversity and Inequality: Power, Status, and Numbers." *Annual Review of Sociology*, 33: 473–501.

Douglas, M. (1966/2002) *Purity and Danger*. London and New York: Routledge.

Driessen, H., & Jansen, W. (2013) "The Hard Work of Small Talk in Ethnographic Fieldwork." *Journal of Anthropological Research*, 69 (2): 240–263.

Ehrenreich, B. (2001) *Nickel and Dimed: On (Not) Getting by in America*. New York: Metropolitcan Books.

Elias, N. (1939/1996) *The Civilizing Process*. Jephcott, E (trans.). Oxford: Blackwell Publishing.

Elliott, C. S., & Long, G. (2016) "Manufacturing Rate Busters: Computer Control and Social Relations in the Labour Process." *Work, Employment and Society*, 30 (1): 135–151.

Elliott, J. R., & Smith, R. A. (2004) "Race, Gender, and Workplace Power." *American Sociological Review*, 69 (3): 365–386.

Emerson, R. M., Fretz, R. I., & Shaw, L. L. (1995) *Writing Ethnographic Fieldnotes*. Chicago: University of Chicago Press.

Enzensberger, C. (1968/2011) *Größerer Versuch über den Schmutz*. München: Hanser Verlag.

Eriksen, T. H. (2013) *Garbage. Waste in a World of Side Effects*. Oslo: Aschehoug.

Fantasia, R. (1988) *Cultures of Solidarity*. Berkeley: University of California Press.

Farvaque, N. (2013) "Developing Personal and Household Services in the EU: A Focus on Housework Activities." Report for the DG Employment, Social Affairs and Social Inclusion.

Fetterman, D. M. (2010) *Ethnography: Step-by-Step*, 3rd ed. Los Angeles: Sage.

Fischer, M., & Makropoulos, M. (Eds.) (2004) *Potsdamer Platz: Soziologische Theorien zu einem Ort der Moderne*. München: Wilhelm Fink Verlag.

Foucault, M. (1977) *Discipline and Punish – The Birth of the Prison*. Sheridan, A. (trans.). London: Penguin Books.

Fournier, V. (1999) "The Appeal to 'Professionalism' as a Disciplinary Mechanism." *The Sociological Review*, 47 (2): 280–307.

Freud, S. (1908) *Character and Anal Eroticism*. S.E. 9.
  (1919) *The Uncanny*. S.E. 17.

Galič, M., Timan, T., & Koops, B. J. (2016) "Bentham, Deleuze and Beyond: An Overview of Surveillance Theories from the Panopticon to Participation." *Philosophy & Technology*, 30 (1): 9–37.

Gallie, W. B. (1956) "Essentially Contested Concepts." *Proceedings of the Aristotelian Society, New Series*, 56: 167–198.

Garsten, C., & Jacobsson, K. (Eds.) (2004) *Learning to be Employable: New Agendas on Work, Responsibility and Learning in a Globalizing World.* Basingstoke: Palgrave MacMillan.

Geertz, C. (1957) "Ritual and Social Change: A Javanese Example." *American Anthropologist,* 59 (1): 32–54.

(1973) *The Interpretations of Cultures.* New York: Basic Books.

Goffman, E. (1956) "The Nature of Deference and Demeanor." *American Anthropologist,* 58 (3): 473–502.

(1959/1990) *The Presentation of Self in Everyday Life.* Edinburgh: The Bateman Press.

(1963/1990) *Stigma: Notes on the Management of Spoiled Identity.* London: Penguin Books.

(1967) *Interaction Ritual: Essays on Face-to-Face Behaviour.* Garden City: Anchor Books.

(1971/2017) *Relations in Public: Microstudies of the Public Order.* New York: Routledge.

(1983) "The Interaction Order." *American Sociological Review,* 48 (1): 1–17.

Gold, R. (1958) "Roles in Sociological Field Observations." *Social Forces,* 36 (3): 217–223.

Goldberg, D. T. (2000) "Racial Knowledge." In Back, L., & Solomos, J. (Eds.) *Theories of Race and Racism.* London: Routledge, 154–180.

Göttlich, U., & Winter, R. (2004) "Postfordistische Artikulationen von Stadtarchitektur, Konsum und Medien." In Fischer, M., & Makropoulos, M. (Eds.) *Potsdamer Platz: Soziologische Theorien zu einem Ort der Moderne.* München: Wilhelm Fink Verlag, 81–106.

Gouldner, A. M. (1954) *Patterns of Industrial Bureaucracy.* Glencoe: The Free Press.

Graham, S. (2016) *Vertical: The City from Satellites to Bunkers.* London and New York: Verso.

Grey, C. (1998) "On Being a Professional in a 'Big Six' Firm." *Accounting, Organizations and Society,* 23 (5/6): 569–587.

Grömling, M. (2007) *Branchenportrait Gebäudereiniger-Handwerk.* Köln: Institut der deutschen Wirtschaft Köln.

Grossman, H. (2006) "The Beginnings of Capitalism and the New Mass Morality." *Journal of Classical Sociology,* 6 (2): 201–213.

Haggerty, K. D., & Ericson, R. V. (2000) "The Surveillant Assemblage." *British Journal of Sociology,* 51 (4): 605–622.

Hall, J. R. (1992) "The Capital(s) of Cultures: A Non-holistic Approach to Status Situations: Class, Gender, and Ethnicity." In Lamont, M., & Fournier, M. (Eds.) *Cultivating Differences: Symbolic Boundaries and the Making of Inequality.* Chicago: University of Chicago Press, 257–288.

Hall, S. (2000) "Old and New Identities, Old and New Ethnicities." In Back, L., & Solomos, J. (Eds.) *Theories of Race and Racism.* London: Routledge, 144–153.

Hammersley, M., & Atkinson, P. (2007) *Ethnography: Principles in Practice*, 3rd ed. London: Routledge.

Hannerz, U. (2006) "Field Worries: Studying Down, Up, Sideways, Through, Backward, Forward, Early or Later, Away and at Home." In Coleman, S., & Collins, P. (Eds.) *Locating the Field: Space, Place and Context in Anthropology.* London: Bloomsbury Academic, 23–42.

Hanser, A. (2012) "Class and the Service Encounter: New Approaches to Inequality in the Service Work-place." *Sociology Compass*, 6 (4): 293–305.

Hard, R. (2004) *The Routledge Handbook of Greek Mythology.* London: Routledge.

Hatton (2017) "Mechanisms of Invisibility: Rethinking the Concept of Invisible Work." *Work, Employment and Society*, 31 (2): 336–351.

Heyl, B. (2001) "Ethnographic Interviewing." In Atkinson, P., Coffey, A., Delamont, S., Lofland, J., & Lofland, L. (Eds.) *Handbook of Ethnography.* London: Sage, 369–383.

Hirschhauer, S. (1999) "Die Praxis der Fremdheit und die Minimierung von Anwesenheit. Eine Fahrstuhlfahrt." *Soziale Welt*, 50: 221–246.

Hochschild, A. R. (1983/2003) *The Managed Heart: Commercialization of Human Feeling*, 20th ed. Berkeley: University of California Press.

(2016) "Foreword: Invisible Labor, Inaudible Voice." In Crain, M., Poster, W., & Cherry, M. (Eds.) *Invisible Labor: Hidden Work in the Contemporary World.* Oakland: University of California Press, xi–xiv.

Hodson, R. (2001) *Dignity at Work.* Cambridge: Cambridge University Press.

Hodson, R., Welsh, S., Rieble, S., Jamison, C. S., & Creighton, S. (1993) "Is Worker Solidarity Undermined by Autonomy and Participation? Patterns from the Ethnographic Literature." *American Sociological Review*, 58 (3): 398–416.

Holvino, E. (2010) "Intersections: The Simultaneity of Race, Gender and Class in Organization Studies." *Gender, Work & Organization*, 17 (3): 248–277.

Hughes E. C. (1951) "Mistakes, a Problem in the Sociology of Work." In Specht, K. G. (Ed.) *Soziologische Forschung in Unserer Zeit.* Wiesbaden: VS Verlag für Sozialwissenschaften, 123–129.

(1958/2012) *Men and Their Work.* London: Forgotten Books.

(1976) "The Social Drama of Work." *Mid-American Review of Sociology*, 1 (1): 1–7.

(1984/2009) *The Sociological Eye: Selected Papers*. New Brunswick: Transaction Books.

Hughes, J., Simpson, R., Slutskaya, N., Simpson, A., & Hughes, K. (2016) "Beyond the Symbolic: A Relational Approach to Dirty Work through a Study of Refuse Collectors and Street Cleaners." *Work, Employment and Society*, 31 (1): 106–122.

Islam, G., & Zyphur, M. J. (2009) "Rituals in Organizations: A Review and Expansion of Current Theory." *Group & Organization Management*, 34 (1): 114–139.

Janssens, M., & Steyaert, C. (2019) "From Diversity Management to Alterity Politics: Qualifying Otherness." http://openarchive.cbs.dk/bit stream/handle/10398/8127/8791023122.pdf?sequence=1 (accessed March 2019).

Janssens, M., & Zanoni, P. (2014) "Alternative Diversity Management: Organizational Practices Fostering Ethnic Equality at Work." *Scandinavian Journal of Management*, 30 (3): 317–331.

Jenkins, R. (2008) *Social Identity*, 3rd ed. London: Routledge.

Jermier, J. M., Knights, D., & Nord, W. R. (Eds.) (1994) *Resistance and Power in Organizations*. London: Routledge.

Kanter, R. M. (1977) *Men and Women of the Corporation*. New York: Basic Books.

Karafyllis, N. C. (2013) *Putzen als Passion. Ein philosophischer Universalreiniger für klare Verhältnisse*. Berlin: Kadmos.

King, D. K. (1988) *Multiple Jeopardy, Multiple Consciousness: The Context of a Black Feminist Ideology*. Chicago: University Chicago Press.

Koestenbaum, W. (2011) *Humiliation*. New York: Picador.

Kolb, K. (2014) "Status Shield." In Ritzer, G. (Ed.) *The Blackwell Encyclopedia of Sociology*. Blackwell. https://doi.org/10.1002/9781405165518.wbeoss329.pub2 (accessed September 2020).

Korczynski, M. (2003) "Communities of Coping: Collective Emotional Labour in Service Work." *Organization*, 10 (1): 55–79.

(2009) "The Mystery Customer: Continuing Absences in the Sociology of Service Work." *Sociology*, 43 (5): 952–967.

Korczynski, M., & Evans, C. (2013) "Customer Abuse to Service Workers: An Analysis of Its Social Creation within the Service Economy." *Work, Employment and Society*, 27 (5): 768–784.

Koschmann, M. A., & McDonald, J. (2015) "Organizational Rituals, Communication, and the Question of Agency." *Management Communication Quarterly*, 29 (2): 229–256.

Kracauer, S. (1963/1995) *The Mass Ornament: Weimar Essays*. Levin, T. Y. (trans. & Ed.). Cambridge: Harvard University Press.

Krajewski, M. (2018) *The Server: A Media History from the Present to the Baroque*. Iurascu, I. (trans.). New Haven: Yale University Press.

Krause, P. (2015) "Einkommensungleichheit in Deutschland." *Wirtschaftsdienst: Zeitschrift für Wirtschaftspolitik*, 95 (8): 572–574.

Kreiner, G. E., Ashforth, B. E., & Sluss, D. M. (2006) "Identity Dynamics in Occupational Dirty Work: Integrating Social Identity and System Justification Perspectives." *Organization Science*, 17 (5): 619–636.

Kristeva, J. (1982) *Powers of Horror*. New York: Columbia University Press.

Kunda, G. (2006) *Engineering Culture*. Philadelphia: Temple University Press.

(2013) "Reflections on Becoming an Ethnographer." *Journal of Organizational Ethnography*, 2 (1): 4–22.

Kunda, G., & Ailon-Souday, G. (2006) "Managers, Markets, and Ideologies: Design and Devotion Revisited." In Ackroyd, S., Batt, R., Thompson, P., & Tolbert, P. S. (Eds.) *The Oxford Handbook of Work and Organization*. Oxford: Oxford University Press, 200–219.

Kvale, S. (1996) *Interviews: An Introduction to Qualitative Research Interviewing*. London: Sage.

Lamont, M. (1992) *Money, Morals, and Manners: The Culture of the French and American Upper-Middle Class*. Chicago: University of Chicago Press.

(2000) *The Dignity of Working Men: Morality and the Boundaries of Race, Class, and Immigration*. Cambridge: Harvard University Press.

Lamont, M., & Molnar, V. (2002) "The Study of Boundaries in the Social Sciences." *Annual Review of Sociology*, 28: 167–195.

Lamont, M., Silva, G. M., Welburn, J., Guetkow, J., Mizrachi, N., Herzog, H., & Reis, E. (2016) *Getting Respect: Responding to Stigma and Discrimination in the United States, Brazil and Israel*. Princeton: Princeton University Press.

Lamphere, L., Zavella, P., Gonzales, F., & Evans, P. B. (1993) *Sunbelt Working Mothers: Reconciling Family and Factory*. Ithaca: Cornell University Press.

Laporte, D. (2002) *History of Shit*. Cambridge: MIT Press.

Latzke (2015) *Wert und Werte von arbeitsintensiven Dienstleistungen. Die Markt- und Qualitätskonstruktion in der Gebäudereinigungsbranche*. Wiesbaden: Springer VS.

Lawrence, T. B. (2004) "Rituals and Resistance: Membership Dynamics in Professional Fields." *Human Relations*, 57 (2): 115–143.

Leana, C. R., Mittal, V., & Stiehl, E. (2012) "Organizational Behavior and the Working Poor." *Organization Science*, 23 (3): 888–906.

Lefebvre, H. (1974/1991) *The Production of Space*. Oxford: Blackwell.

Leidner, R. (1991) "Serving Hamburgers and Selling Insurance: Gender, Work, and Identity in Interactive Service Jobs." *Gender and Society*, 5 (2): 154–177.

(1993) *Fast Food, Fast Talk*. Berkeley: University of California Press.

Léné, A. (2019) "Job Satisfaction and Bad Jobs: Why Are Cleaners So Happy at Work?" *Work, Employment and Society*, 33 (4): 666–681.

Leo, P., Steinbeis, M., & Zorn, D.-P. (2017) *Mit Rechten reden: Ein Leitfaden*. Stuttgart: Klett-Cotta.

Lessenich, S. (2013) *Die Neuerfindung des Sozialen: Der Sozialstaat im flexiblen Kapitalismus*. Bielefeld: transcript Verlag.

Link, B. G., & Phelan, J. C. (2001) "Conceptualizing Stigma." *Annual Review of Sociology*, 27: 363–385.

Lintott, S. (2016) "Superiority in Humor Theory." *The Journal of Aesthetics and Art Criticism*, 74: 347–358.

Llewellyn, N., & Hindmarsh, J. (2013) "The Order Problem: Inference and Interaction in Interactive Service Work." *Human Relations*, 66 (11): 1401–142.

Lloyd, A. (2016) "Understanding the Post-Industrial Assembly Line: A Critical Appraisal of the Call Centre." *Sociology Compass*, 10: 284–293.

Lorbiecki, A., & Jack, G. (2000) "Critical Turns in the Evolution of Diversity Management." *British Journal of Management*, 11 (1): 17–31.

Lukes, S. (1975) "Political Ritual and Social Integration." *Sociology*, 9 (2): 289–308.

Lundberg, H., & Karlsson, J. C. (2011) "Under the Clean Surface: Working as a Hotel Attendant." *Work, Employment and Society*, 25 (1): 141–148.

Lupton, B. (2000) "Maintaining Masculinity: Men Who Do Women's Work." *British Journal of Management*, 11 (1): 33–48.

Lynd, S. (2014) *Doing History from the Bottom Up: On E.P. Thompson, Howard Zinn, and Rebuilding the Labor Movement from Below*. Chicago: Haymarket Books.

Lyon, D. (2001) *Surveillance Society: Monitoring Everyday Life*. Buckingham: Open University Press.

(2003) "Surveillance as Social Sorting: Computer Codes and Mobile Bodies." In Lyon, D. (Ed.) *Surveillance as Social Sorting: Privacy, Risk and Digital Discrimination*. London: Routledge, 13–31.

MacDonald, C., & Korczynski, M. (Eds.) (2009) *Service Work: Critical Perspectives*. New York: Routledge.

Makropoulos, M. (2004) "Ein Mythos massenkultureller Urbanität. Der Potsdamer Platz aus der Perspektive von Diskursanalyse und

Semiologe." In Fischer, M., & Makropoulos, M. (Eds.) *Potsdamer Platz: Soziologische Theorien zu einem Ort der Moderne*. München: Wilhelm Fink Verlag, 159–188.

Mann, S., Nolan, J., & Wellmann, B. (2003) "Sousveillance: Inventing and Using Wearable Computing Devices for Data Collection in Surveillance Environments." *Surveillance & Society*, 1 (3): 331–355.

Martin, A. W., Lopez, S. H., Roscigno, V. J., & Hodson, R. (2013) "Against the Rules: Synthesizing Types and Processes of Bureaucratic Rulebreaking." *Academy of Management Review*, 38 (4): 550–574.

Marx, G. T. (2003) "A Tack in the Shoe: Neutralizing and Resisting the New Surveillance." *Journal of Social Issues*, 59 (2): 369–390.

Massey, D. (2005) *For Space*. London: Sage.

Massey, D. S. (2007) *Categorically Unequal: The American Stratification System*. New York: Russell Sage Foundation.

Massumi, B. (1995) "The Autonomy of Affect." *Cultural Critique*, 31: 83–109.

Mauss, M. (1950/1990) *The Gift: The Form and Reason for Exchange in Archaic Society*. London: Routledge.

May, T. (1999) "From Banana Time to Just-in-Time: Power and Resistance at Work." *Sociology*, 33 (4): 767–783.

McCabe, D., & Hamilton, L. (2015) "The Kill Programme." *New Technology, Work and Employment*, 30 (2): 95–108.

Meara, H. (1974) "Honor in Dirty Work: The Case of American Meat Cutters and Turkish Butchers." *Sociology of Work and Occupations*, 1 (3): 259–283.

Menninghaus, W. (2003) *Disgust: The Theory and History of a Strong Sensation*. Albany: State University of New York Press.

Miller, I. W. (1997) *The Anatomy of Disgust*. Cambridge: Harvard University Press.

Millmann, G. (2014) *Ist Putzen Stress? Psychische Belastungen am Arbeitsplatz am Beispiel von Beschäftigten in der Gebäudereinigung*. Hamburg: disserta Verlag.

Monahan, T. (2011) "Surveillance as Cultural Practice." *The Sociological Quarterly*, 52 (4): 495–508.

Müller, M. (2019) "Night and Organization Studies." *Organization Studies*, 40 (10): 1513–1527.

Mumby, D. (2005) "Theorizing Resistance in Organization Studies: A Dialectical Approach." *Management Communication Quarterly*, 19 (1): 19–44.

Newlands, G. (2020) "Algorithmic Surveillance in the Gig Economy: The Organization of Work through Lefebvrian Conceived Space."

Organization Studies. https://doi.org/10.1177/0170840620937900 (accessed September 2020).

Newman, K. S. (2000) *No Shame in My Game: The Working Poor in the Inner City*. New York: Vintage Books and Russell Sage Foundation.

Nisim, S., & Benjamin, O. (2010) "The Speech of Services Procurement: The Negotiated Order of Commodification and Dehumanization of Cleaning Employees." *Human Organization*, 69 (3): 221–232.

Nowobilska, M., & Zaman, Q. M. (2014) *Potsdamer Platz: The Reshaping of Berlin*. Heidelberg: Springer.

Ortmann, G. (2003) *Regel und Ausnahme. Paradoxien sozialer Ordnung.* Frankfurt a. M.: Suhrkamp.

Otis, E. M., & Zhao, Z. (2016) "Producing Invisibility: Surveillance, Hunger, and Work in the Produce Aisles of Wal-Mart, China." In Crain, M., Poster, W., & Cherry, M. (Eds.) *Invisible Labor: Hidden Work in the Contemporary World*. Oakland: University of California Press, 148–168.

Otto, B. D., & Strauß, A. (2019) "The Novel as Affective Site: Uncertain Work as Impasse in Wait Until Spring, Bandini." *Organization Studies*, 40 (12): 1805–1822.

Paetzold, R. L., Dipboye, R. L., & Elsbach, K. D. (2008) "A New Look at Stigmatization in and of Organizations." *Academy of Management Review*, 33 (1): 186–193.

Paulsen, R. (2015) *Empty Labor: Idleness and Workplace Resistance.* Cambridge: Cambridge University Press.

Portillo, S. (2012) "The Paradox of Rules: Rules as Resources and Constrains." *Administration & Society*, 44 (1): 87–108.

Poster, W. R. (2011) "Emotion Detectors, Answering Machines, and E-Unions: Multi-Surveillances in the Global Interactive Service Industry." *American Behavioral Scientist*, 55 (7): 868–901.

Poster, W. R., Crain, M., & Cherry, M. A. (2016) "Conclusion." In Crain, M., Poster, W., & Cherry, M. (Eds.) *Invisible Labor: Hidden Work in the Contemporary World*. Oakland: University of California Press, 279–292.

Pullen, A., Rhodes, C., & Thanem, T. (2017) "Affective Politics in Gendered Organizations: Affirmative Notes on Becoming-Woman." *Organization*, 24 (1): 105–123.

Rancière, J. (2010) *Dissensus: On Politics and Aesthetics*. Corcoran, S. (trans). London: Bloomsbury Publishing.

Reagin, N. R. (2007) *Sweeping the German Nation: Domesticity and National Identity in Germany, 1870–1945*. Cambridge: Cambridge University Press.

Resch, C., & Steinert, H. (2004) "Der Potsdamer Platz aus der Perspektive der Kritischen Theorie: Die Widersprüche von Herrschaftsdarstellung – Bescheidenes Großtun als Kompromiss." In Fischer, H., & Makropoulos, M. (Eds.) *Potsdamer Platz. Soziologische Theorien zu einem Ort der Moderne*. München: Wilhelm Fink Verlag, 107–138.

Riach, K., & Warren, S. (2015) "Smell Organization: Bodies and Corporeal Porosity in Office Work." *Human Relations*, 68 (5): 789–809.

Richer, Z. (2015) "Toward a Social Topography: Status as a Spatial Practice." *Sociological Theory*, 33 (4): 347–368.

Rodriguez, J. K., Holvino, E., Fletcher, J. K., & Nkomo, S. M. (2016) "The Theory and Praxis of Intersectionality in Work and Organisations: Where Do We Go From Here?" *Gender, Work & Organization*, 23 (3): 201–222.

Rollins, J. (1985) *Between Women: Domestics and Their Employers*. Philadelphia: Temple University Press.

Rosen, M. (1988) "You Asked for It: Christmas at the Bosses' Expense." *Journal of Management Studies*, 25 (5): 463–480.

Rosette, A. S., Carton, A. M., Bowes-Sperry, L., & Hewlin, P. F. (2013) "'Why Do Racial Slurs Remain Prevalent in the Workplace? Integrating Theory on Intergroup Behavior." *Organization Science*, 24 (5): 1402–1421.

Roy, D. F. (1959) "'Banana Time': Job Satisfaction and Informal Interaction." *Human Organization*, 18: 158–168.

Sanders, T. (2004) "Controllable Laughter: Managing Sex Work through Humour." *Sociology*, 38 (2): 273–291.

Sandler, D. (2003) "Incarnate Politics: The Rhetorics of German Reunification in the Architecture of Berlin." *Invisible Culture*, 5. https://ivc.lib.rochester.edu/incarnate-politics-the-rhetorics-of-german-reunification-in-the-architecture-of-berlin/ (accessed September 2021).

Sassen, S. (2001). *The Global City: New York, London, Tokyo*. Princeton: Princeton University Press.

Sauder, M. (2005) "Symbols and Contexts: An Interactionist Approach to the Study of Social Status." *The Sociological Quarterly*, 46 (2): 279–298.

Sayer, A. (2007) "Dignity at Work: Broadening the Agenda." *Organization*, 14 (4), 565–581.

Schmidt, F. A. (2017) "Digital Labour Markets in the Platform Economy. Mapping the Political Challenges of Crowd Work and Gig Work." https://library.fes.de/pdf-files/wiso/13164.pdf (accessed June 2020).

Schürmann, L. (2013) *Schmutz als Beruf. Prekarisierung, Klasse und Geschlecht in der Reinigungsbranche*. Münster: Westfälisches Dampfboot.

Schwartzman, H. B. (1993) *Qualitative Research Methods: Ethnography in Organizations*. Newbury Park: Sage.

Sennett, R., & Cobb, J. (1972) *The Hidden Injuries of Class*. New York: Alfred A. Knopf.

Sewell, G. (1998) "The Discipline of Teams: The Control of Team-Based Industrial Work through Electronic and Peer Surveillance." *Administrative Science Quarterly*, 43 (2): 397–428.

Sewell, G., & Barker, J. (2006) "Coercion versus Care: Using Irony to Make Sense of Organizational Surveillance." *Academy of Management Review*, 31 (4): 934–961.

Sewell, G., & Taskin, L. (2015) "Out of Sight, Out of Mind in a New World of Work? Autonomy, Control, and Spatiotemporal Scaling in Telework." *Organization Studies*, 36 (11): 1507–1529.

Sherman, R. (2007) *Class Acts: Service and Inequality in Luxury Hotels*. Oakland: University of California Press.

Shortt, H. (2015) "Liminality, Space and the Importance of 'Transitory Dwelling Places' at Work." *Human Relations*, 68 (4): 633–658.

Silverman, D. (2000) *Doing Qualitative Research: A Practical Handbook*. London: Sage.

Simpson, R. (2004) "Masculinity at Work: The Experiences of Men in Female Dominated Occupations." *Work, Employment & Society*, 18 (2): 349–368.

Simpson, R., Hughes, J., Slutskaya, N., & Balta, M. (2014) "Sacrifice and Distinction in Dirty Work: Men's Construction of Meaning in the Butcher Trade." *Work, Employment and Society*, 28 (5): 754–770.

Simpson, R., Slutskaya, N., & Hughes, J. (2012) "Emotional Dimensions of Dirty Work: Men's Encounter with Taint in the Butcher Trade." *International Journal of Work Organisation and Emotion*, 4 (2): 195–212.

Śliwa, M., & Riach, K. (2012) "Making Scents of Transition: Smellscapes and the Everyday in 'Old' and 'New' Urban Poland." *Urban Studies*, 49 (1): 23–41.

Slutskaya, N., Simpson, R., Hughes, J., Simpson, A., & Uygur, S. (2016) "Masculinity and Class in the Context of Dirty Work." *Gender, Work and Organization*, 23 (2): 165–182.

Soylu, S., & Sheehy-Skeffington, J. (2015) "Asymmetric Intergroup Bullying: The Enactment and Maintenance of Societal Inequality at Work." *Human Relations*, 68 (7): 1099–1129.

Spradley, J. P. (1980a) *Participant Observation*. New York: Holt, Rinehart & Winston.

(1980b) *The Ethnographic Interview*. New York: Holt, Rinehart & Winston.

Staab, P. (2014) *Macht und Herrschaft in der Servicewelt.* Hamburg: Hamburger Edition HIS.

Staples, W. G. (2014) *Everyday Surveillance. Vigilance and Visibility in Postmodern Life.* Lanham: Rowman & Littlefield.

Star, S. L., & Strauss, A. (1999) "Layers of Silence, Arenas of Voice: The Ecology of Visible and Invisible Work." *Computer Supported Cooperative Work,* 8: 9–30.

Strati, A. (1999) *Organization and Aesthetics.* London: Sage.

Stryker, R., & González, R. J. (Eds.) (2014) *Up, Down, and Sideways: Anthropologists Trace the Pathways of Power.* New York: Berghahn.

Der Tagesspiegel (1997) "Bauarbeiter legen mit massiven Protesten Berlins Mitte lahm." www.tagesspiegel.de/politik/bauarbeiter-legen-mit-massi ven-protesten-berlins-mitte-lahm/8658.html (accessed September 2021).

   (2016) "Der Potsdamer Platz ist verkauft." www.tagesspiegel.de/ wirtschaft/immobilieninvestor-in-berlin-der-potsdamer-platz-ist-verkau ft/12786574.html (accessed February 2018).

Tatli, A., & Özbilgin, M. F. (2012) "An Emic Approach to Intersectional Study of Diversity at Work: A Bourdieuan Framing." *International Journal of Management Reviews,* 14 (2): 180–200.

Taylor, P., & Bain, P. (1999) "'An Assembly Line in the Head': Work and Employee Relations in the Call Centre." *Industrial Relations Journal,* 30 (2): 101–17.

Thanem, T., & Wallenberg, L. (2015) "What Can Bodies Do? Reading Spinoza for an Affective Ethics of Organizational Life." *Organization,* 22 (2): 235–250.

Thompson, E. P. (1966) *The Making of The English Working Class.* New York: Vintage Books.

Tilly, C. (1998) *Durable Inequality.* Berkeley: University of California Press.

Tölle, A. (2010) "Urban Identity Policies in Berlin: From Critical Reconstruction to Reconstructing the Wall." *Cities,* 27 (5): 348–357.

Tracy, S., & Scott, C. (2006) "Sexuality, Masculinity and Taint Management among Firefighters and Correctional Officers: Getting Down and Dirty with 'America's Heroes' and the 'Scum of Law Enforcement'." *Management Communication Quarterly,* 20 (1): 6–38.

Trice, H. M., & Beyer, J. (1984) "Studying Organizational Cultures through Rites and Ceremonials." *Academy of Management Review,* 9 (4): 653–669.

Tuan, Y. (1977) *Space and Place: The Perspective of Experience.* Minneapolis: Minnesota Press.

Turner, V. W. (1969) *The Ritual Process.* Chicago: Aldine.

Tyler, M. (2011) "Tainted Love: From Dirty Work to Abject Labour." *Human Relations,* 64 (11): 1477–1500.

Van Maanen, J. (1979) "The Fact of Fiction in Organizational Ethnography." *Administrative Science Quarterly*, 24 (4): 539–550.

(1991) "The Smile Factory: Work at Disneyland." In Frost, P. J., Louis, M. R., Lundberg, C. C., Martin, H., & Moore, L. F. (Eds.) *Reframing Organizational Culture*. Newbury Park: Sage, 58–76.

(2011a) "Ethnography as Work: Some Rules of Engagement." *Journal of Management Studies*, 48 (1): 218–234.

(2011b) *Tales of the Field*. Chicago: University of Chicago Press.

Van Maanen, J., & Barley, S. (1984) "Occupational Communities: Culture and Control in Organizations." *Research in Organizational Behavior*, 6: 287–365.

Veblen, T. (1899/2003) *The Theory of the Leisure Class*. Electronic Classics Series, Pennsylvania State University. https://discoversocialsciences.com/wp-content/uploads/2018/02/veblen_theory-leisure-class1.pdf (accessed September 2020).

Wasserman, V., & Frenkel, M. (2015) "Spatial Work in between Glass Ceilings and Glass Walls: Gender-Class Intersectionality and Organizational Aesthetics." *Organization Studies*, 36 (11): 1485–1505.

Watson, H. (2006) "Berlin's Empty Heart." *Architectural Design*, 76 (3): 100–103.

Watson, T. (2011) "Ethnography, Reality, and Truth: The Vital Need for Studies of 'How Things Work' in Organizations and Management." *Journal of Management Studies*, 48 (1): 202–217.

Weber, M. (1930/1976) *The Protestant Ethic and the Spirit of Capitalism*. Parsons, T. (trans.). London: George Allen & Unwin.

(1946/1991) "Politics as Vocation." In Gerth, H. H., & Wright Mills, C. (trans. & Eds.), *Max Weber: Essays in Sociology*. New York: Oxford University Press, 77–128.

(1978) *Economy and Society: Outline of Interpretive Sociology*. Roth, G., & Wittich, C. (Eds.). Berkeley: University of California Press.

West, C., & Zimmerman, D. H. (1987) "Doing Gender." *Gender and Society*, 1 (2): 125–151.

Williams, C. (Ed.) (1993) *Doing Women's Work: Men in Non-Traditional Occupations*. London: Sage.

Willis, P. (1977) *Learning to Labour: How Working Class Kids Get Working Class Jobs*. London: Hutchinson.

Winiecki, D., & Wigman, B. (2007) "Making and Maintaining the Subject in Call Centre Work." *New Technology, Work and Employment*, 22 (2): 118–31.

Wrzesniewski, A., & Dutton, J. E. (2001) "Crafting a Job: Revisioning Employees as Active Crafters of Their Work." *Academy of Management Review*, 26 (2): 179–201.

Wulf, H. A. (2016) *Faul! Der lange Marsch in die kapitalistische Arbeitsgesellschaft*. Norderstedt: Books on Demand.

Ybema, S., Yanow, D., Wels, H., & Kamsteeg, F. H. (2009) *Organizational Ethnography: Studying the Complexity of Everyday Life*. London: Sage.

Zerubavel, E. (1993) *The Fine Line*. Chicago: Chicago University Press.

Žižek, S. (2000) "Enjoy Your Nation as Yourself." In Back, L., & Solomos, J. (Eds.) *Theories of Race and Racism*. London: Routledge, 594–606.

Zukin, S. (2010) *Naked City: The Death and Life of Authentic Urban Places*. Oxford: Oxford University Press.

Index

differentiation among cleaners, 82–84
  workers' embrace of, 99–101
dignity of cleaners. *See also* dramas of
    dignity, for cleaners
  cleaning as route to, 8–10, 48–49,
    60–62
  client-cleaner encounters and
    protection of, 115
  face-to-face client-cleaner
    confrontations and, 115–118
  materiality of dirt and, 78–79
  resistance to surveillance and,
    142–145
  undermining of, 148–152
  upperworld as threat to,
    124–126
  valorization of cleaning as path to,
    99–101
  work ethic of cleaners and, 75–76
dirt
  cleaners' experience of, 63–64
  detection skills of cleaners for,
    64–65
  materiality of, 78–79
  persistence of, 76–78
  wealth and exclusivity linked to,
    109–110
dirty work, characterization of cleaning
    as, 9–10, 42–43
disgust
  cleaners' feelings of, 65–69
  humor and, 69–72
diversity of cleaning workforce, 7–8
  CleanUp's emphasis on, 43–45
Doormen (Bearman), 122
Douglas, Mary, 40, 64
dramas of dignity, for cleaners, 8–10,
    80–82, 99–101, 148–152. *See also*
    dignity of cleaners
dropouts, as cleaners, 59–60

economic conditions, persistence of
    East and West differentiation
    concerning, 51
education levels, class identity and,
    86–87
elevators, client-cleaner encounters in,
    111, 113–115, 121–122
environmental issues, detergents and,
    67–68

equipment
  cleaners' competition over, 28–33
  quality issues with, 76–78
ethical issues in research
  participant as observer status and,
    161–170
exclusivity, cleaners' annexation of,
    106–107

face-to-face confrontations, client-
    cleaner encounters as, 115–118
Fanon, Frantz, 111
foreign workers
  in cleaning industry, 41
  racism concerning, 91–99
foremen
  client encounters with, 102–105
  inspection rounds by, 131–133
  responsibilities of, 22, 75
  surveillance of workers by, 128–133,
    135–138
Foucault, Michel, 129n.3
Freshfields, 17

garbage collection point, workplace
    conditions in, 25–28
Geertz, Clifford, 94
gendered division of labor
  in cleaning, 41, 47–48
  stereotypes about, 87–91
German cleaners, racism among,
    91–99
German reunification, persistence of
    East and West differentiation and,
    51
gifts from clients, 119–122
gloves, cleaners' reliance on, 67–68
Goffman, Erving, 103–104, 111–115,
    123
Graham, Stephen, 19–20
guest workers *(Gastarbeiter)*, cleaners
    as, 50–54

Hall, Stuart, 83–84
health concerns of cleaners, 47, 49, 53
  aches and injuries from work, 72–74
  detergents and, 67–68
  exposure to dirt and filth and, 65–69
Hidden Injuries of Class (Sennett &
    Cobb), 8

service workers (cont.)
  community in Potsdamer Platz of,
    33–35
  invisibility of, 152–153
  third-party service-work providers of,
    20–24
  verticalized urbanization and
    invisibility of, 20
sexism
  in cleaners' culture, 35–38
  recruiting and promotion policies at
    CleanUp and, 87–91
sexual flirtations, cleaners' engagement
  in, 33–35, 87–91
shame, dirt as source of, 78–79
Sherman, Rachel, 125n.57, 126n.63
shit
  cleaners' attitudes about, 65–72
  wealth and exclusivity linked to,
    109–110
skin contact with dirt, cleaners'
  anxieties concerning, 65–69
smells, cleaners' awareness of, 65–69
smoking areas, workers' use of, 25–28,
    33–35
social drama of work, 8–9
  client encounters with cleaners,
    102–105
  confrontations with surveillance,
    134–142
  differentiation in workers
    interactions and, 99–101
  face-to-face client-cleaner
    confrontations and, 115–118
  non-person status of cleaners and,
    110–113
  outside social interactions, 80–82
  personal encounters between workers
    and clients and, 110–122
  work-related interactions, 52–53,
    82–84
The Social Drama of Work (Hughes),
    99–100
Sony Corporation, 17
spatial segregation
  essentially contested space and, 35–38
  in Potsdamer Platz, 12–14
  surveillance avoidance and, 138–142
  of upper and underworlds of
    cleaners, 35–38

Statue of Liberty, 153–156
status shield, client encounters with
    workers and, 103–104
stigmatization of cleaning
  class identity and, 86–87
  cleaners' resistance to, 78–79
  dignity and, 8–10
  public perceptions linked to, 42–43
  work ethic as antidote to, 142–145
support networks for migrant workers,
    54–56
surveillance
  cleaners' tactics against, 127–128,
    151–152
  confrontations with, 134–142
  disciplinary power of, 129n.3
  invisibility of cleaning as resistance
    to, 135–142
  observation *vs.*, 145n.39
  Potsdamer Platz system for, 128–133
  refusal of cleaners to care about,
    134–135
  reverse surveillance, 138–142
  turning off by cleaners of, 135–138
  visibility of, 145–146
  work ethic despite resistance to,
    142–145
Surveillance Society (Lyon), 131
Systemrelevante Berufe (system-
    relevant occupations), 157–160

theft of cleaners' belongings,
    28–33
The Theory of the Leisure Class
    (Veblen), 112–113
Thompson, E. P., 9n.29, 150
toilets, cleaners' anxieties over exposure
    to, 65–69
Tom (CleanUp account manager)
    (pseudonym)
  cleaners' relationship to, 59–60
  client interactions with, 117
  diversity management and, 91–99
  offices of, 20–24
  recruiting and promotion policies,
    87–91
  teamwork advocated by, 82–84
tourism, Potsdamer Platz and, 18–20
traceless cleaning, cleaners' techniques
    for, 76–78

Printed in the United States
by Baker & Taylor Publisher Services